RIOT

RIOT

A Behind-the-Barricades
Tour of Mobs,
Riot Cops,
and the Chaos
of Crowd Violence

Loren W. Christensen

PALADIN PRESS • BOULDER, COLORADO

Other Books by Loren W. Christensen
  Deadly Force Encounters (with Alexis Artwohl)
  Far Beyond Defensive Tactics
  Gangbangers
  On Combat (with Lt. Col. Dave Grossman)
  Skid Row Beat
  Skinhead Street Gangs
  Surviving Workplace Violence
  Warriors: On Living with Courage, Discipline and Honor

Riot: A Behind-the-Barricades Tour of Mobs,
Riot Cops, and the Chaos of Crowd Violence
by Loren W. Christensen

Copyright © 2008 by Loren W. Christensen

ISBN 13: 978-1-58160-635-5
Printed in the United States of America

Published by Paladin Press, a division of
Paladin Enterprises, Inc.
Gunbarrel Tech Center
7077 Winchester Circle
Boulder, Colorado 80301 USA
+1.303.443.7250

Direct inquiries and/or orders to the above address.

PALADIN, PALADIN PRESS, and the "horse head" design
are trademarks belonging to Paladin Enterprises and
registered in United States Patent and Trademark Office.

Visit our Web site at www.paladin-press.com

Front cover photo credit: REUTERS/Andy Clark. Riot police fire tear-
gas at protesters outside the World Trade Organization conference in
Seattle, Washington, November 30, 1999.

Contents

Acknowledgments

The idea for this book came from my son, Dr. Dan L. Christensen. Yes, he does have a doctorate, and yes, I'm bragging. I had just wrapped up a couple of books and was searching for a new project when Dan mentioned that a year earlier he had suggested that I write a book on riots, though I couldn't recall our conversation since memory is the fourth thing that fades when you reach my age.

"You've been in a lot of them," Dan said. "It would be a good project for you."

I thought about it for about 30 minutes and then called my friend Jon Ford, editorial director at Paladin Press.

"Funny you should call," he said. "We're just finishing production on a book called *Riot Prevention and Control* by Charlie Beene. It's targeted at law enforcement, but I was thinking we need another book on the subject, one for a broader audience. One that takes the reader inside of a riot and shows what it's like on both sides. And I was thinking of you to do it."

Two great minds—Dan's and Jon's—thinking alike, leaving me to do all the work.

And it was indeed a tough project, but it was made a little easier by so many helpful people.

First, a big hug to my significant other, Lisa Place, for her support over the many grueling months it took to write *Riot*, and for her compassion whenever I had a long day of research and writing with little usable material to show for it. There were many days like that.

My deepest thanks to:

Dr. Dan Christensen	Jon Ford
Lisa Place	Lawrence Kane
Mark Mireles	Monya LeBlanc
Bill Valentine	Rick Anderson
Joshua Trevino	John Hoffman
Lt. Col. Dave Grossman	Wim Demeere
Martin Cooper	Drew Anderson
Bob Del Torre	Charles Beene
Sara Ortega	

And to those people who didn't want to be mentioned by name because of their particular circumstances.

Thank you all for your encouragement, invaluable information, and for telling me about your experiences.

Introduction

"The Los Angeles riots were not caused by the Rodney King verdict. The Los Angeles riots were caused by rioters."

—Rush Limbaugh

"A riot is the language of the unheard."

—Martin Luther King, Jr.

The first time I thought about a riot—what it is, what it involves, its extraordinary power, its single mind—was when I found myself smack in the middle of one. The year was 1969, and I was serving as a military policeman in the U.S. Army in my third year of service, assigned to street patrol in war-torn Saigon, Vietnam.

My partner and I had received a radio dispatch to a street disturbance. In police parlance, a "disturbance" can be a fight between two people, an excessively loud radio, or an annoying barking dog. This time, the disturbance was a riot: hundreds of

South Vietnamese people, college-age mostly, running through the streets, setting fires, damaging property, hurling Molotov cocktails, and smashing windows. We never did find out the cause. We assumed it was over something that Saigon's crooked government had done, or something it would not do. Or, perhaps, since most of the rioters were of draft age, they were afraid of and angry about the never-ending war.

• • • • •

We are just a couple of blocks away from where the "disturbance" is happening when dispatch upgrades the call. "Be advised that the situation is now a riot. Dozens, maybe hundreds involved."

Even from two blocks away, we can hear the screams, commands barked through megaphones, and the unidentifiable sounds of mayhem. Dispatch is talking to us again: "Be advised that all involved are indigenous people. It's a Vietnamese police problem. Stay out of it, and make sure no Americans get involved."

No sweat, my partner and I are thinking as he slows the Jeep. Few Americans get into this part of Saigon anyway.

The sounds are louder now, like something you would hear from outside of a sports arena. No, it's different. There are cheers, but some of the roar sounds . . . angry? What the heck was . . . ? An explosion? The next sound we know: the burp of an M16 on full auto. We pull around the corner onto a wide street.

On both sides are the usual open-front shops, noodle carts here and there, a few limp, sad trees struggling to survive in one of the most polluted cities in the world, and zillions of bicycles and mini Honda scooters parked wherever there is space. And hundreds of people running amok. My partner stops our Jeep in the middle of the street as we attempt to absorb the pandemonium before us. We get out, lean against the hood, and watch . . . and what a show it is.

Masses of people sweep down the street like a tsunami. In front of them: carts, bicycles, motorcycles, street signs, garbage cans. In their wake: overturned carts, twisted bicycles, fallen motorcycles, bent or uprooted traffic signs, strewn garbage, and flattened garbage cans. The mob gives us wide berth, though some venture within a few feet to shout an anti-American slogan or two. "Go home American MP! We don't want you in our country!" We manage to laugh at that. OK, no problem. We're on the next plane.

At times, the air fills with flying missiles: sticks, rocks, trash cans, bicycles, bricks, bottles, and flaming Molotov cocktails. The targets are buildings and cars. Few are directed at us, probably out of respect for the M16s we hold at the ready. When the occasional rock or bottle does arc toward us, we just duck or sidestep out of the way.

The noise is horrendous and frightening, a cacophony of screams, shouts, sirens, blaring horns, whistles, breaking glass, fireworks, and bursts of automatic gunfire, full mags fired into the air by angry and frightened Vietnamese police.

Our role as casual spectators changes quickly to one of hyper-vigilance as the violence around us intensifies and grows mad with disorder. To the left, cheers; to the right, screams; behind us, a burst of fireworks; to the front, gunfire. Wafting tear gas chokes and blinds us. Waves of people move away from us and then toward us. Faces peer down from rooftops: first one, then two, then 50. One hurls a brick, another a Molotov cocktail. Then, a storm of bricks and firebombs. Flaming bottles break and fires splash across streets and sidewalks all around us.

Out of the corner of my eye, I see something flying my way. It's a Molotov cocktail. Before I can even jump away, it hits the spare tire attached to the back of the Jeep about three feet from where I'm standing. It bounces off at an angle and lands 15 feet away on the pavement, where it bursts into flames and sprayed glass. If it had exploded on the tire, my face would have an entirely different look today.

We send out an urgent call for more American MPs, Vietnamese police, and Vietnamese soldiers. Dispatch orders us to

move out of the hot zone to a place where we are less likely to
have to engage. We do so. Gladly.

• • • • •

I didn't know it then, but I would be involved in many more
riots during my 29 years in law enforcement. What enthralled me
in 1969 was the same thing that continued to enthrall me over the
years, whether the riot was happening in a minority neighborhood
involving dozens of enraged people, during a drunken party with a
hundred or more alcohol- and drug-fueled 20-somethings, or at an
anti-war riot with thousands of angry protestors of every age.
Throughout my career, I would find riots exciting, frightening,
adrenaline pumping, empowering, and maddening. Sometimes
these feelings came one at a time; sometimes they came all at once
like a thundering and destructive tornado.

Though some of the riots I experienced were terrifying in their
scale and intent, I must admit that I liked working them as a police
officer, probably as much as other cops hated them. Some officers
like robbery-in-progress calls, and some like the thrill of a car
chase. I liked a good riot. However, just because it was one of my
favorite jobs on the bureau doesn't mean that it didn't frighten me.
Most of the time it did. But that never stopped me from wading
right into the thick of things, more so when I was a young hot dog
than when I was an older and wiser veteran.

Beside the rush of going head-to-head with an angry mob, I
also found the whole phenomenon fascinating. A riot reveals so
much about people, those on both sides of the police barricades. I
definitely learned a lot about myself, some of which was not that
good to know.

Riot examines the nature of riots and strives to give you a
sense of what it's like to be in one. It examines the psychological
influences that affect everyone involved, from street cop to bottle
thrower to business owner, and how these feelings can be so pow-

erful. The book looks at the many kinds of riots—race, sports, prison—and, for lack of a better term, oddball riots that, while strange and maybe a tad amusing, are nonetheless destructive, injurious, and deadly.

In Chapter 1, "Riot: The Basics," we begin by looking at the elements of a riot. We'll examine how one typically starts, its chaos, how it's sometimes fun for rioters, the misunderstanding the various players have of one another, specific triggers that can lead to a riot, how a peaceful crowd can change to a mob, a few of the psychological factors that mobs possess, and the difficult job the police have and how they, too, can be susceptible to crowd psychology.

No matter what the initial motivation of a riot, most eventually entail people clashing with the police. In Chapter 2, "Perceptions," we examine how each side of a conflict sees the other—sometimes accurately, most often inaccurately—and how that influences the situation. The way players physically appear to each other is a critical aspect of perception. The police wear uniforms of authority, while many protestors wear a "uniform" of sorts, too. We examine how each side sees this emblematic attire, and we look at the power that it possesses. Lastly, we look at the many influences that affect witnesses' perceptions.

At the time of my first riot in Saigon, I didn't know the name for the way in which mobs of people act as if they were of one mind. Today, we have the descriptive word "groupthink," a term that describes exactly what I saw and have seen many times since. We examine this phenomenon and all its elements in Chapter 3, "Crowd Psychology."

While the information in Chapter 4, "The Power of Anonymity," is an aspect of psychology and could therefore fit into Chapter 3, it's so significant that it needs a separate chapter. Anonymity is the driving force that allows some rioters and police officers to act out in ways they normally would never consider. The power of a force called "deindividuation" helps people to "hide" within a crowd. Interestingly, calling out the name of an individual who is acting under a seemingly anonymous cloak can instantly snap him back to reality.

Chapter 5, "Sports Riots," begins our examination of various types of riots. We start out with a cop's-eye-view of what it's like to be in the middle of a sports riot, followed by a brief examination of a few big riots that have occurred during and after major sporting events. From there, we debunk the belief that violent sports are a catharsis for viewers, then get into the myriad reasons why otherwise normal people act out so stupidly in the stands and on the streets outside the arena.

In Chapter 6, "Race Riots," we look at a subject about which everyone has an opinion: Do we all harbor latent racism? We discuss that before reviewing a few of the big race riots that exploded in the turbulent 1960s. Then, after a rundown of the so-called Rodney King riots in Los Angeles in 1992, we present an instructive interview with a tell-it-like-it-was Los Angeles cop who reveals what it was like to work the many long days during the deadly, destructive anarchy. We then look at the elements that are usually present in a race riot and follow that with an examination of the media's role. From there, we look at the issue of censorship and the way political correctness can sometimes present a false reality.

In Chapter 7, we're off to the big house to look at prison/jail riots. After reading a powerful quote that is both crude and truthful about life behind bars, we examine a few of the major prison riots that have occurred over the last few decades. Is racism a prime motivator behind most prison riots? We examine the answer. Then, veteran prison official and author Bill Valentine graciously answers my questions about a riot he experienced, as does another veteran corrections officer, Monya LeBlanc, who tells what it was like to be in a military prison riot.

One of the largest riots in the United States in recent years took place at the World Trade Organization (WTO) gathering in Seattle, Washington, in 1999, and in Chapter 8 we examine what happened there. More than 50,000 protestors came to the rainy city to voice their concerns about the WTO, and a significant portion of them tore it up. We look at all the elements that rocked Seattle's businesses, police department, and people. One protestor, who was there and actively involved, holds nothing back as he tells of his experience. We finish the chapter by looking at the WTO riots that occurred in Cancun and Hong Kong in the years since the big one in Seattle.

In Chapter 9, "Miscellaneous Riots," we review those that don't fit into the sports, racial, and prison categories. As you shall see, they, too, can be spontaneous, destructive, injurious, and deadly. In fact, some of these riots have had tremendous impact on our country and culture, and on other countries and cultures around the globe, taking lives and damaging property to the tune of millions of dollars.

Significant historical riots are encapsulated throughout the book: labor, race, political, prison, sports, and others. Friedrich von Schlegel wrote in *Athenaeum* that "A historian is a prophet in reverse." While it's arguable that these riots happened when times were considerably different from those we live in now, it's not a stretch to see how similar events can easily happen again. In fact, they do, nearly every week somewhere in the world. It's important, therefore, to look at major riots of the past that have, in some cases, defined the era in which they occurred. Perhaps W. H. Auden said it best when he wrote in *The Dyer's Hand*, "Man is a history-making creature who can neither repeat his past nor leave it behind."

It was amazing how many riots happened during the months I spent researching and writing this book. At times there was a riot occurring somewhere virtually every day, and always once or twice a week. There were labor riots in France, riots throughout Europe over the disrespectful cartoons of the Prophet Muhammad, the Los Angeles jail riots, and the World Trade Organization riots in Hong Kong, to name just a few of the big ones. There were lots of medium-size riots, too, and a few small ones. Many of them I discuss in the following pages or just mention briefly to give you a sense of their spontaneity and destructiveness to property and lives. Conversely, many recent and historical riots don't appear within these pages. I don't mean to be disrespectful to those who lived through those events. They have been omitted simply because similar ones are discussed.

Are there more riots today than at any time in recent years? It certainly seemed like it to me as I worked on this book, though admittedly I might have had tunnel vision. For sure, the world today is in turmoil with wars, catastrophic natural disasters, political upheavals, gas shortages, and mass starvation. But haven't there always been these problems? Could it be that these horrific things just seem more prevalent since we live in the so-called information age? Today, when something happens on a remote iceberg, we hear about it within minutes on one of the 24-hour news channels or through continually updated web sites. Sometimes they show it to us *as* it happens.

I'll leave it to others to decide if there are more riots today than in the past few decades. Instead, in the following pages you will learn what a riot is, why it happens, how it happens, who participates, and what it feels like to be in the middle of one. It's my hope that after reading this book, you will never read about a riot in the newspaper or watch one on the television news the same way again. It's also my hope that should you find yourself in one, on purpose or accidentally, you will have a greater understanding of its dynamics and of its dangers.

Chapter 1

Riot: The Basics

Sixty police officers, all wearing heavy jackets and helmets and holding riot batons, stood at the ready along one side of the Hilton, four neat rows of 20 officers, one row behind the other. One officer, a veteran of many demonstrations and street riots, stood in the front row, his eyes following a lieutenant who paced nervously as he waited for the word to move.

The riot was around the corner, and the officers in waiting could hear its sounds: curses, screams, the beating of a drum, whistles, bodies slamming against each other. Clouds of smoke and tear gas wafted along the sidewalk on drunken air currents produced by the high rises.

A voice shouted from all the portable radios in desperate surround sound. "We're outnumbered . . . send four squads . . . Fifth and Taylor . . . now!"

"We're on," the lieutenant barked to the formation. "Helmet shields down. We're going in."

For whatever reason, the veteran officer in the front row turned and caught the eyes of a cop in the last row; young, probably fresh out of the academy. The rookie's eyes were large, wet, darting, with lots of white. The unlined skin around them was tight, seemingly on the verge of tearing. The jaw vibrated. So did the head. The restless eyes stopped on the old cop's weathered face for a moment, not seeing him. Then they darted away.

States differ on their legal definitions of a riot, but not by much. Mostly it's a matter of word choice or a discrepancy in the number of people involved. Here is a general definition that serves our purpose in this book.

1. A violent and turbulent peace disturbance perpetrated by six or more people acting together.
2. An assembly of people who are out of control, causing injury, or endangering the physical safety of others, or their own, threatening or causing property damage, and often violating laws.
   People involved in a riot have the power through violence to disturb the public peace and safety, thus necessitating police action.

There are other prerequisites required to establish a criminal charge of "riot," and the interested reader is encouraged to research that information by specific state. But with every violent riot—sports, race, political—there is a corresponding expert on CNN explaining why it happened.

"It was all about social rage."

"Young, drunken fans needing a release."

"It was just ugly racism."

"Anger at the government."

"Lack of jobs."

"The voice of the oppressed."

While there might be some truth in such simple explanations, it's also true that these conditions are always present in society. There is always some degree of social rage, especially the kind brought on by subtle and not so subtle racism. There are always intoxicated people at college and professional sporting events.

Unemployment is always with us to some degree. So what was it about last night that made 400 people destroy a city block, set bonfires in the street, and overturn police cars?

THE NATURE OF A RIOT

To answer the question of why a riot happens, we need to look at the many elements that make up its formation and life. We need to understand how various influences, causes, and participants combine in a number of ways to set violence in motion.

The Formation of a Riot

A riotous mob is born when members of a crowd are no longer concerned about laws and authority and follow their leaders (whether formally or informally designated) into unlawful and disruptive acts. Mob behavior is highly emotional, usually unreasonable, and likely to erupt into violence. A mob can form from almost any crowd when certain conditions exist, such as when:

- A group gathers to vent their grievances or protest an issue.
- The group's anger is redirected from the issues to those people who represent the issues.
- The group grows in size as curious bystanders, sympathetic onlookers, and opportunists join their ranks.
- Skilled agitators from within the crowd, or opportunistic agitators from outside of it, take advantage of the moment to incite people to commit irrational actions.
- Some members of the crowd sway others to act out criminally.
- Two or more groups with opposing views come into contact and face off.

The Triggers of a Riot

For our purposes here, let's define "trigger" as a necessary condition for a riot. Although those listed here are considered major events, we will see that a trigger can also be something as seemingly insignificant as an inconsiderate dog, a police traffic stop in a volatile neighborhood or, as what happened in my community recently at a nearby park, drunken picnickers. The trigger is pulled and chaos explodes. Typical ones in the United States include:

- a large sporting event in a major city
- a high-profile jury trial
- a shooting by a white police officer in a minority neighborhood
- a rally by a hate group, such as skinheads and the Ku Klux Klan
- a meeting of abortion proponents and opponents
- a high-profile rap concert
- an event in which opposing street gangs are present
- a racial incident in prison
- a presidential visit to a large city
- a labor strike
- a Democratic or Republican national convention
- an antiwar rally

From Crowd to Panicked Mob

While a panicked crowd might not overturn police cars and set fires in the middle of intersections, it often exhibits many of the same characteristics as rioters do. Here is a typical progression that can turn a peaceful crowd into a dangerous, riotous mob.

- People in the crowd believe that there is some kind of danger, such as fire, smoke, tear gas, or someone with a gun or bomb.
- People cannot disperse quickly enough as the danger gets closer, so they act out in desperation.
- People believe erroneously or know accurately that there is only one escape route, or that an exit is available, though one is not.
- People become crushed at the front as those in back force their way forward.
- People fight those who entrap them at their front and rear.

The above are typical precursors to a riot, but there are many other types of incidents that fall outside these parameters. Consider these recent examples from around the world.

An eclipse. Hundreds of Muslim youths in the northern Nigerian city of Maiduguri attacked and set fire to hotels, bars, and brothels after seeing that the moon was beginning to disappear. They attacked mostly Christian targets, blaming the eclipse on "the preponderance of sinful activities in the city."

A funeral. In the West Bank town of Bethlehem, Palestinian students threw rocks at Israeli soldiers and rioted after they had paid their respects to the family of an 8-year-old boy killed by troops earlier. The soldiers used tear gas to quell the unrest.

A death. In Palm Island, 65 kilometers from Townsville in Queensland, Australia, residents rioted and attacked the police station after a second person within a year died while in police custody. Rioters set fire to the courthouse and jail. More than 80 extra police officers flew in to restore peace.

A concert. In Bahrain, religious protestors chanted "No to unclean tourism" as they clashed with riot police over the presence of Lebanese singer Nancy Ajram performing at the exhibition center, a woman considered sultry and provocative. Between 150 and 300 Shiite Muslims rioted to prevent concertgoers from entering the arena. They set tires, threw rocks, and broke car windows.

A raid. In Belfast, Northern Ireland, 40 police officers were injured and 10 cars and a double-decker bus burned when Protestant militants rioted for five hours. They were protesting police raids on Protestant paramilitary figures, the last one done shortly before the riot.

A sale. In the northern part of London, nine ambulances responded to 20 cases of heat exhaustion, injuries, and a stabbing when 4,000 people crushed into a department store for a special midnight sale. People physically fought over discounted sofas, fell to the floor from the pressing wave of bodies and were injured during the course of a struggle with other shoppers. When employees posted signs on the windows that the store was no longer open, the crowds tried to smash through the windows.

A traffic accident. In Zhengzhou, China, severe fighting broke out between Han Chinese and Chinese Muslims. Although the cause was unclear, it appears that a traffic accident between members of the two ethnic groups might have caused the riot. Up to 5,000 people clashed, fighting with clubs and setting fire to each other's homes. The unconfirmed body count was 148.

A Web site. During riots in France in 2005, police charged three youths, all in their mid-teens, with inciting violence through their web sites, which they used to urge people to join the riots and attack police stations.

Happy Riots?

Sometimes a trigger can be a happy moment, starting what some pundits call, a "good-news riot." This is often associated with sporting events. It used to be common for fans of the losing team to riot in anger or clash violently with fans of the winning team. Today, it's become quite common for the streets to be set ablaze by jubilant fans from the winning side. This means that police officers in every city that hosts a major game must now gear up in anticipation of large, intoxicated crowds demonstrating their joy by destroying things and falling off light poles.

The Suddenness of a Riot

It was almost the end of our shift on a blisteringly hot summer day when a radio call dispatched my partner and me to a neighborhood problem involving a dog that had been "watering" someone's roses. "Easy call," my partner said with relief, though his proclamation would prove to be inaccurate. "Let's handle it quickly and head in to the precinct and out of this heat."

Most everyone on our beat had remained inside their homes throughout the day to escape the oppressive weather, so it was a surprise to see about 50 people in the street in front of the complainant's address, all of them screaming, fistfighting, and chasing one another through the yards. Before we could even get out of the patrol car, another half-dozen vehicles screeched to a stop in the middle of the street, their occupants spilling out to join in the fray.

We had no idea what was going on beyond what we were told in the radio call, but we suddenly found ourselves in the middle of whatever it was. We tried to separate combatants, but for every one group of fighters we pulled apart, two more battles erupted in the street and yards. Half the 100 combatants were friends of the mutt's owner, and the others were friends of the woman whose roses the dog had sprinkled. More than a dozen police came to help pull people apart and handcuff those who resisted.

Before there was peace, several people went to jail and a few received injuries, including me when a man swung a 2 x 4 at a neighbor but hit my arm instead.

All over a dog with an indiscriminate whizzer. Or was it? Perhaps there had been neighborhood problems between the warring factions, and this was just one more incident. While the dog might have been the trigger, other forces had been coming together over the long summer. It had been miserably hot for several days. People were unable to sleep night after night so that each day's routine aggravations compounded. Fatigue, oppressive weather, and a continual problem between two groups were ripe for a trigger. That's when the dog bounded onto the scene.

The Spontaneity of a Riot

A riot is rarely planned. The general exception occurs during some well-planned political demonstrations, when agitators (they are usually said to be from another city) organize resistance and lead the charge of destruction and mayhem. We know there is some truth to this because protestors often rehearse how to respond to police commands, how to resist the police, what to say when arrested, how to force the police to carry them bodily to the custody vehicles, and even how to continue to be uncooperative in jail. This preparation is for the inevitable confrontation with the police, whatever form that might take, including an all-out riot. Still, it's accurate to say that riots are seldom planned.

Rather, most riots explode out of an event, such as a celebration after a sporting event, a perceived racial incident by the police, a controversial jury verdict, a heated protest, or any of the other triggering conditions listed above. Generally, leaders in the mob surface as the disturbance unfolds, especially when the initial event is spontaneous, such as the aforementioned fracas over the dog. In that case, the leaders were two women, both of whom were loud, agitated, and able to rally their friends and relatives to attack the other side.

Organized Crowd Tactics

In the book *Riot Prevention and Control* (Paladin Press, 2006), author Charles Beene, a retired captain with the San Francisco Police Department, comments on protestors' preparation to meet with the police:

In activist training sessions prior to major demonstrations, protestors learn, among other things, how to go limp when police try to remove them, how to craft pithy sound bites for TV reporters while being dragged away in cuffs, and when to call their lawyers. They are taught how to handle medical emergencies and maintain "jail solidarity." They learn how to monitor and record the actions of police officers with eyewitness testimony and cameras. And they practice extensively before the actual event. After the disastrous WTO protest in 1999, one Seattle police spokesman said the episode taught them a "hard lesson by a well-trained and equipped adversary."

In many of the downtown riots in which I was involved, those leaders who the police determined to be the primary agitators didn't agitate at all but remained in the background, away from the fray. They knew that the police try to remove agitators because more times than not, their absence quiets those who remain. If they did agitate, they did so by conveying directions to others, who would then pass along the information to those on the front lines.

This often reminded me of Civil War commanders who would watch a battle from a high vantage point and give orders to young officers, who would run pell-mell into the fight to pass them along to the colonels, captains, and lieutenants on the battlefield.

In *The Strategy of Conflict* (Harvard University Press, 1960, 2006), Thomas Schelling expounds upon the notion of leaderless action when he writes:

> It is usually the essence of mob formation that the potential members have to know not only where and when to meet but just when to act so that they act in concert. Overt leadership solves the problem; but leadership can often be identified and eliminated by the authority trying to prevent mob action. In this case, the mob's problem is to act in unison without overt leadership. To find some common signal that makes everyone confident that, if he acts on it, he will not be acting alone. The role of "incidents" can thus be seen as a coordinating role; it is a substitute for overt leadership and communication. Without something like an incident, it may be difficult to get action at all, since immunity requires that we all know when to act together.

In my experience, Schelling's term "incident" can be a thrown bottle, a rock hurled through a window, or a protestor tackling a police officer. It is an action that "stirs the pot," escalating the situation quickly and seemingly spontaneously. In the case of the aforementioned neighborhood riot, the repeated confrontations between the owner of the roses and the owner of the dog collectively served as an incident that "gave permission" to the others to clash. Once we got the two separated and their screaming quieted, the other brawls ceased or lessened in intensity. But when one of the women suddenly bolted around the officers and charged screaming and cursing into her adversary, others in the mob were once again given permission to restart their clashes. After we finally got the two women into two police cars and whisked them away, the situation quieted.

When a Protestor Errs

Sometimes a demonstrator will misread the signs. Finding the crowd too peaceful, he decides to escalate the situation to anarchy and riot, believing that that is what the leaders and other demonstrators want. So he throws a bottle through a window or gets inches away from a police officer's face and screams threats and foul names. What he doesn't know is that no one has followed his lead and that he is acting all by himself. Before he realizes it, the long arm of the law reaches out, grabs him by his collar, and takes him away to jail. I saw this happen many times, and it never failed to crack me up.

I saw this sort of unplanned escalation occur many times at street demonstrations, alcohol-fueled parties, sporting events, and rock concerts. They were riots born quickly from one incident that was either a deliberate provocation or a misunderstanding by the police or the crowd. (Such misunderstandings will be discussed in more detail at the end of the chapter.)

Here is a generic example of how I saw many events deteriorate into rioting. Say 50 demonstrators have blocked pedestrian traffic into a government building by sitting down and linking arms. There are two other groups of about 50 protestors each doing the same thing at other entrance points to the building. The police arrive at one entrance and warn the demonstrators several times that they will be arrested if they don't get up and move. The demonstrators ignore the police warning and then jeer and insult them verbally. After the time limit passes for them to disperse, they again ignore the police warnings and remain steadfast.

The police move in. Since there are TV news cameras pointed at them, the protestors scream and carry on as if being beaten. These horrific sounds are powerful agitators to the police, uninvolved observers, and even other protestors who know that it's falsification done for effect. Even when protestors don't physically fight, they are often instructed to be uncooperative with the police and to force officers to pick them up and carry them.

Tweak a Pinkie and Save a Vertebra

On one occasion, about 20 protestors sat in a circle outside of a senator's fourth floor office blocking foot traffic and chanting noisily. After we ordered them to leave several times and they ignored us, we moved in and handcuffed their wrists behind their backs. We then escorted them one or two at a time into an elevator in which we all stood quietly listening to the gentle music as we descended to the first floor.

As they had preplanned, when the elevator doors opened to a horde of news cameras in the lobby, each protestor screamed and dropped to the floor as if the officer had done something awful to them. After the fourth or fifth time, I showed the other officers how to hold onto the handcuffed arrestee's little finger so that when the protestor tried to drop his body, his weight would shift painfully to his pinkie and thus stop him from going any farther.

It worked like a charm. Every time the protestors went to drop, the acute pain in their little fingers forced them back to an upright position. This stopped them from presenting a false image to the press, and it prevented officers from having their backs wrenched from trying to hold up dead weight.

Several women, children, and obese people have sat down at the front of the formation so the news cameras can capture the moment as the police struggle to get them to stand. The protest leaders hope that viewers at home will be shocked and enraged at the sight of uniformed cops physically removing mothers, children, and those with physical limitations.

The officer in charge gives a direct command to the protestors to get up and move. They ignore the order and underscore their disregard by jeering and catcalling. The officer in charge then orders the officers to pick up the children and use pain compliance on the adults should they refuse to budge. This is legal force since the protestors are disobeying lawful commands by physically balking against police officers' efforts to move them.

Say a female protestor is especially vocal when the police try to pick her up. She might be hamming it up for the cameras, or her verbal protests might be real should she be new at this and therefore unaware that the police are legally authorized to use physical force to remove her. Since her screams are particularly piercing, the news crews rush forward to capture the moment.

Another protestor, sitting a few feet away, curses loudly, shouts at the officers to stop brutalizing her, and then scrambles to his feet to come to her rescue. An officer grabs him, and they tussle for a moment before they both fall on several protestors, who yell and struggle to untangle themselves. In the eyes of other officers, who look over after the two have fallen, it appears that one of their own is in peril. They charge in and begin grabbing people, who resist because they don't understand why they are being manhandled by the cops. Additional police are called in, while protestors from the other two entrance points come to the aid of their "abused" friends. The situation quickly escalates into a full-scale riot.

The Chaos of a Riot

Reading about a riot in the newspaper or even seeing it on the evening news doesn't convey its exhilarating and frightening force, nor the overwhelming sense of helplessness when caught in its eye. Screams, sirens, the thud of batons on bodies, amplified police commands, angry chants, exploding firecrackers, the clatter of horse hooves, the beating of drums, chopper blades, breaking glass, the roar of flames. The stench and thick smoke from burning debris, the sweat of fear, the sting of wafting tear gas. An army of bodies surging into each other, cursing, crying out in pain, falling. Professional agitators roving in back, lines of helmeted riot police moving up a street in a hauntingly rhythmic step, a circle of cops subduing a thrashing protestor, news media scrambling for position.

There are moments in some riots when all is chaos and it seems, especially when you're smack in the middle of it, that the social order has ended and all is anarchy and pandemonium. Here, an anonymous police officer makes an observation of a time during the riot that exploded in Los Angeles after the acquittal of four officers charged for the beating of Rodney King. To this officer, all social order had indeed collapsed.

> There were a lot of looters and rock and bottle throwers being beaten back by the police. Hell, at first the National Guard was shooting people for running through roadblocks. There were a lot of gunfights that were never investigated, and the ones that were got only a cursory look. The use-of-force shooting policy for reporting went out the window during the first four days. That's how it is during these kinds of mass actions. It was like fighting building-to-building in a combat zone. In fact, we were. The detectives were not going to send a team to investigate; they would get shot on the way into the scene. Hey, there were firemen being shot and shot at. There were officers getting into shootings with looters, and if there was no one dead, they were instructed to fill out a simple report.

The Joy of a Riot

While there is certainly merit to the above explanations as to why people engage in riot, I've heard participants say things like "It's fun," "It's exciting," or "It's a rush."

It might have been antiwar sentiment that brought those Saigon students together in protest that I discussed in the introduction, but the fuel for their destructiveness was the joy of riot. It was frightening to experience a hailstorm of Molotov cocktails, bricks, and stones while the rioters laughed and carried on jubilantly. I remember wondering if they had forgotten the cause that brought them together, or if it had shifted to the background while they seemingly played so dangerously.

During the early 1990s, I was a member of an arrest team that assembled each time President George Bush or Vice President Dan Quayle came to town, and they came often. On every visit, the protestors came out in force, and each time they ripped up the streets. It was their anti-Bush sentiments that brought them out, but their focus transitioned quickly from their disagreement with the president's policies to how to best vandalize property and fight the police. They carried out their resistance with lots of laughter, cheering, dancing to street drummers, or just dancing to no music at all. It was party time for many of them; it was obvious in their faces, their bodies, and their actions.

A friend—let's call her Anne—lives in France and has participated in several large demonstrations there. In 1997, there were several large protests, some with as many as 40,000 participants, over such issues as the reform of a university curriculum, an increase in public school tuitions, and changes to the public health system. One protest in which Anne took part occurred in a large city in southern France. Although the event was huge, it was peaceful—that is, until agitators infiltrated and began to riot, just for the sake of rioting.

> The youths came from the ghettos. Those kids weren't students or public workers, and they were not interested in the use of civil rights. They would just take advantage of the fact that they were in the middle of a crowd to start the breaking and the burning. They would break the stores windows to steal electronic gadgets, clothes, shoes, and food. The burning of cars and things was done for the fun. Whenever the youths would see police officers or cars that actually were escorting us for protection (and implicitly agreeing with us since they were public employees, too), they would insult them and start throwing stones or Molotov cocktails at them. The policemen would answer back by throwing tear gas and begin making arrests.

To be fair, just as not every person in a crowd participates in riotous behavior, not everyone carries on as if the whole event is a big party. While working on this book, I attended several antiwar protests in downtown Portland, Oregon. There were the usual mix of people who wanted their voices heard in protest of the war, and there were those who came to party. I'm always amused by those middle-aged people, perhaps parents of young men and women serving in Iraq, who appear to be caught off-guard by people dancing in the street and taunting police officers along the marching route. Their expressions seem to ask: *How is dancing, blowing whistles, and verbally harassing the police going to bring the troops home?*

Consider the riot in Los Angeles after a jury acquitted the four police officers accused of beating Rodney King. The cause? "Another blatant example of racism," the experts said. "Mass unemployment in the black community," others insisted. "Oppression by the police," some argued. All these causes sound logical and no doubt were part of what triggered the riots that destroyed so much, hurt so many, and left indelible images in our minds. However, there was also a lot of serious partying going on, as was evident in much of the news footage of the disorder. The jury system might indeed be imperfect, there might indeed be racism throughout our institutions, and there might indeed be incidents of heavy handedness by the police, but for sure, many of those rioters were having a blast looting, vandalizing, and committing street crimes.

The Participants in a Riot

In *Riot Prevention and Control*, Capt. Charles Beene lists five types of troublemakers found in a typical mob. They are, in brief:

Followers. Sometimes called "suggestables," these people go along with what's going on. A store window is broken, so they figure they might as well steal the stuff in the store.

Encouragers. They don't join in the unlawful activity, but they do not readily leave either. They may shout encouragement to the crowd or police. They just want to see and hear the action. When confronted, they might respond with something like, "I'm not doing anything wrong, officer."

Opportunists. These types are usually of a low social status (i.e., poor, uneducated). They act on impulse and are easily convinced that burning and looting are the things to do. Their attitude is, "The police can't catch us all," so they take advantage of the situation to engage in unlawful behavior that they otherwise might not do.

Criminals and thugs. These are opportunists, too, but they are more deliberate in their intentions and actions. Like professional agitators, they show up in crowds with the specific goal to encourage trouble. Then, while the police are engaged, they move down the street and begin smashing windows and engaging in other crimes. Serious criminals might direct their attention to banks and gun stores. Many times, gangs will come to the scene of trouble and, knowing their rivals will be there, attack them, feeling the police will be too busy to interfere.

Psychopaths. These people are unpredictable and are set off by emotions. They suffer from a mental disorder in which they perceive reality but do not understand social or moral responsibility. They commit crimes or engage in bizarre behavior for instant gratification. They completely disregard the welfare of others and therefore can be very dangerous.

POLICE RESPONSE TO RIOTS

A brief look at police preparations for a planned, large-scale protest illustrates the multifaceted organization that goes into law-enforcement handling of crowd events. The task of a police agency during a planned demonstration is to ensure the safety of people on both sides of the issue and to safeguard property. This is rarely an easy job given that protestors and those protested against have strong feelings about the issue in question and certainly about each other. The police try hard to accommodate both sides prior to the event, though frequently one or both refuse to give an inch. The police gather information as to the mood and intent of both sides by simply talking with them, or they get it from informants.

If the demonstration is, say, in front of a courthouse, the agency will post a line of officers in front of the primary entrance points, at the corners of the building, behind it, and even on the rooftops. Officers on rooftops are often those who know the leaders by face and can notify arrest team leaders on the street of their location if these individuals begin to agitate the crowd to an unlawful level. By posting police at these locations, they form a perimeter that the demonstrators cannot cross. The police give the protest leaders this information in advance so they know they will be arrested for trespass if they violate it; sometimes it's given the day of the event, via bullhorn.

Larger masses of officers form, a block or two away from the protest site, ready to respond should the situation deteriorate. City buses are used to transport squads of officers to the site and to transport arrested persons to jail.

Depending on the location of the event, the police establish a command post in a nearby parking lot, hotel room, or a room at the closest police precinct. The command post is manned by police leadership and others assigned to facilitate those in charge and those on the front lines. Command officers make the decision when to send in more troops, when to move perimeter lines, when to call officers in from home, and when to release officers after the situation quiets.

As is the case in many situations in police work, in crowd control you're damned if you do and damned if you don't. When the police respond to a demonstration with a large contingent of officers, only to have the protestors sing a few songs and wave their signs, people criticize the agency for overreacting. However, when the police send too few officers and the demonstration suddenly explodes into violence, the public, politicians, and news media quickly condemn the agency's lack of preparation.

Old Tactics for Modern Times

According to military historian James Dunnigan, author of *The Perfect Soldier*, some tactics used against rioters by law-enforcement agencies around the world are actually thousands of years old. With some variations, they look like this . . .

An advancing line of officers, sometimes carrying shields, sometimes armed with clubs of some sort, stand shoulder to shoulder facing the rioters. To advance, each officer stamps his right foot onto the pavement and then drags his left one forward, creating a sound that is at once eerie and rhythmic: *Clomp! Draaag. Clomp! Draaag*. The visual and audio effect is that of a machine, and it has a powerful psychological effect on the mob. Sometimes riot officers systematically bang their clubs against their shields as they stomp forward, imitating another ancient psychological tactic.

When soldiers use this tactic, it's common for them to be armed with fixed bayonets. They point their weapons toward the mob, then stomp, drag, and jab their sharp-tipped rifles in a rhythmical and menacing forward advance.

These tactics, borrowed from history, are powerful motivators for the riotous crowd to move and disperse.

I wonder what people would say if American officers responded as did the Sardinian police militia during a soccer riot at the World Cup matches in 1990. Hundred of English fans flew to the matches with, what critics argue, the intent to cause problems. Due to the massive number of fans in the stadium, the police decided not to spread themselves thin but rather use the officers at their disposal to surround a group of ruffians, beat all of them to a bloody pulp with clubs, and then move on to do it again with a new group. They didn't arrest many of them, thus saving the officers and the courts hassle, time, and money. Nor were the troublemakers allowed to move to other parts of the stadium to join forces with other rowdy fans. Because of the beatings and the attrition, the riotous conditions soon ended.

Consider how the authorities gained control of rioting between Hindus and Muslims in 2002 in and around Ahmedabad, India. First, a large mob of Muslims firebombed a train carrying Hindu activists, and then Hindu rioters torched homes and businesses in a mainly Muslim village, which burned alive at least 25 people. To restore order, thousands of Indian troops patrolled the streets in an effort to quell the violence. They had orders to shoot to kill rioters on sight and, in fact, opened fire at least once on Hindu mobs that attacked Muslims with swords and sticks. This tactic worked: by Saturday, Indian police said there were no new major outbreaks of further violence.

When I worked as a military policeman in Saigon, radio dispatch sent several of us to a large fire in a densely populated area of the city to ensure that Americans stayed out of the vicinity. Within minutes, the fire spread to 70 buildings, many of which were residences or businesses. After fire hoses proved to have little effect, helicopters flew to the scene to dump huge containers of water on the spreading flames. As it turned out, the hurricane of winds generated by the chopper blades fanned the fire even more, and the tons of water that smashed onto the flimsy structures crushed them to the ground before they had a chance to burn.

People who lived and worked in the area went berserk as they tried to save trapped people and their possessions. It didn't take long before opportunists began looting. The South Vietnamese Army (ARVN) was on the scene, their M16s set on full automatic. From my partner's and my position, we saw ARVN MPs repeatedly spray rounds over the heads of fleeing people, some of whom were just victims of the fire running for their lives. In other areas, ARVN troops received orders to shoot looters.

Such harsh punitive responses are not likely to happen in the United States (well, maybe by storeowners and homeowners), nor is it being suggested that the police shoot rioters. Since the U.S. Constitution recognizes the rights of Americans to exercise freedom of speech, the freedom to assemble, and freedom of the press, law enforcement must work hard to do their "damned if you do, damned if you don't" job. That is the nature of police work.

Special Riot-Control Units

Many police agencies around the country have created specialized units under such names as Rapid Response Team, Tango Team, and Rapid Tactical Response to handle riot situations. These teams consist of intensely trained officers in highly effective riot-control procedures. Typically, a team will consist of a team leader, a point officer with a weapon that discharges beanbags or other nonlethal rounds, and officers with shields and aerosol agents, such as tear gas, pepper spray and batons.

Sometimes these teams remain out of sight until the situation has gotten to such an extreme that they must be called in, a decision made by a supervisor observing the fray. On command, the line of regular officers already on the scene open a space to allow the marching riot-control team, who look like an invading army from Mars, to pass through and advance smoothly yet aggressively toward the crowd. The psychological effect can be daunting and most often scatters rioters.

Although their techniques are modern and sophisticated, controlling riotous people remains, as it has for hundreds of years, one of the toughest jobs in law enforcement.

Leadership Role

There are few jobs more difficult than being part of the command structure during a violent riot. Careers can be made and destroyed by a right or wrong decision in the heat and confusion of total pandemonium. There were many times when I witnessed those in charge refuse to make decisions, concerned they would do the wrong thing and suffering the ramifications later. I never saw a commander get into trouble over this, but I did see several lose the respect of the line troops. In some cases, the front line officers were forced to make their own decisions. When they were good ones, the command got the credit, but when they were poor, the line officer got into trouble.

When responding to a crowd disturbance, those in charge must consider:

- How credible is the intelligence information about the nature and development of the riot?
- How many officers should be involved?
- Should off-duty officers be brought in on overtime?
- Should auxiliary officers be called up?
- Should the National Guard be notified?
- Is there room in the jail to handle mass arrests?
- Should businesses and residences in the target area be notified?
- Should fire department and ambulance personnel be present?
- Where will the police agency's media contact be positioned?
- What information should be given to the media?
- Will media coverage of police readiness exacerbate the problem?

Cops: The Human Element

As much as police leaders think that training will turn the troops into well-oiled machines, the reality is that they remain human. Is it possible to train them to work and respond in perfect coordination? Sure. Is it possible to train them to overcome all the weaknesses and frailties of the human condition? Don't bet on it. Just as mobs can be swept into violence by psychological influences—anonymity, impersonality, suggestion and imitation, emotional contagion, and release from repressed emotions (all discussed in later chapters)—frontline riot control troops can be so influenced as well.

It's paramount that fatigue be taken into consideration when determining the ability of officers to deal objectively with abusive language, taunting, flying missiles, spittle, shoves, and kicks. Officers are likely to suffer from increased anxiety and fatigue when forced to remain on duty, especially in riot formation for extended periods. Then when they see their fellow officers get hurt, their tension needles blip into the red zone, tweaking their psyches. Suddenly they are in a war zone, and the rioters are the enemy. As one officer admitted, "Yes, one gets a sense of satisfaction when an attacker's action is thwarted by a swift baton blow to his thigh."

There were times when my fellow officers and I were on post for 12 to 14 hours without a break, without water, and without using a restroom. During a couple of the big anti-Bush riots downtown, we worked from 6 AM to 2 AM. After 14 hours of intensity, squad leaders, sergeants, and lieutenants can have trouble controlling troops pushed to their physical and emotional limits. In fact, supervisors can have trouble controlling themselves. No one, especially a rioter who just got caught throwing a bucket of paint at a police car, wants to be arrested by officers who are fatigued, angry, frustrated, and hungry . . . and desperately need to go to the bathroom.

How bad can it get? Consider my workday when I was with a 10-officer arrest team during one of the bigger riots in our jurisdiction. First, we swooped in to help 200 officers gain control of a huge mob on Broadway. Once we had yanked out a few of the troublemakers, we ran three blocks to deal with a mob setting fires on 5th Avenue. Then we ran to a mob trashing a car on 7th Avenue. Then we dashed over to help two squads of officers getting overwhelmed on 8th Avenue. When that was under control, we loaded into police cars and sped to officers who were surrounded by protestors on 2nd Avenue.

This would go on hour after hour without rest, without water, without food, and without time to let the adrenaline subside. Then some scrawny, hapless, anarchist-type would throw a firecracker at my overtaxed squad and would be surprised that his arrest lacked warmth, care, and big hugs.

Agencies need to consider the fact that officers need rest, food, and water. When the department doesn't do the right thing for the officers, their immediate supervisors, usually sergeants and lieutenants, need to beg, borrow, and steal to ensure that their troops get these necessities. That said, officers must realize that there might be times when getting these things is going to be difficult, if not impossible, which brings us back to training. Not only do officers and supervisors need to train in good tactics, crowd

War Chant

One officer told me about a large riot he worked that involved about 250 officers and around 3,000 protestors. He said that at one point he was with about 100 officers standing down in a large, empty building no more than a block away from where several squads of fellow officers were clashing intensely with violent protestors.

Those inside stood or sat in squads of 15, waiting anxiously as they listened to the battle outside and to the confusion of excited radio transmissions of sergeants and lieutenants yelling for additional officers. As each sergeant in charge of a squad ordered his people out onto the street, he would shout something like, "Squad six! Let's go!" Those officers would quickly form a column and exit the building.

At one point, there were about four squads, 60 officers, waiting for their turn to go. Someone, probably to burn off nervous energy, began rhythmically thumping the end of his baton on the cement floor. Thump . . . thump . . . thump. A second officer did the same, and then a third. Then five were doing it. Ten. Fifteen.

Someone started a chant: "Let's go! Let's go!" Then there were 20 people thumping and chanting. Thirty. Those who at first had shaken their heads with mock disgust when the thumping and chanting began now joined in. Then 40 officers, 50, finally all 60. The tribal sound echoed eerily in the cavernous building and filled every officer with red-hot adrenaline.

When a lieutenant bellowed above the din for the rest of the sergeants to form up their officers and head out the door, there erupted a collective cheer that had to have sent some rioters outside running.

psychology, and teamwork, but they also need to learn how stress, fatigue, anger, and frustration can affect a person's judgment, no matter how well trained.

Consider a team of exhausted riot cops in one anonymous city who caught several looters inside of a major department store. The thieves were first startled at the sight of the officers, who in their riot gear looked more like Klingons from the *Star Trek* TV series. Then they were startled in the extreme when the tired-looking officers locked the doors, trapping the looters inside with them. "Then the enforcement action began," one officer said candidly and without apology.

When Officers Get Out of Line

There were times when an overly aggressive police officer or sergeant in charge of a squad of 10 officers would ignite peaceful protestors into a riot. As mentioned earlier, sometimes all it took to weaken the integrity of a police line and set off a problem was for one undisciplined officer to break ranks to "deliver some payback."

I remember one cop dashing from our formation to chase after a protestor who had been kicking passing cars. The officer ran like a crazy man, zigzagging through the mass of people, and then leapt through the air and tackled the man's head as if he were a steer in a rodeo. The momentum sent them both crashing to the concrete in a writhing pile. A television news team captured the entire episode, and the station showed it repeatedly for days after. While the incident got a few laughs back at the precinct, not all officers thought it was funny. Many felt that the footage made the police look like they were out of control. One officer was for sure.

I once served under a sergeant who had a vindictive nature. The problem was that he used his position as squad leader to make all of us look antagonistic and stupid. For example, there were many times when we positioned ourselves on a high vantage point so we could look down and see a mass of demonstrators. "See that guy wearing the orange tie-dyed t-shirt by that truck," he would say excitedly, pointing in the direction of one protestor

All

Too often, an entire group catches the blame for the actions of one of its members.

When one cop makes a bad decision, breaks the law, or is slow to respond, many proclaim, "All cops are dumb," "All cops are crooked," or "All cops are lazy."

When one protestor throws a rock at a window, pushes a cop, or refuses to move, many proclaim, "All protestors are vandals," "All protestors are assaultive," or "All protestors are uncooperative."

Mark Twain said, "Every generalization is dangerous, especially this one."

among hundreds. "He threw a tomato at me earlier today. Let's go get him now."

While throwing a tomato at the police is illegal, going after the culprit when he is with 200 of his violent, cop-hating comrades doesn't show great wisdom.

Combating a riotous mob is a tough task for law enforcement. It's almost always a no-win situation since the protestors, arrestees, press, and citizens see the actions of law enforcement through their own experiences and prejudices. Some will applaud them, and some will criticize them.

Such is the nature of police work, and such is the nature of mob violence.

MISUNDERSTANDINGS

It's not uncommon for the police and protestors to misunderstand each other. While there are neutral people on both sides (i.e., those who have not been somehow tainted toward the other), there are those who are affected by preconceived notions, sometimes greatly. The slightest action by someone or several people on the opposing side is perceived through a lens of fear, prejudice, or absolute hatred. This can have a powerful influence on how the confrontation unfolds.

A crowd, high on the excitement of the moment or intoxicated on alcohol or drugs, see the police move into their midst. While there are some people there who have never had a bad experience with the police and therefore view them somewhat neutrally, others have had run-ins with the cops and thus see them in a negative light. To the latter, the officers' uniforms, weapons, authoritative presence, and powers of arrest conjure negative feelings ranging from distrust to dislike to fear to hate.

The police see things differently. Most officers don't like moving into a mass of people to break up a fight, disperse a protest, or close down a beer party. They know how their uniform affects some people, especially those who detest them and all that they represent. Some officers go into a situation without preconceived negative views about the crowd because at one time they, too, protested issues or engaged in rowdy parties. Other officers, however, because of previous bad experiences in such settings, approach with a high level of vigilance.

Now there are two groups of people, each side with members who are suspicious and apprehensive of the other. The setting is tense, noisy, and confused, with a number of people on both sides anticipating the worst from the other. Then, when something happens in the crowded setting—say, a person from one group bumps someone from the other group by accident—the situation can escalate in the blink of an eye.

It can be argued that the police are trained professionals and should not jump to conclusions. However, imagine for a moment that you're at the scene as a police officer. You're outnumbered in a noisy, chaotic, tense setting. All eyes are on you. Some eyes hate you, some think you're a joke, and some are relieved that you're there. Suddenly you're bumped from behind, which causes you to stumble forward, to the accompaniment of sneers and cheers of several in the crowd. You have no idea if it was done by accident or on purpose. What would you do? If you ignore it, you risk showing weakness and thus encouraging someone else to do it again. If you grab the person who pushed you, you risk manhandling someone who might have bumped you by accident. It's a tough call. Since you don't know for sure, maybe you should just shout loudly above the din, "Did you really mean to do that, sir?" The crowd will laugh at you, of course, jeer some more, and watch to see what you're going to do next.

When you're in uniform, the ball is always in your court; all eyes are on you as you consider what to do. It's a little like a popular game show in which a moderator asks contestants questions and, as they struggle to answer them, they are bombarded with distractions. Sometimes a scantily clad model throws them to the floor, or someone pours a bucket of paint over their heads. In a riot, or in the midst of an agitated crowd on the brink of rioting, one or more officers must decide a course of action while the mob jostles and jeers them and, in more serious cases, strikes them with missiles, pushes them, spits on them, and throws urine on them.

Sometimes one person in a peaceful demonstration can push the envelope and ignite a falling-dominoes effect of misunderstandings. Let's say that there are 200 people singing "We Shall Overcome" when a crowd member, acting on his own agenda, throws something that hits a building, a passerby, or a police officer. Three officers move quickly into the protestors and apprehend the person, who resists by twisting away from their grasp. When the police grab him more vigorously to overcome his resistance, cries of "police brutality" fill the air from three or four people in the immediate vicinity, people who might not have seen the protestor throw the object. (Note: Agitators will often cry "police brutality" even when officers are not taking any action at all. They do this in the hope that demonstrators in the back will think that officers acted brutally somehow, and then rush forward to strike out at the police.)

Others in the crowd cannot see what is happening, so they jockey for better position, an action that knocks one of the officers off balance. As he stumbles to catch himself, he reaches out at the closest person he thinks responsible, and that person jerks away, shouting his innocence. Additional officers push people aside to get to the disturbance. This offends those who are pushed, some of whom are innocently in the way and others who are deliberately blocking the officers' path. One or two of them push back, one hard enough to constitute a charge of harassment. Two officers grab that person. There is more pushing, grabbing, shouting, and screams as additional police cars wail their arrival. What began as a peaceful demonstration has, within seconds, escalated into a riotous melee between protestors and police.

Is this type of misunderstanding rare? Not at all. I saw it happen repeatedly at virtually every riot I experienced. For the police, responding to a riot situation, or a mass of people on the verge of riot, isn't a clear, methodical, and absolute process like an investigation on the popular television program *CSI*. It's chaotic, a confusion to the senses, which are getting bombarded with urgent data. Add to this the stress of being in the hot seat, being the one looked at, the one on whom the situation hinges, and it's a wonder the police can function at all. But they do, and most do it very well.

PSYCHOLOGICAL INFLUENCES
ON COLLECTIVE BEHAVIOR

We conclude this chapter with a list of five psychological influences that affect all parties involved in a mass civil disturbance: the rioters, their target(s), and the police. They will be discussed in detail in subsequent chapters, but they are mentioned briefly here because they are so basic to all that is a riot.

Impersonality. This is a phenomenon in which someone sees all members of a certain group as being all good or all bad. For example, some violent protestors might see all police as bad. Or, in a race riot, all members of a particular race might consider those of another race as all bad. (It's for this reason that a police force should consist of a mix of races and ethnicities. This helps them better understand those involved in racial disorder and thus respond only to violations of the law rather than the race or ethnicity of the people.)

Anonymity. The mass and oftentimes short life of a mob tends to make many of its members feel anonymous and faceless. This phenomenon causes people to act without conscience, believing that the moral responsibility for their actions belongs to the entire mob. Officers trying to control the mob are also susceptible to this, which can lead certain members to act out on feelings they normally suppress (more on this below).

Suggestion and imitation. The massiveness of a mob causes many of its members to forget they are individuals and makes them susceptible to following others like sheep. There is a powerful instinct to follow the crowd, and only those with deeply ingrained convictions are strong enough to repulse this urge. This influence can affect police officers in a riot as well. Whenever one officer violates policy or procedure, there likely will be others who imitate his actions.

Emotional contagion. The size and activities of the mob generate a building emotion that is felt and influenced by each member. Often called "collective emotion," even bystanders can be caught up in the wave and soon find themselves involved. Police officers, too. A squad's anticipation can be palpable as they wait on a side street to go into battle.

Discharge of repressed emotions. As a result of the other four influences listed here, certain individuals feel a sense of freedom to discharge any repressed emotions they harbor, including rage, hate, revenge, and a need to destroy. Some police officers might harbor feelings of contempt for a particular race, ethnicity, sexual preference, or lifestyle, which can lead them to act more harshly during a civil disturbance.

The good news is that these five psychological influences don't impact everyone. The bad news is that those who are influenced by them can cause serious confusion, destruction, and injury on both sides.

Sources

Legal-Explanations.com.
"Eclipse triggers Nigeria riot," by Barnaby Phillips, BBC News, January 10, 2001.
"Boy's funeral triggers a riot" by Nasser Shiyoukhi, *The Columbian*, November 17, 1997.

"Australia: Aboriginal death in custody triggers Palm Island Riot," by Mike Head, World Socialist Web Site, www.wsws.com, December 3, 2004.

"Sultry Nancy Ajram triggers fundamentalists riots in Bahrain," author unknown, Associate Press, www.haharnet.com.

"Violence escalates in India," author unknown, CNN.com/World, March 2, 2002.

"Anti-gay church protests at soldiers' funerals," author unknown, MSNBC, www.msnbc.msn.com/id/9102443/, August 28, 2005.

"Villages cordoned off following ethnic riots in Central China," author unknown, *The Manila Times*, www.manilatimes.net, November 3, 2004.

"40 hurt in Protestant militant riot in Belfast," author unknown, MSNBC, www.msnbc.msn.com/id/8824982/, August 5, 2005.

"I-chaos: Man stabbed in store riot," author unknown, www.eveningtimes.com, October 2, 2005.

Chapter 2

Perceptions

"It is the mind which creates the world about us, and even though we stand side-by-side in the same meadow, my eyes will never see what is beheld by yours, my heart will never stir in the emotions with which yours is touched."

—George Gissing,
The Private Papers of Henry Ryecroft

A warrior is often defined as one who does what needs to be done; a person who lays his life on the line for others; one who moves toward the sound of gunfire while everyone else flees. More and more people refer to police officers as warriors, although not everyone sees it that way. Here is an anonymous blog writer's perception of the term:

> Warrior cops??? Give it a break with the warrior cop
> title. The term warrior applies to honorable and patriotic mili-
> tary personnel who serve in combat. A so-called warrior cop
> is generally nothing more than a thug who manages to have

the law on his side. The Nazi Gestapo is a good example. I
see the warrior profession as an honorable one . . . being an
honest cop is also an honorable profession . . . put the empha-
sis on honest.

But that perception works both ways. Some demonstrators see
themselves as warriors: men and women with the guts and determination to go toe-to-toe with the government, big industry, abor-
tionists, the police, or whoever. Yet many in law enforcement see
demonstrators as lawbreakers, losers who need a cause to feel
important, children of the '60s trying to relive their glory years, or,
in police parlance, simply "assholes" who cost taxpayers money
for police overtime and vandalism to city property.

Which brings us to one of the great philosophical questions in
life: Is it possible for us to know another point of view in the same
way that we know our own? In the context of this book, is it possible for a group of protestors and their target—be it the military,
law enforcement, big business, loggers, or the president of the
United States—to perceive the issue in question the same way?
How about individual protestors? Will each one see the cause the
same way? How about cops? Will every officer in a squad see a
protest or their police department's mission the same way?

What about people in the community? After National
Guardsmen shot several rioting Kent State students in 1970, killing
four, townspeople in nearby Kent were shocked. That is, some
were. Others not only agreed with the actions of the troops but
thought the soldiers should have shot even more students. Read the
editorial section of the newspaper in the days that follow a riot and
you will find some letter writers who agreed with the protestors
and some who agreed with the way the police handled them.

COPS AND PROTESTORS: LIKE CATS AND DOGS

Before we get deeper into the question of different perceptions, we need to acknowledge a fundamental reality of the relationship between cops and protestors. Like cats and dogs, it's in their nature to clash. During my years in law enforcement, I cannot recall protestors and police agreeing on much of anything. Even when the police were assigned to maintain peace so protestors could voice their dissent about, say, a corporation buying land, the police would inevitably be the victim of catcalls and verbal insults (oftentimes from both sides).

There were many times when I was assigned with other officers to provide a police presence at a protest that I hadn't a clue what the protest was about, and I didn't care enough to find out. I was just there for two or three hours, doing my job as peacemaker. Other times I was assigned to an event where I agreed with the demonstrators. Still, my fellow officers and I were called "trigger-happy Gestapo thugs," "boot-stomping Nazis" (for the record, we wore black Adidas running shoes), and a host of other names. All this while we simply stood on the sidewalk or sat in police cars watching the event. Of course, police officers cannot retaliate and call the protestors names, but that didn't keep me from having my private thoughts about them.

Writer Josh Trevino describes a similar example that he witnessed during a violent protest in Scotland. The clash pitted helmeted, shield-carrying police officers on foot and horseback against young protestors who Trevino described as "dirty, disheveled, and profane; and almost all dressed in black."

The opponents slammed into each other. The mob of anarchists surged behind a volley of thrown garbage as the police responded with well-coordinated manuevers of officers, horses, and smashing batons. "It was a fearsome sight, seeing the lines clash," Trevino writes. "The outcome was never in doubt: some of the kids were trampled, some thrown bodily back a surprising distance, and some fled in pure fear. All deserved it. As swiftly as it began, the police line halted just shy of my alley [from where Trevino watched], having cleared perhaps a hundred feet of Rose Street." As the police ranks tightened their formation in preparation for the next clash,

Trevino makes this observation about an isolated episode amidst the chaos:

> Into my alley, some women dragged another woman, this one elderly and evidently in a seizure. She twitched and moaned on the pavement, eyes rolled back into her head, and one of the girls began shrieking at the impassive line of [officers]. "Do something! Help her! We pay your salaries! Do your job!" She was immune to irony, and for all I know, the cops were too: they did not move.
>
> According to her companions, the old woman, one of the anarchists, had been thrown into a seizure by the shock of the police charge. Male anarchists walked back up to the police line to berate the cops: "So this is how you treat the elderly! Fascists! I hope you're proud!" A few gathered about the gagging, twitching old woman to take amateur videos of the fruits of police state brutality. Two anarchist women, clad in black but with orange crosses pinned to their shirts, moved forward to render first aid.
>
> The foot police sealing me and a platoon of anarchists into our alley opened ranks, and two cops, in full armor but without shields or batons, strode confidently among us. Ignoring threats and curses, they walked to the old woman in seizure, knelt down, and began to render aid. In a flash, it became clear why the cavalry had charged as it did: with their flanks and rear secure, the police could render aid. Having been among them long enough to get a sense of their nature, I have no doubt that lone policemen amongst the crowd would have been assaulted mercilessly even in their mission of mercy; now, though, they could do good work unhindered. The anarchists, excepting two, withdrew from the old woman. The couple remaining spoke in low voices to the cops, and they worked together to calm the stricken woman. The rest milled about, cowed and perhaps even shamed.

What happens all too often when protests turn violent is that after the first brick is thrown or the first arrest made, the primary motive of the gathering is cast aside as the protestors seemingly forget about the initial target of their discontent and focus solely on doing battle with the police. Chants against big corporations change to cries about a police state, fascist cops, and that old song, police brutality. The mind-set of the police changes from that of carefully monitoring a large mass of people who were voicing their discontent about, say, corporate America, to one of hypervigilance, a heighted sense of threat, an increased startle reflex, and irritability over being called names and getting struck with flying missiles.

Consider this violent clash in Toledo, Ohio, in October 2005 between black street gangs and the police. It started out as a march by white supremacists demonstrating against black gangs. When angry black gangbangers interrupted their march, it took only seconds before the street ignited into violence between the two sides. The clash between whites and blacks was short-lived, because as soon as the police interceded, the situation evolved quickly to that of the gangs fighting the cops, which would continue for four hours, long after the white supremacists had gone home. When it was over, 65 people went to jail, several officers were injured, and an unknown amount of property incurred damage.

Look at another 2005 incident in Alexandria, Egypt, where thousands of Muslims rioted outside a Coptic Christian church to condemn a play they deemed offensive to Islam. The police attempted to stop the protestors from approaching the church, and the mob turned on the officers and threw rocks at them. They quickly moved from denouncing a play to fighting the police. Before it was over, 53 rioters were arrested, one police car was set on fire, eight others were damaged, 90 people were injured, and one died after being trampled and inhaling tear gas.

Of course, there is much more involved here than innate cat-and-dog personalities. What causes police and protestors to come to an event with preconceived notions of the other group's outlooks, motives, and agendas? Let's have a look.

TAKE 1: PERCEPTIONS AND A POLICE SHOOTING

As I write this, five days have passed since a police officer shot and killed a man who attacked him with a knife on a downtown street in my city, Portland, Oregon. The man had been screaming, yelling, and threatening people for some time before someone called 9-1-1. He somehow overpowered the first officer on the scene and wrestled him into a chokehold. A moment later, three more officers pulled up in their cars and rushed toward the scuffle with their guns drawn. A few paces before they got to their comrade, the officer broke free. The berserk man lunged at the four with his knife, missed, backed off, and then lunged again. On his third attempt to stab them, one of the officers fired, and the man fell dead.

Several citizens witnessed the entire incident, all of whom reported the man's actions as I have related them here. They all agreed that the first officer had been in trouble. One witness said he was about to come to his aid when the other officers arrived on the scene. The witnesses confirmed that the officer didn't fire until the man attempted to stab them a third time.

However, a web site for local and global activists saw it differently. Actually, they didn't see it at all. Their perception of what happened was driven entirely by their belief that there is a massively coordinated conspiracy that connects what they call the "corporate media" and "info-tainers" (the media), "militarized right-wing nutjobbers" (the police), and "the police state" (the government) to hide the truth and sanction "totalitarian repression" by killing the homeless and minorities.

It's unknown how many of these people who have such negative opinions about the police have actually faced an enraged person armed with a knife. What is known, however, is that their perceptions, their preconceived notions of the officers who were there—men who were faced with their own mortality and forced to make a split-second decision—caused them to believe that the cops acted not only wrongfully but criminally. (In fact, according to their web site, their perception of the *witnesses* was that they, too, were part of this huge conspiracy.)

I have talked with activists in Cop Watch, an organization that monitors police activity for evidence of wrongdoing, and they have told me that they believe that there is never, *never,* a situation in which the police should use deadly force. It's always about choice, they said, and they believe that the police "always" choose to kill. With such a mind-set, with such a perception of reality, is it not surprising that they perceive any use of force by the police as negative, unnecessary, and criminal?

HOW PROTESTORS AND POLICE VIEW EACH OTHER

Allow me to speak for protestors for a moment. I think I'm qualified to do so, at least in a general sense, since during my nearly 30 years on the police force, I talked with countless activists and anarchists, listened to their speeches, read their literature, and was a target of their taunts, curses, and thrown objects. In the eyes of most activists, the police embody rules, structure, and societal control. They see police officers, as a group, as representing oppressive authority, big government, and heartless corporations. They see individual officers as brutal, stupid, quick on the trigger, and easy to bait into overreacting. Many times I heard protestors single out uniforms, badges, and guns as evidence of the true nature of the "fascist police." These are significant symbols that represent everything that they despise in their world. (More on this below.)

My French friend Anne, whom I mentioned in Chapter 1, participated in many demonstrations in her country. In one large march, the police were there to protect thousands of people as they protested against what they believed to be unfair reforms in education and health care. Problems began when "ghetto kids" infiltrated the demonstration for no other purpose than to riot and clash with the police. In her words:

The Police Baton: A Symbol, a Weapon

In *Riot Prevention and Control*, Capt. Charles Beene provides excellent insight into perceptions of the police baton:

The police baton is perhaps the most recognizable symbol of police response to crowd disturbances. It can be a powerful symbol of police authority, as when a line of officers, professional and firm, advance on a violent mob, beating their tactical shields with their batons as they move in to restore order. It could also be seen as a negative symbol of police brutality, as when officers wildly rush into a crowd and strike anyone in the vicinity with their batons, whether they are lawbreakers or innocent bystanders. It all depends on the commanders' ability to manage the scene and their troops, and the extent and quality of the training provided to officers prior to civil disturbances.

I believe that, at least for the marchers, the police were not a threatening presence, but a protective one. For the ghetto kids, the police and any uniformed person were a symbol of the government "racism," repression and authority. In fact, the ghetto kids have been known to throw stones at firefighters and ambulances when they go to the ghettos to rescue someone. During the demonstration, they would wear masks and threaten to beat us up if we said anything or tried to stop them.

So how do the police see the protestors? Just as protestors lump police officers into one group, many officers lump all protestors together. Here is how a reporter in the November 13, 2003, edition of south Florida's newspaper *Sun-Sentinel* paraphrased a Miami police spokesperson in an article titled, "Police describe some of the Miami free trade protestors as anarchists":

They have no leaders, so they often spend hours in meetings trying to reach consensus among each and every one of them. They like punk music and the color black. They hate Starbucks, [corporate] logos, and any symbols of "corporate greed." They're young idealists and older intellectuals; they're loosely organized yet highly mobilized. They're anarchists—best known for the mayhem and destruction left in their wake at Seattle's World Trade Organization meeting four years ago. Police see them as bored, rich white kids who only want to cause trouble.

PERCEPTIONS OF APPEARANCE

When we communicate, we employ more than just words. Statistics from Stanford University show that 7 percent of what we communicate comes from our words, 38 percent from our voice tone, and 55 percent from our body language. Included in body language are such things as the way we stand and walk, our posture, how we use our hands as we communicate, how we comb our hair, and how we dress.

We look for clues about others from their appearance, especially clothing. How one dresses provides a quick way to determine someone's sex, status, membership in particular groups, legitimacy, authority, and occupation. Clothing and physical appearance can be important in the initial development of social relationships. Psychologists tell us that physical appearance, including clothing, is most often how we form a first impression of someone. Some believe it has an even greater effect than a person's personality.

The uniform worn by police officers elicits stereotypes about the officers' status, authority, attitudes, and motivations. It instantly tells everyone that the person wearing it has powers of arrest, powers to use force, even deadly force, and the authority to establish order. The police uniform can have an extraordinary psychological and physical impact on some citizens. Depending on their

Instant Opinion
Research shows that we form an impression about people within three to seven seconds of seeing them. It further shows that when that impression is negative, it takes time and effort to change the opinion.

background, it can bring forth emotions ranging from respect to fear to anger to hatred.

As a military policeman in Saigon and as a street cop in Portland, I was attacked verbally and physically simply because I was in uniform. There were times when grown men wept as I approached them, including tough Green Beret soldiers on two separate occasions in Vietnam. There were people who ran from me when they had not broken the law. Others called me names as I walked or drove past them, and there were people who pointed their fingers at me and went "Bang!"

Many protestors dress in military fatigues (rather ironic since they detest the military and war), bandannas (sometimes over their faces), chains, boots, stocking caps, and gloves. Some have mops of longish hair or dreadlocks. Cops often call this "the protestor look" or "the protestor uniform," laughing that in their struggle to not conform, they assume a look that conforms to half the people at any protest in the country. Of course, not all protestors look like this, but many do. Since they make up a healthy percentage of those who require police attention, is it any surprise that officers perceive all people who dress this way as troublemakers?

Just as the protestors say, "The fascist police are here with their uniforms, badges and guns," many police officers say, "The agitators are here with their military clothing, signs, video cameras, and bandannas to keep from being identified while they rampage."

It just makes sense. Based on the experience of protestors, the people who pepper sprayed them, dragged them by their armpits to paddy wagons, and shot their legs with rubber bullets were not store clerks from Macy's. They were cops. Likewise, based on the experiences of the police, seldom has a nicely dressed young man thrown a trash can through a department store window.

The Power of a Uniform

There *is* power in the police uniform. During my years on the PD, I saw officers come into the precinct thousands of times wear-

"You like me? What's wrong with you?"

On occasion, citizens would walk up while I was in uniform and thank me for being out on the front lines for them and their family. But these episodes shed an interesting light on police perceptions of the public.

Statistics show that the majority of people like and respect the police and understand that the job is a dangerous, stressful, and thankless one. It's my opinion, however, that these people aren't vocal about how they feel, or at least not as vocal in the public forum as those who dislike the police.

Year after year, I heard the grumblings of those who perceived anything and everything the police did as wrong, brutal, incompetent, illegal, and a whitewash. Whether the negativity came from a drunk I was wrestling into the backseat of my police car, from a scathing editorial written by the editor of the largest newspaper in the city, from the 5 o'clock news, or from my own mother on a couple of occasions, I heard it virtually every day. I expected it. I became conditioned to it. It was part of doing business.

So how did I perceive those people who would go out of their way to walk up to me and say thanks for my good work and sacrifice?

My immediate perception was to wonder what they wanted. What were they hiding? Why were they trying to manipulate me? Why were they kissing up?

Sometimes, after talking with them for a while, my suspicions proved to be right: they were up to no good. More times than not, however, they passed my litmus test, which revealed that they were indeed being thankful to the police department.

It always bothered me that I had greater trust in those who made it absolutely clear that they detested the police. Those kind and grateful citizens who liked us and appreciated what we did first had to get past my negative perceptions of them before I could accept their words of respect and gratitude.

ing shorts, Hawaiian shirts, and sandals, or dirty overalls and boots from having just worked their land, or sweat pants and tank tops from their sessions at the gym, all of them exuding an aura of relaxed casualness. But as each one shed their civilian clothes in the locker room and began to slip on uniforms and pistol belts and swipe a brush over the tops of their shoes, there began a transformation. By the time they were fully dressed and had holstered their weapons, they stood a little taller, their shoulders seemed broader, their aura more businesslike, and their demeanor more authoritative. A similar effect occurs when an officer slips on the tools of riot control. The helmet and shield, gloves, pepper spray, and riot baton necessitates a different mind-set, focusing the officer's attention on the extreme discipline and, if necessary, combat to come.

The Power of the Exterior

When I was a young police officer in the 1970s, I occasionally worked undercover in various types of demonstration infiltrations, narcotics cases, and prostitution stings. Though the hippie era was mostly gone, for some the long hair, shaggy beard, boots, and military jacket look was hard to put to rest. Whenever I worked an undercover job, I would go without shaving for a few weeks, let my hair grow to my shoulders, and wear parts of my old army uniform, including my tattered Vietnam jungle boots.

Every time I worked these details, I felt a not-so-subtle change come over me. My police presence, attitude, and outlook disappeared almost immediately as I took on a laid-back, slovenly, even rebellious demeanor. I would talk and walk in the manner of a person who functioned on the streets with other people living on the fringe of society. I even looked at uniformed officers as not being as cool as me, and I hung out mostly with other undercover cops who looked and acted the same as I did.

I never worked undercover for more than a few weeks at a time, so I don't know if this outlook, this persona taken on for the purposes of the mission, would have eventually passed. I do know that with some of my police pals who spent many months and even years undercover, it became increasingly difficult to see their police persona, at least the one they displayed when in uniform. I was always glad to get out of these assignments and once again don the blue. I didn't like myself very much when I played these roles. I'm a straightlaced guy at heart, I guess.

There have been cases where undercover officers went in too deeply for too long and had trouble coming out of it psychologically. While there is much more to it than just the clothing one wears and the mannerisms one exhibits, I found these exterior elements to be powerful pieces of the puzzle.

Similarly, there *is* power in the protestor's uniform. One could argue that the typical activist look—army fatigue jacket, cargo pants, stocking cap, and heavy boots—provides some degree of audacity and boldness for people to act out. There is a subtle psychology that occurs when putting on military-type clothing, though for some it's not so subtle. After all, cargo pants and military jackets are action clothing. Even sunglasses can free an individual to be aggressive since they hide the eyes, the essence of the person. Facemasks and hoods that cover the entire head also embolden the protestor to act out as if he were invisible. If it's taken to the next level—donning padded clothing and motorcycle helmets to absorb the impact of riot batons, or gas masks to blunt the effect of tear

A Warrior's Uniform

A friend once took me to a martial arts seminar at a local college in San Francisco. As we began undressing in the locker room of the physical education department, a man who looked to be in his 70s shuffled into our row, nodded to us, and placed a bag on the bench. He was short, bent in the shoulders, and moved as one would expect a 70-year-old man to move. I assumed he was part of the janitorial staff, so I went back to talking to my friend and getting dressed.

A few minutes later, I glanced over at the old man, who was now slipping on white karate pants. It took a second for that to register in my mind, because I had expected him to change into janitor-type clothes. Then I saw his red belt lying on the bench next to his white karate jacket. In Japanese martial arts systems, a red belt denotes the rank of ninth- and tenth-degree black belt, a level that takes 40 or 50 years to acquire, and one that few people achieve legitimately. I would learn later that this man was Professor Duke Moore, a karate and jujitsu master who had been training since the 1930s and head of the organization hosting the seminar.

Equally amazing was that, as Professor Moore put on his uniform, the "old man" dissolved and a warrior leader emerged. He stood straighter, taller, and took on all the authority of General Patton. There were 200 participants attending the seminar that day, half of whom were experienced black belts. Even if Professor Moore had not been in front of the formation leading the training, his uniform and powerful sense of presence left no doubt that he was the commander in chief.

gas—then you *know* these people are arriving at an event pumped to do battle with the cops.

Mislabeling

These preconceived notions about the appearance of members in each group can lead to significant cases of mislabeling, of making assumptions about an individual without having all the facts. This is a function of the "impersonality" concept we touched on in Chapter 1 and will explore further in Chapter 3 (as the "out-group" phenomenon). The "enemy" is depersonalized, lumped together as a monolithic group rather than a collection of individuals. Thus, to someone who is antiauthority and who especially dislikes law enforcement, the police uniform labels the officer as a heavy-handed, ignorant Gestapo figure. He gets the label even though he may have just come from a call where he gave CPR to an unconscious baby and spends his off-duty hours working with troubled kids. Likewise, some police officers will automatically label the protestor wearing army fatigues, steel-toed boots, and hair in dreadlocks as an anarchist type who will likely destroy property as soon as the demonstration is in full swing. He gets the label though he is really a social worker for street people who appreciates and vocally supports the tough job the police do in the community. He just happens to dress funky.

VIOLENCE: NOT ALWAYS WHAT IT SEEMS

Another philosophical question that needs to be addressed in this chapter is this: Do our perceptions of things, events, and people allow us to experience the world as it truly is? By definition, perception is awareness through the senses and, as such, is often tainted by one's experience or lack of experience and the naiveté that can spawn. In the context of this book, we need to understand that people view violence through the prism of their life experiences, and it very much affects how they perceive the actions of protestors and police during a riot.

My year in Vietnam working as a military policeman was virtually one big bar brawl interrupted by the occasional rocket attack. It was 12 months of solid violence, where hand-trembling, jaw-quivering fear was a daily factor, one to which I grew accustomed. My fellow MPs and I would engage in suppressing a 20-minute brawl, complete with flying chairs, overturned tables, and pools of blood, and then brush ourselves off, sit down, and lunch on a bowl of noodles.

A year after I got home, I joined the Portland Police Bureau and, right out of the academy, they sent me to the roughest part of the city. My first night consisted of calls to two tavern brawls, a nasty car wreck into a river, and three violent family fights, one of which concluded with the shotgun slaying of an abusive stepfather by his angry stepson. While some rookies were shocked at just how violent and inhumane people could be, I was not, nor were the handful of other Vietnam vets working street patrol for the first time. Our experiences in a war zone had conditioned us, numbed us even, to what shocked and horrified others.

Most people live sedate, violence-free existences. Sure, they have seen some violence on cable news, albeit sanitized and brief, but most go about their lives oblivious to the ugliness and pure savagery of people who want to hurt other people. This reality was brought home to me when, early in my police career, I was on patrol with a civilian ride-along. She was a student in her mid-30s taking night classes at the university to finish her degree. She wanted to add a little color to a sociology paper she was writing by including her experience riding with a street cop.

At that time, I worked a busy beat populated by street thugs. Not only was it typical to investigate several bloody assaults during the week, I almost always got into at least one or two "beefs" (police parlance for resisting arrest situations) in the same five-day period. Some were minor scuffles, while others were knock-down, drag-out, roll-over-the-hood-of-the-car type of fights. When I had finally got the person under control, I'd handcuff him, stuff him into my car, drop him off at jail, and then speed off to the next call. Just routine, ma'am.

A couple hours into the shift in which the ride-along was with me, dispatch sent me to assist with a violent teenager in custody at a neighborhood recreation center.

"I don't know if I want him arrested," the center's manager said as he walked us to the office. "Maybe you can just talk to him. He's trying to pick fights in the gym, and I just want him off the premises. A couple of my people are holding onto him."

The kid sat radiating hostility, arms folded, angry eyes glaring at the far wall, ignoring me as I stepped into the small office. He wore a Metallica t-shirt and tattered jeans, his dirty-blond hair hanging to mid back. "What's going on today, son?" I asked as the two rec center employees released their grip on his arms.

"I ain't talking to you, asshole," he mumbled through clenched teeth as he stood and started moving toward the door. He deliberately banged shoulders with me as he passed.

"Hey, come here," I said, which only made him move even faster toward the door. I grabbed at his shoulder as he yanked it open, but he jerked away from me. I grabbed again, this time a handful of his stringy hair, and jerked him backwards about five stumbling steps until his legs banged against the chair. Still using his hair, I yanked him down onto the seat. "I need to find out what happened here before I know if you're free to go," I said calmly. He struggled to get up, but I held him tightly by his roots. "Do we have an understanding, son?"

He stopped struggling and I released my grip, though I kept my hand at the ready on the back of the chair. "Okay," he said after a long while. He eventually apologized to the center's manager and said something about having a bad day. We chatted for a few minutes, after which the manager said he would not press charges. We sent him on his way, and my ride-along and I left shortly after.

Although she had been bombarding me with questions about police work before the call, she now sat quietly, looking at her intertwined fingers. Ten minutes passed before she spoke again.

"Do you ever get used to it? The violence, I mean?"

"Violence?" I asked. "You mean like a shooting?"

"Like that fight. With the kid just now."

"I'm sorry. I guess I don't know what . . .You mean when I made the boy sit down? That was a fight to you?"

I was not trying to be macho. It was just that I had already filed the incident in the back of my mind as no big deal.

"I've just never been around violence like that. It's frightening. Horrible."

I started to tell her that that was nothing, not even close to being a fight. Now, that bar brawl two nights ago, *that* was a fight. But I didn't say it. If she thought my pulling the kid's hair to make him sit down was violence, there was no way she could comprehend the pool table thrown through the window, followed by the badly beaten bartender.

After talking with her for a while, I understood that her perception of how I stopped the kid from escaping had formed in a mind that lacked experience with violence or even had comprehension of it. My perception of that brief encounter was filtered through eyes and a mind that had a few years of police experience in a rough area of town and, before that, what seemed like 20 years in Vietnam condensed into 12 months. The difference in our perceptions was immense.

Did this woman think my actions were wrong? I don't remember her saying it overtly, but I do recall a little twist of the mouth and a sniff of disdain. I never saw what she wrote about the incident.

There are many people like this woman. While there is certainly nothing wrong with being naïve in a certain area, it's important to understand that it does affect perception.

Here is another example of how one's perception of an incident can be based on incomplete information. One warm summer afternoon, my partner and I were cruising a downtown Portland street watching the crowded lunchtime sidewalks. Two bicycle patrol officers suddenly streaked by, jumped off their bikes, and grabbed a 20-something woman by her arms. Two people nearby on the jammed sidewalk took off like startled deer and disappeared around the corner of a building. Not knowing what was going on, we pulled to the curb and got out.

"She just scored some heroin from those two guys," one of the bike officers called to us as he and his partner tried to control the screaming and kicking woman. "She's trying to swallow the packet. Grab her legs."

A crowd of shoppers and businesspeople gathered as I grabbed one thrashing leg and my partner, after taking a hard heel in the chin, grabbed the other. We held on as best we could as the two bike officers restrained her arms and tried to force her jaw open. They needed to retrieve the evidence to make the drug arrest.

"Stop it! Stop it right this instant!" The shrill commands were coming from an elderly woman dressed in expensive clothes and clutching shopping bags from Saks Fifth Avenue. "This is a disgrace!" she cried, slapping one of the bike officer's arms. "Four big men assaulting this poor woman. I'm going to call your chief about this."

The woman's outburst caught us all by surprise for a moment. The senior bike officer, known to be a smooth talker, recovered first.

"Ma'am," he said as he continued to hold the struggling woman's scab-covered arms. "I'm sorry this is upsetting you on this beautiful day. But you see, we just watched this woman make a dope deal and now she's trying to swallow the evidence. We don't want her to do that because if she does and the bag bursts in her stomach, she will likely die. I've arrested her before, and I know her to have AIDs. Maybe you can help by sticking *your* hand into her mouth and getting the heroin for us."

The elderly woman shook her head quickly as if to rid herself of her erroneous perception and accept reality. "Oh," she said.

"Well, thank you." She walked away quickly, as did all the others who had gathered to watch.

We retrieved the heroin and lodged the young woman in jail.

TAKE 2: PERCEPTIONS AND A PROTEST

A week after the police shot the man who attacked them on the sidewalk with a knife, local activists announced on their web site that they would hold a protest the following Friday at the Portland Police Memorial, a beautiful monument near the Willamette River that honors those officers who have given their lives in the line of duty. The protestors said they were going to unveil something to honor people shot by the police. I went to see what would unfold.

Nothing did. The protestors were there in their uniforms: fatigue pants and jackets, backpacks, skateboards, dreadlocks, and angry expressions. Actually, one of them didn't fit in. He was about 50 years old, hair trimmed short, wearing a nice shirt and khaki pants. He held a sign that read, "Justice."

The police were there, too, dressed in their regular uniforms. Some had attentive expressions, and others looked bored as they stood silently near the memorial watching the protestors. Once the police and protestors realized the event was not going to erupt, they began to talk to one another about the perceptions each had of the shooting. Though the conversation was cordial, I doubt it swayed either side.

There was one, lone protestor who acted out a little. He looked to be about 20, slender, wearing baggy shorts, t-shirt, and a blue bandanna covering his face. As the officers and other protestors chatted, he danced all about them to music only he could hear and scrawled slogans on the sidewalk in colored chalk. Though the young man was virtually under the officers' feet, they didn't react to his baiting. They hardly gave him a glance.

Coincidentally, a TV news crew was nearby doing a story on an unrelated event. When I asked the reporter if they were going to cover the protest, she glanced over at the protesters and shrugged with a look of disgust.

You have to wonder how onlookers—many of whom rolled their eyes and shook their heads as they strolled by on that warm evening—would have perceived this event had the protestors not been wearing their uniforms. How would things have been different had they all shown up wearing regular street clothes like the older man with the "Justice" sign? Would onlookers and the TV reporter have taken them more seriously and maybe moved in closer to hear what they had to say?

What if the police had overreacted by pushing the protestors away from the memorial site and pepper sprayed those who balked? Might many of the passersby been angered by such tactics and even sided with the protestors? I'm guessing yes. For sure, the TV crew would have been ecstatic as their cameras rolled.

But none of that happened because:

- The protestors likely perceived the professional demeanor of the officers as nonthreatening to them.
- The officers perceived the protestors as nonthreatening to them.
- Each side perceived the other as being open to dialog and took advantage of it by engaging in civil discussion.
- The one protestor who did try to agitate the police failed because officers perceived him as only wanting their attention, which they would not give him.
- The location was in an upscale part of Portland, where people came to enjoy the rolling lawns, riverscape, boats, and fine sidewalk dining. Since most people in the area supported the police, they perceived the appearance and actions of the protesters with disfavor.
- The TV crew had seen it all before and knew how protestors used them to get their message out. They perceived the small number of protestors, the antics of one antagonist,

and the professionalism displayed by the police as a non-newsworthy event.

This entire event was all about perceptions. While each group—protestors, police, passersby, and media people—likely perceived the others through a prism of their personal experiences and the way in which they understood those experiences, except for the one protestor dancing about, no one reinforced their stereotypes. In a perfect world, such events (we cannot say it was a nonevent since it did accomplish something by virtue of nothing happening) would occur more frequently than those that reinforce bad perceptions. Sadly, it's not a perfect world.

It's safe to say that the negative perceptions that many protestors have about the police and the negative perceptions that many police officers have about protestors are not going away anytime soon. They will remain as long as their perceptions of each other are reinforced with nearly every demonstration, certainly with every demonstration that turns riotous.

Sources

"Perhaps they'll sing after the revolution," by Josh Trevino, Spot-on, www.spot-on.com.

Chapter 3

Crowd Psychology

"I am the people—the mob—the crowd—the mass.
"Do you know that all the great work of the world is done through me?"

—Carl Sandburg,
I Am the People, The Mob

In *Rioting in America* (Indiana University Press, 1999), Paul A. Gilje recounts how in 1934, a radio announcement and newspaper stories reported that a black man would hang in the state of Florida. The mood was both celebratory and vengeful. Even the sentencing body proclaimed that, "All white folks are invited to the party." They did come, too, somewhere between 3,000 and 7,000 of them from 11 Southern states. All were white, and all were hungry for a lynching.

"First they cut off his penis," news reporters at the scene reported to the nation. "He was made to eat it. Then they cut off his testicles and made him eat them . . . Then they sliced his sides and stomach with knives and every now and then somebody would cut off a finger or toe."

The frenzied crowd burned him with red-hot irons and then hung him until he was nearly dead. The lynchers later dragged his body from a car to the front of his alleged victim's house so that she could come out and plunge a knife into his heart. Later, the lynched body hung in the courthouse square. People sold photographs of the man and displayed parts of his body.

The above is an extreme example of man's inhumanity to man, one that clearly reveals in an extraordinarily frightening way how a mob functioning under the illusion of unanimity can turn into a one-mind, destructive organism against someone they see as not of their kind. Additionally, it shows how a frenzied mob rationalized, in a collective and sick fashion, the morality of their vengeful actions. In this chapter, we examine these forces closer.

EARLY EXPOSURE TO THE POWER OF INFLUENCE

For the most part, I was a straightlaced teenager in the early 1960s. I followed the rules in high school, and if I misbehaved at all, it was when I ran in the hall or was tardy for class, heavy stuff like that. That was how my parents raised me. I would not have thought about doing anything improper—at least on my own volition.

One day in my senior year, word spread that there was going to be a book slamming protest during seventh-period study hall. All 100-plus students hated the teacher because he strictly enforced the "you have to study while in study hall" rule. To show our disdain for the mean man's unreasonableness, everyone slammed their heaviest book on the floor exactly at 2:30.

While this little act of civil disobedience was not on the level of looting appliance stores and overturning police cars, it was a big deal for me and, I'm guessing, for many other kids in my school. It was a perfectly coordinated act of rebellion, though the teacher just laughed and told us to get back to our studies.

Still, it had empowered us. A few weeks later, several hundred of us held a sit-down strike in the hallway just outside the dean's office in protest of some school issue that we perceived as being unfair.

Now, with two successful protests under my belt, I was practically an anarchist. Were dreadlocks, black clothing, and a face bandanna next?

No; those would be my only experiences as a protestor. In all future ones at which I would be present, and there would be many, I would represent law enforcement. Nonetheless, my limited experience as a protestor made me think about the power of influence. That is, how the power of several people—more than 100 in the first instance and hundreds in the second—could get me to do something that I would have never done by myself.

After high school, it would be five years before I was in another demonstration. This time it was a big one, in Saigon, Vietnam. There I saw masses of violent protestors move as one body, like schools of fish turning this way and that in perfect harmony, as if they shared one mind. I saw 20 people on a rooftop with rocks, bricks, and Molotov cocktails on the ledge before them. Some watched the rioting below while others looked left and right, as if waiting for a signal. I didn't see one given, but suddenly the rooftop mob acted as if they had all received an order telepathically. First, a single flaming Molotov cocktail arced high off the roof and exploded into a wall of fire on the street. An instant later, the air filled with rocks, bricks, sticks, and more firebombs.

Down on the streets and off to the left, a hundred people surged, destroying food carts, bicycles, scooters, trash cans, and street signs. To the right, a larger mob poured down the sidewalk, then out into the street, and then onto the sidewalk again. One person would launch a bottle or rock through the air and a moment later, 20 others would do the same, as if the first thrower's action had given them permission to proceed.

To my young soldier's eyes, this seemingly one-mind action was at once intriguing and frightening. It was a phenomenon that I would see occur in violent mob action repeatedly in the many riots

I worked as a cop. As will be discussed later, I saw it happen within the police ranks, too.

Crowd Defined
There are four types of crowds:

- Casual (e.g., vacationers on a beach in summer; people strolling through a county fair)
- Conventional (e.g., people gathered at an outdoor jazz festival; a group watching a movie)
- Expressive (e.g., people cheering at a sporting event; a group swaying at a rock concert)
- Acting (e.g., violent rioters, destructive mobs)

While this book mostly is concerned with an acting crowd, history shows that the first three types can turn violent quickly. We will look at many such cases throughout this book.

GROUPTHINK

Several interchangeable terms define how a disorderly crowd thinks, as if it were one organism. Such terms as "groupthink," "mobthink," "collective hysteria," "mob mentality," and "herd behavior" all reference to some degree the phenomenon of individuals in large groups thinking and acting as one. Those who use the term "herd psychology" often call such people "sheeple," a good name for those who momentarily lose their ability to think on their own and follow others mindlessly.

I like the term mobthink, because to my mind it best describes how people think after they have moved from being a casual, conventional, or expressive crowd to a disorderly and destructive acting crowd—a mob committing acts of violence. However, apparently I'm in the minority, because there doesn't appear to be much written on mobthink, at least by that terminology, though there is a great deal of material that uses the word groupthink. So let's use that term. Let's be sheeple and go along with the group, if you will.

Social psychologist Irving L. Janis (1918–1990), a research psychologist at Yale University and a professor emeritus at the University of California, Berkeley, coined the term groupthink, which describes certain systematic errors by groups when making collective decisions. Janis wrote in *Victims of Groupthink* that a crowd of people affected by its influence will ignore alternatives and take irrational actions that dehumanize other groups. Irving said that a group is especially vulnerable to groupthink when its members have similar backgrounds, when they are insulated from outside opinions, and when there are no clear rules for decision making.

Irving wrote of eight symptoms of groupthink:

1. Illusion of invulnerability
2. Unquestioned belief in their inherent morality
3. Collective rationalization of the group's decisions
4. Shared stereotypes of the "out-group," especially opponents
5. Self-censorship: members withhold criticism
6. Illusion of being unanimous
7. Direct pressure on dissenters to conform
8. Self-appointed "mindguards" who protect the group from negative information

When the above symptoms exist within a group, there is a strong likelihood for groupthink to occur. It's especially likely when the group is highly cohesive and feels a decision has to be made right away. When all members are in solid agreement, they are less inclined to look at alternative courses of action. Groupthink can lead to carelessness, unreasonable thinking, and irrational decision making.

Allow me to comment on each of Professor Janis's eight symptoms of groupthink based on what I have seen in violent demonstrations, as well as from what I have seen as a member of a large police agency. As you will see, many of these symptoms are interrelated.

Illusion of Invulnerability

Members of a group feel that their numbers and their beliefs make them indestructible to outside forces.

Among the Rioters

Now, I must admit that I've never asked a rioter, "When you and 200 of your closest friends surged into the baton-wielding, pepper-spraying police ranks, did you feel a sense of invulnerability?" However, it's easy to agree with Janis when, as a cop, you're on the receiving end of such a surge. You can see it in the faces of the rioters, hear it in their shouts, and feel it when they smash into you. You are convinced that they are convinced that they are invulnerable.

On one occasion, I was in a line with about 20 other riot cops standing side-by-side after we had just repelled yet another surge from a few hundred anti-President Bush protestors. They had just pushed into us for the third time and were now taunting us in preparation for another assault. One protestor, his face glowing with excitement, chest heaving, fists clenched, stepped in close to me and peered into my face mask. "You gonna hit me with your stick?" he asked with a big smirk. "Come on. Are you gonna hit me with your stick?"

Now, riot police are not supposed to respond to verbal taunts, but my lieutenant was busy at the far end of our formation dealing with other protestors who were shouting and threatening. No one could hear me except for this one person, whose face was just inches from mine.

"Yes," I said, looking hard into his eyes. "I *am* going to hit you." Then in my best, tight-lipped, Clint Eastwood voice, I added, "And you got to ask yourself: 'Can I handle the pain?'"

The protestor's smirk disappeared, his eyes widened, and he backed away from me, slowly at first, uncertain, frightened, and deflated. He then spun and disappeared quickly into the mob. I saw him briefly a few minutes later, cowering behind others, and then he was gone. In a span of 10 seconds, he went from feeling invulnerable to very, very vulnerable.

My psychology 101 take of our exchange is that, for the brief moment it took me to comment, the protestor no longer felt that he was an anonymous part of a mob but rather an individual standing face-to-face with another individual, who similarly no longer felt that he was part of a mass of blue. With just a quick exchange of words, his world changed to a situation of *mano-a-mano*, one guy vs. one guy, him vs. me. I had even underscored the personal aspects by telling him that *I*, an individual from the blue mass, was going to administer pain to *him*, an individual from the mob.

The change on his face, his expression, was one of enlightenment: *I'm no longer an anonymous member of the mob. I'm no longer invulnerable. Out of this blue mass, I had to select the one crazy cop, a guy with hard eyes, a whispery voice, who promises to hurt me* (and I want to believe that he also thought, *A guy who looks and talks a lot like Clint Eastwood*).

With his new revelation, he disappeared, never seen by me again.

Retired San Francisco Police Captain Charles Beene tells of an incident when a crowd of 300 ready-to-go-berserk basketball fans learned that they were, indeed, not invulnerable.

> I called out a highly trained and highly disciplined tactical crowd control squad consisting of one sergeant and seven officers. The officers went on line and used the "10-mile stare" to avoid a verbal clash with the protestors, but still one rioter got in an officer's face and screamed all the "muthaf . . . er" phrases.
>
> I ordered the crowd to disperse, but they refused. This

was exciting to them, 300 rioters vs. eight officers. I then commanded the squad to clear the street. As the eight stepped forward, one baton struck an elbow and shattered it. The sound was loud, and everyone for a block around heard it.

That was the end of one riot as the 300 retreated over cars, under them, and through hedges. They all heard the breaking of the bones in that guy's elbow and they wanted no part of that.

The illusion of invulnerability had been shattered right along with one rioter's elbow.

Among the Police

Can the police experience a sense of invulnerability? Of course. They are human, just like the protestors. Some regular uniformed officers feel it when they are wearing vests and helmets, and some riot officers feel it when they are wearing their full protective riot regalia. Some feel it when they are standing or moving side-by-side with their fellow officers, each protecting the officer to their left and right. Group unity. Group power. Group invulnerability.

Most veteran officers would agree that the feeling of invulnerability fades quickly, especially the first time a missile of some kind bounces off their helmets. Or the first time an officer gets separated from the others and is suddenly facing a horde of frenzied rioters. Or the first time the mob calls him out by name . . .

I specialized in white supremacy crimes when I worked in the Gang Enforcement Team of the Portland Police Bureau, spending most of my time among skinhead street gangs. As a media spokesperson on such crimes, skinheads knew my name and face, which meant I was the target of their rage.

At one riot, I was part of a line of officers wearing heavy jackets to protect us from thrown acid or urine, and helmets with face shields to protect our faces from flying missiles. As such, we were unidentifiable. We all looked the same.

Early in the event, we were facing about 80 people, 20 to 30 of which were skinheads taking advantage of the chaos to add some of their own. They began to chant . . . not just any chant, but this one: "We want Christensen! We want Christensen!"

Some of the other officers on the line thought it was funny to step back and leave me out there for a moment, but I was not as amused. I didn't volunteer to identify myself, and the moment quickly passed as events changed. However, for a few seconds upon hearing my name called, and then for a second or two when my prankster buddies took a step back, I knew what vulnerability in a crowd was all about.

Unquestioned Belief in Their Inherent Morality

This symptom of groupthink follows the thinking that if everyone feels the same way about something, it must therefore be right. Included in this is a sense of good guys vs. bad guys, with both sides thinking that they are, of course, the good guys.

Among the Rioters

Few groups are as intense in their sense of morality as are the pro- and anti-abortion protestors. Both sides come together through a common belief in religion, politics, philosophy, and motherhood. Both groups believe down to the marrow of their bones that what they hold to be true *is* the truth. The right truth. The moral truth. They protest for it, clash violently for it, and, in the case of antiabortion extremists, blow up clinics for it, shoot doctors for it, and then go to jail without an ounce of remorse or regret for what they did. After all—so they think—their correct beliefs and their correct decisions to act on them are in everyone's interests. This is a powerful and daunting belief system for the police, the courts, and those on the opposing side to deal with.

The phenomenon is not restricted to the abortion issue. Think of how a similar sense of righteousness has fueled the violent actions of Islamic fundamentalists, protestors against the World Trade Organization, and scores of other groups.

Among the Police

Most people who go into police work have a powerful, innate sense of right and wrong, and the first year or two of training instills that sense deeply into the marrow. The police believe that they must abide by their sworn oath to enforce the laws, maintain order for the good of all, and, in the case of mass disobedience, reestablish that order. As such, most officers feel morally obligated, even at risk of their own lives, to do what needs to be done to serve the people.

Collective Rationalization of a Group's Decisions

Members of a group will collectively justify their decisions and actions out of certainty that they are right, no matter what they hear to the contrary.

Among the Rioters

In the context of many riots, the mob believes that they are absolutely right no matter what others outside the group say or no matter what the evidence shows. Members continuously feed each other data that supports their belief and the rightness of their cause.

A group of protestors will march against, say, a perceived racist act by a city bureau while, at the same time, have a second agenda to prove that the police are brutal thugs. No matter what the city bureau says to show that the accusation of racism is incorrect and no matter how calm the police are, the group will not change their course of action or thinking.

I have stood leaning against a police car with a group of other officers a block away from a protest, talking about how we would rather be somewhere else. Still, just the fact that we were in view of the protesters would ignite them into shouting such things as, "What are you going to do, Gestapo? Beat us with your clubs and shoot us with your guns?" By the time they had worked their way over to taunt and call us names to our faces, they had fueled each other into a frenzy, to such a degree that they acted as if we *had* indeed just beaten them.

Among the Police

For the police, this one is closely tied with the previous symptom. The police believe their actions are right because they are acting on the side of the law, the foundation of their existence, and what mostly holds our society together.

Out-Group Stereotypes

To underscore differences, especially the negatives of the other group, each side creates demeaning labels for the other.

Among the Rioters and the Police

Members of a violent protest group look at the police and think, "racist," "fascist," "stupid," "puppet." Members of the police group look at the protestors and think, "hippy," "leftist," "anarchist," "stupid," "puppet." Notice the similarities.

This manifestation of us vs. them psychology can also play itself out within each group. Within most every group, there are people who aren't afraid to think for themselves. Let's call them mavericks. Among the protestors, there might be a maverick with a close relative who is a police officer. Within the police department, there might be an officer who was an activist in college and still supports certain causes today. These people will likely disagree with the stereotypes of the other side perpetuated by their peers. When this happens, others within their group might turn on them and make accusations that they are being supportive of the opposing side and therefore possessing some of that group's stereotypical traits.

"Maybe he's a narc," several protestors might say behind the back of one who has spoken in support of the police. "Narc" is a derivative of "undercover narcotics officer," meaning that the person might be a civilian informant for the police or an actual undercover officer. Labeling someone a narc can have serious consequences for the accused, ranging from distrust to ostracism to murder.

"You a granola eater, too?" a police officer says to his partner after the partner mentions that he agreed with the antiwar message of a protest. "Granola eater" is slang for an activist, vegetarian, or anyone who follows a so-called hippy lifestyle. Once word gets around about the accused officer's stance, others will look at him with distrust and disdain; some might even refuse to work with him.

Self-Censorship

When it appears that everyone in the group has a unanimous mind-set, it can be awkward, even dangerous, to voice a different opinion, as described above. Most members won't dissent for fear others will perceive them as a rebel, a person apart from the rest of the group. To remain in the group, it's best to keep differing opinions to one's self.

Among the Rioters

As a member of a rioting crowd, it would take an unusual level of fortitude to confront a group of your peers who were engaging in criminal activity with which you disagreed, such as busting store windows or assaulting passersby. Not only might you not prevent others from doing something that you know is wrong, you might become overwhelmed by the moment and join in. It's not uncommon for the police to arrest a vandal during a riotous protest and, when asked why he broke out a bank window, the suspect cannot answer because he doesn't know why. Some will admit that, though they knew it was wrong, they still went along with the crowd. They knew that if they had tried to prevent the other protestors from acting out, the others would have ostracized them and possibly thrown them through the window themselves. Captain Beene said that he arrested protestors on more than one occasion who told him, "I don't know why I smashed that window. I guess it just seemed like the thing to do at the time. I did what I normally would not do."

Among the Police

There were several times at demonstrations when a sergeant in charge of the arrest team of which I was a member would order us to wade into the crowd and nab a particular person, or to encircle a half-dozen protestors he had deemed were doing something wrong. I didn't always agree with his decision for any number of reasons, but I kept silent because to have verbally spoken out against the order would have caused a conflict at a volatile time. It would have disrupted the continuity of the team and would definitely have not been a good career move.

The Illusion of Unanimity

In order for self-censorship to work, each member must perceive that there is a consensus in the group. This collective sense of everyone being unanimous is often a false perception, but it has to work for the group to function well together.

Among the Rioters

Sgt. Bob Del Torre, San Francisco Police Department (ret.), says, "I have worked over 500 demonstrations in my 33-year police career, and I've arrested these types of violent protestors. However, I have seen very few people after they have been arrested who still want to fight for their cause. The majority become quiet and reserved. They turn into small, frightened kittens, where moments before they felt that they were hard-charging tigers in concrete jungle warfare. Many of them will admit later to the police that they didn't want to break the law, *but they felt that the others in their group believed that doing so was needed to make a statement.*" [Emphasis added.]

Among the Police

It's a little different in the quasi-military structure of a police agency. The leadership assumes and demands that there be unanimity among the troops. If there is dissent, leadership expects that the officer or officers will nonetheless keep their mouths shut and perform as ordered. Should an officer break from the unanimous group and, say, prevent another officer from arresting a protestor, he would be ostracized by the others, face severe disciplinary action from the police administration, and likely be "talked to" out in the parking lot by his immediate peers.

Direct Pressure on Dissenters

When an individual dares, bravely or foolishly, to think outside the group, other group members or its leaders will quickly apply pressure to that person to conform. The rule is simple: no dissenters. If the group cannot get the individual to conform, then the group works to discredit him and even to force him out.

Among the Rioters

It's not uncommon for a group of protestors to think that a dissenter in the group is a narc. I've spent a little time undercover in such groups, and never have I seen people who are more paranoid. Of course, the fact that I was in the group made their paranoia somewhat valid. Still, many of them felt that law enforcement, especially the FBI, secreted themselves into their ranks not only to gather intelligence information but also to instigate problems among the protestors and encourage trouble out in the street during protests. Some even believe that undercover officers are responsible for breaking windows and starting fires to discredit the protestors.

Among the Police

Group dynamics within the police ranks are considerably different because individual members must follow orders no matter what their personal convictions. If an officer is adamantly opposed to working a demonstration, say, in support of abortion rights, he has the option of talking to his immediate supervisor about his concerns and his desire not to be involved. Depending on the police agency, this action carries with it a risk of being ostracized or, at the least, getting a reputation of being outside of the group.

I worked for a while with a devoutly religious partner who had profound beliefs against homosexuality. Nonetheless, there were times when we had to work security for the annual gay parade, a five-mile march that drew thousands of gays, straight supporters, and angry people who didn't like them. The sergeant and lieutenant quickly snuffed any issues my partner voiced about the mission. "It's a direct order," they said. "You *will* do it."

On rare occasions, a new recruit with a strong religious conviction that he could not take a life even in self-defense would somehow slip through the complicated and sophisticated hiring process. In such extreme cases, pressure to change from other officers or direct orders from supervisors won't work. Instead, the agency would declare him a dangerous liability to himself, the citizens he swore to protect, and his co-workers who depend on him to save their bacon in a crisis. The only option is to terminate.

Self-Appointed Mindguards

These are individuals within the group who work to prevent others from receiving opposing views and information.

Among the Rioters

Whenever there is a police-involved shooting in my city, and before the public is given any details, local protest groups spring into action, writing negative comments on Internet blog sites, picketing city hall with "police brutality" and "police killer" signs, and bombarding city newspapers and all the alternative newspapers with angry, accusatory letters. This response is guaranteed when the shooting victim is any person of color or is mentally ill.

Information that surfaces in the following days demonstrating that the shooting was unavoidable and necessary to protect the lives of the officer and nearby citizens is ignored or dismissed by the groups as a conspiracy by the police, media, government, and even witnesses. Should an individual in the group comment about or seriously ponder evidence that justifies the shooting, he is quickly bombarded by members as to how such info is fabricated as part of a conspiracy by the all-powerful government. The goal of the group is to feed information to these individuals quickly in order to retain continuity and restore the illusion of unanimity.

Among the Police

In the police group, an individual officer with a dissenting opinion will find himself bombarded with information to the contrary from the others. It also happens in situations that don't involve a protest. For example, say an officer working the traffic division doesn't feel that drunk drivers should be incarcerated because he believes they suffer from a disease and should therefore be given medical treatment. Other officers will verbally assail him with data as well as war stories as to why this is not a good belief. The officer's immediate supervisor, usually a sergeant, will also talk with him in an attempt to maintain a sense of unanimity among the troops. The sergeant will likely not mention the dissenter to the division captain so as to maintain the boss's sense of unanimity among his people.

When an officer's dissenting opinion involves, say, an antiwar demonstration, in that he is in support of the protest, he will be fed data from his fellow officers as to the violent and criminal nature of the protestors.

IN-GROUP, OUT-GROUP

To be able to kill another human being in times of war, it's helpful to dehumanize the enemy. It's easier to pull the trigger when one views the opposing army as gooks, rag heads, imperial-ists, barbarians, blue-eyed devils, krauts, nips, and so on. Hearing this and saying it repeatedly underscores the enemy's differences, their less-than-human qualities, their evilness, their opposition to what is good and what is right, and the belief that they exist out-side your group, a group that does have human qualities, is good, and is right. Dehumanization is a device used by fighting men and women since the dawn of history for one basic reason: it works.

Now, I cannot speak for all protestors and all police officers, but I'll go out on a limb and say that while dehumanization is cer-tainly done in the civilian world, it occurs on a much smaller scale than it does among combat troops. I've talked with many police officers who have been forced to kill in self-defense of themselves or others, and never have any of them said they dehumanized their assailant before shooting him, or even spoke in such terms after the incident. I have never talked with rioters who have fired on civilians, police, or firefighters during riots, so I cannot say what was in their minds when they leveled the barrel of the gun and pulled the trigger. If I had to guess, I would say that these criminal snipers, in their rage, hate, utter callousness, or even infectious excitement, did indeed dehumanize their targets.

For the course of this discussion, "in-groups" and "out-groups" are more apropos terms than "dehumanizing" and are, in fact, the ones most often used in academia. The in-group is your group, one that consists of one or more people with similar charac-teristics, such as the same nationality, religion, politics, sex, or cause. The out-group consists of people who don't share any of these characteristics.

The in-group will often label the out-group negatively (inferi-or, stupid, lazy, aggressive, etc.), even when the out-group isn't doing anything that a neutral party would consider bad. As noted earlier, there were times when I was standing with several officers watching people exercise their constitutional right to protest. Suddenly, they would turn on us with taunts, insults, and antics in an attempt to bait us into confronting them. Then they would throw things at us. The irony was that as they hurled fruit, bottles, fire-crackers, and street barricades our way, they would shout that we were brutal fascists, that we abused the law, and that we enjoyed hurting people. But to them, they were the in-group and we were the out-group, so their behavior was justified.

From the perspective of some police officers and their in-group, all protestors (the out-group from the vantage point of the police) are anarchists out to disrupt peace and order. They are seen as counterculture types who need a cause to define themselves, to feel special, and to be heard. As such, these officers see them as aggressive, stupid, and hostile to law and order.

Some in-group members will view the out-group as the cause of all their problems. Many in the police view protestors not only as being responsible for disrupting peace, damaging city and pri-vate property, and draining tax money, but for causing them to lose their days off and work long, overtime hours. Many protestors view the police as guardians of whatever it is that they are against. This is illustrated perfectly with the abortion issue, where many in the pro-life group see the police as taking sides with the pro-choice group, while many on the pro-choice side see the police as siding with the pro-lifers. Similarly, environmental activists arrest-ed for blocking loggers from cutting trees see law-enforcement as being in partnership with those big corporations that want to destroy forests.

A common device for maintaining the integrity of a group, and to highlight all that the in-group is about, is to create a conflict with an out-group. Just about the time that an in-group loses inter-est in the out-group or, perhaps, thinks of the out-group's members as "not so bad," renewed conflict fans the embers of the differ-ences and once again everyone remembers why they don't like the out-group.

Just because individual members of an in-group share similari-ties does not mean that there is not conflict. But all differences

Scapegoating

A scapegoat is someone selected to bear the blame for something bad. Scapegoating occurs when a person or group is deemed responsible for one or more problems. Scapegoating is a powerful tool of propaganda and has been used by many groups to demonize others:

- In the middle of the last century, Nazis blamed Jews for Germany's economic and political problems.
- White supremacists today believe that minorities are the cause of rampant crime in America and are a financial drain on the economy.
- Some blacks blame the government for infusing drugs into their communities.
- Some people blame Hispanic immigrants for draining the resources of social services.
- Not too long ago, people accused Vietnamese immigrants of taking jobs from "real" Americans, though few wanted those jobs anyway.

within a group will evaporate in the face of a common enemy. Thus two cops who dislike each other will stand side-by-side and battle members of an out-group. Likewise, two protestors who don't get along will raise their fists in anger and rebellion at a common cause. The Chinese sage Mencius said eons ago, "Brothers who may quarrel within the walls of their home will bind themselves together to drive away intruders." The point of this axiom is that any threat from the out-group, real or imagined, strengthens the unity of the in-group, no matter what infighting is going on within that group.

Sources

Victims of Groupthink: A Psychological Study of Foreign Policy Decisions and Fiascoes, by Irving L. Janis, Houghton Mifflin, 1972.
"Groupthink," Wikipedia, en.wikipedia.org/wiki/Groupthink.
"What is groupthink?" Psychologists for Social Responsibility, www.psysr.org.

"In-groups and out-groups," by Heidi Burgess,
www.beyondintractability.org.

Chapter 4

The Power of Anonymity

"I believe I have never felt more excited, more powerful and more invincible than when I was marching in the middle of a crowd of 35,000 people. I think those feelings are connected with the loss of any sense of my identity, my gender, race, politics, and so on. In exchange, I became a part of a human tsunami."

—Anne

A mob has incredible power to influence, change, and empower the personalities of its members. Not only can it change a personality, at least momentarily, it can enable the individual to act in ways he would never consider when alone. This is such a powerful aspect of crowd dynamics that it requires a brief chapter of its own.

DEINDIVIDUATION

The transforming effect that a mob can have on individuals is termed by some psychologists as "deindividuation," which is defined as the loosening of a person's normal behavior constraints to the extent that they feel free to act on impulse, to act abnormally, even to act criminally. Deindividuation occurs when a person loses his individual identity and gains the social identity of the group or, in the case of this book, the mob. It requires two elements:

- anonymity
- diffused responsibility

The larger the mob, the greater the effects of anonymity and diffused responsibility.

The size and energy of a large group promotes a sense of anonymity among its individuals. When a large group has formed because of a passionate cause—abortion, war, race, politics—its zeal, its dynamic force, and its mass lead some of its members to lose their sense of individualism. *Some* is an important word here. Some people lose their individualism and act out, but others do not. Think of the last news clip you saw of a post-game riot by basketball fans. The camera's long shot likely revealed a throng of people milling about as a smaller group of people acted out.

The powerful emotions of members of a crowd fuel others around them so that they, too, are charged. Anne, my French friend who has participated in several mass demonstrations in her country, describes the feeling perfectly in the quote at the beginning of this chapter.

For some individuals caught up in the emotion and energy of the moment, their personal sense of what is right and wrong and their responsibility to those beliefs shifts from themselves to the crowd. They find themselves imitating what others are doing—shouting, cursing, running about, vandalizing—actions they would normally never do by themselves. Again, not everyone will act out in this manner, especially those people who are well-disciplined or who have strong convictions against doing so. Weaker individuals, however, are susceptible to conforming to the actions and emotions of others.

Hiding in a Crowd

Certain individuals act out criminally because the mass of the mob hides their actions, or so they believe. When I worked as part of an arrest team during violent demonstrations, each of us would watch the mob for individual criminal acts. When we saw a crime take place, there were times when we could not immediately go into the crowd to nab the culprit because there were too many people and too few of us. However, when the crowd thinned a little between the culprit and us, we moved in quickly to apprehend the person.

This always drew two responses. First, the culprit—who thought he had carried out his crime anonymously—was surprised when grabbed suddenly by three or four burly cops and rushed out of the crowd, his feet barely touching the pavement. But that was just half of his shock. The other was his sudden realization that he was indeed an individual and therefore responsible for his illegal acts.

The second response was from the crowd: it was always one of anger. They didn't see what the person had done, or if they had, they had already forgotten it. (Some crowd members knew why we were making the arrest, but they pretended shock and dismay to stir the emotions of those who didn't know.) When those who were in the dark as to what had happened saw police officers (the out-group) rush into their midst and nab one of their own (from their in-group) who was purportedly just standing there innocently, they exploded with rage.

We eventually stopped using this technique because it usually caused an escalation of violence from the mob, which meant more arrests and injuries on both sides. Until we stopped, however, I must admit that it was fun to see the amazement on the faces of criminals who thought they had acted with anonymity and impunity.

Certainty of Punishment

Law enforcement and social scientists talk about the effectiveness of knowing in advance that illegal conduct will have swift

Following the Lead of Others in the Police Ranks

Police officers, like members of a mob, tend to follow others in their group. One improper act by one officer can result in additional improper acts by others. I'm not talking about throwing bottles through windows as emotionally charged people do in a mob, but rather actions considered improper by the police department, such as acting alone, wading into the crowd without back-up, and breaking formation.

When one officer does it, another will most assuredly go along to back him up, even when the second officer disagrees with the first officer's actions. Then a third officer will come to the aid of the first two. A fourth will observe someone in the mob commit a crime and give pursuit, and someone will go to back him up. Soon, officers are running helter skelter and the police have lost their effectiveness as a combined force.

consequences from the authorities. This is usually referred to as "certainty of punishment," and those who believe that it works argue that it's a powerful deterrent. (There is another aspect to this—certainty of punishment vs. severity of punishment—that we will not get into since it's beyond the scope of this book.)

A law passed recently in my city that states that motorists must reduce their speed to 20 miles per hour in a school zone, and they must do so 24 hours a day. This means that if you're driving in a school zone at 3 AM, you had better slow to 20 or you're going to receive an expensive ticket. People are still complaining about the absurdity of this law, but they are complying because they know the police are enforcing it. Like all traffic laws, this one works great when drivers are sober, but not so great when a driver is under the influence of an intoxicant and believes in his pickled brain that fast is good and the possibility of apprehension is nonexistent.

With rioters, a conflict arises when they are under the influence, too—that is, under the influence of deindividuation when immersed in the frenzy of mass chaos. Under these extreme conditions, certainty of punishment becomes irrelevant, replaced by the joy of believing that their actions are anonymous. They lose their

When Anonymity Is an Illusion

"Rich" (not his real name) was an 18-year-old freshman at the University of Massachusetts who, among many others, found himself arrested during a riot that broke out when the Boston Red Sox lost to the New York Yankees. "I just wanted to have some fun," Rich said when asked why he chose to riot. "Alcohol was definitely a factor in causing me to get arrested. I was just being a complete idiot."

Rich and his roommate had been drinking in his dorm room when the game ended. Since there was a campus area nearby that had been the scene of previous post-game rowdiness, the two joined several other students and proceeded to the site, armed with eggs and toilet paper to throw.

"I was 40 feet within the crowd," he said, believing there was no way anyone would stop him or even see him. "But within three seconds of the egg leaving my hand, I got arrested by a cop who was in the crowd."

individualism and become part of the mob; in their minds, they are unidentifiable, unaccountable, and not responsible. They are convinced that it's impossible for them to be singled out and punished.

COMBATING DEINDIVIDUATION

So if certainty of punishment does not always mitigate the behavior of members of a rowdy crowd, what techniques can be used to direct people to exercise self-control?

One technique is to call a person by name to remind him of his individualism. This seemingly simple act has a powerful psychological effect. It breaks the spell of deindividuation, reminding them of their own identity and, subsequently, their responsibility and accountability for their actions. There were many times in a riot situation where I called out to people I knew; something like, "Hey, Sam! I see you there in that black trench coat. I'm going to be watching you all day. Better watch your step. I know where you live." Sometimes the person acted like the proverbial kid caught with his hand in the cookie jar: he would smile sheepishly and affect an air of innocence, then disappear into the crowd. Other times, his peers looked at him with suspicion, no doubt their paranoid minds wondering how the police—the enemy—knew his name. (The same technique works well to snap police officers back to attention if they begin to succumb to the emotion and intensity of a riot, e.g., "Adams, get back into the formation!" If the officer cannot regain his facilities, a wise leader will send him to the rear and out of the fray until he can get himself under control.)

Sometimes, simply a police presence can reduce the sense of anonymity among crowd members. The steady gaze of a police officer will nearly always put the brakes on thoughts of vandalism and assault by individuals who are merely caught up in the moment (as opposed to being one of the core of instigators and aggressors). There were many occasions in tense crowd situations where I would lock eyes with a likely culprit who I thought had window breaking on his mind. A rock or bottle would drop from his hands and he would turn quickly to lose himself in the crowd. This effect was not long lasting, though, as it was common to catch the same person in a crime later, after a renewed sense of deindividuation led him to believe again that his actions would go unnoticed.

Parents will no doubt recognize this behavior from experiences they have had with their young children. When you're not in your kids' sight, you're out of their minds. The same is true with some violent protestors. When they know the police are watching them, they drop any thought they had of throwing a brick—or at least postpone the thought until they can again lose themselves in the mass of people.

While a strong police presence is a deterrent to deindividuation and the criminal activity it can breed, there is a good argument that it *incites* rioters in some circumstances. The sight of police in riot gear can stir up the emotion and aggression of certain members of a crowd, who in turn whip up everyone else in a hurry. Field commanders need to be perceptive to this potential development and know when to pull officers to a place that is out of sight of the demonstrators but still close enough to respond when needed.

Similar to the gaze of an officer, we know that the unblinking eye of closed-circuit television cameras deter crime. When there is a planned demonstration, say at a city hall, the quick installation of cameras on streetlight poles and rooftops and a public announcement of such might go a long way toward minimizing the belief among some protestors that they can execute criminal acts anonymously. As well, knowing that there are cameras present and taping their every move will make most police officers think twice about using force greater than is necessary.

While the knowledge of the presence of cameras is a strong deterrent against misbehavior on all sides of a demonstration, there remains the issue of excitability. When the situation pushes certain individuals to an extreme level of arousal and their bodies throb with adrenaline, they are likely to act out wrongfully either because they forget about the cameras or because their emotions are so intense that they simply don't care. For the most part, though, cameras are a great deterrent, and we will likely see them used more and more in the future.

Sources

"Rioting: The New Campus Craze," author unknown, CNN.com
    www.cnn.com/2004/EDUCATION/02/26/life.rioting.reut,
    February 26, 2004.
"Keeping an eye—and a camera—on college students," by Jack
    Levin, *Boston Globe*, February 5, 2005.
"What Is Mob Psychology?"
    http://instruct1.cit.cornell.edu/courses/psych470/To_Be_Edited
    /Mob_Psych_MEP.doc.

Chapter 5

Sports Riots

Fan: from the word "fanatic." Fanatic comes from the Modern Latin *fanaticus,* meaning "insanely but divinely inspired."
—Online Etymology Dictionary

According to the Wikipedia online encyclopedia, "Sport consists of physical activity or skill carried out with a recreational purpose: for competition, for self-enjoyment, to attain excellence for the development of a skill, or some combination of these."

Let me add this to the definition. Sport, according to my caustic view, "occasionally includes extreme violence on the playing field, in the spectator stands, in the streets outside the stadium, and into the nearby city. Windows, doors, and street signs will be damaged, cars overturned and set ablaze, and people injured and killed. Riot police will be called in and, when it's over, the 'sport' will have cost the city hundreds of thousands of extra dollars in property damage, police overtime, and lawsuits."

I'm not making light of this. Sadly, this is the harsh reality of too many sporting events these days. I experienced it firsthand when responding to dozens of sports-related riots during my years with the Portland Police Bureau, and many, many other cops can confirm this view.

Officer Cage and Officer Langston are pseudonyms for two police officers who live and work in a major city in the south. They wish to remain anonymous due to the sensitivity of their work assignments. Officer Cage provided me with a lengthy description of their experience during a particularly ugly sports riot.

> My partner, Officer Langston, and I were dressed in plainclothes and had just gotten out of court, but we couldn't get to our car because the streets were blocked by a riot that had broken out in the middle of a large Super Bowl victory parade. There were literally thousands of people. It was hard to tell how many were actually involved, but from where we were, all we could see were black teenagers beating people up.

Mix together a massive number of adrenaline-charged sports fans lining and jamming the streets, the presence of the winning team waving from slow-moving convertibles, a dash of intoxicants, a pinch of racism, then toss in a few roaming street gangs, and you've got a volatile recipe cooking on hot. Cage, who is white, and Langston, who is black, didn't know what caused the mix to boil over, but what they did know was that they were suddenly part of the stew.

> We were about a block and a half from the epicenter of the riot, which had started at the McDonalds on Baker Street, but even where we were it was mass chaos. We could see that everyone was running from the area, or maybe they were coming at us; we didn't know.
> Langston and I began running toward the trouble to see what was going on, but we never made it all the way, because

there were just too many gang members beating up anyone
not black. There were fights everywhere. One of the black
teens was quoted on the news that night as saying, "This is us
getting some of ours back for being slaves back in the day."

Langston and I decided to "Alamo up" by putting
our backs to the wall of some building. To this day I
cannot remember what building it was, but I do remember it was brick.

The mind gets selective when under extreme stress; it remembers
critical things and forgets those it deems irrelevant right then. In the
heat of the moment, the officers' minds didn't care what building
they used for protection, as long as it was made of solid brick.

Verbal communication was difficult due to the yelling,
screaming, and general melee. Langston was right next to me,
and I had a hard time hearing him. We saw a Hispanic girl go
down after getting jumped by a couple of black teenagers; her
friends managed to pull her out of there. We saw uniformed
officers here and there, but there was no coordinated effort.
Mostly, if the cops saw something happening and there were
enough of them, they would move against it.

There have been incidents where uniformed officers in the
confusion of an event have shot plainclothes officers, and few
events are more confused and chaotic than a massive riot—in this
case, a post-Super Bowl parade gone bad: panicking crowds,
marauding gangbangers, and two plainclothes cops, one white and
one black, who, to both the mob and stressed uniformed officers,
were just two more bodies in the insane melee. Cage continues:

Several officers pointed their guns at us before we could
show them our neck badges. Seeing that a blue-on-blue misunderstanding was likely, and that everything was getting too

ugly, we decided to scram out of there. We had no destination in mind other than anywhere else but there.

We hadn't gone far before we came across some tourists, out-of-towners with little children. We latched onto them and began herding them through the massive riot. We were shoulder-blocking people for about three blocks until we found an area that was out of the eye of the storm. If you were in my way, you got KO'd unless you were elderly or a child. With the family safe, we took off to find our vehicle, and then we got the hell out of there.

I found out a long time ago that when I get massively stressed I start to laugh uncontrollably. I was laughing while at the same time I was so very scared. My laughing made Langston laugh, too, especially when I told my friend that I would haunt his black ass forever if he bailed on me in the middle of a race riot.

Martin Cooper recently retired after 30 years of service with the Lancashire Constabulary, a police force in the northwest of England. As a veteran officer, Martin is well experienced in large-

Types of Fan Violence

Sociology professor and author D.S. Eitzen defines three types of fan violence: exuberant celebration, rowdyism, and sports riots.

- Exuberant celebration generally involves fans celebrating their team's win by destroying goalposts, store windows, police cars, and other things.
- Rowdyism is similar to exuberant celebration, but with rowdyism it does not matter which team won: the fans act out using the sports event to vent their hostility and frustration if their team lost, or their joy and sense of empowerment if they won.
- Sports riots refer to violent acts triggered by something that happened on the field. Eitzen links this type of violence to more profound reasons, such as tension between the fans because of economic, ethnic, religious, or political reasons.

scale riots of all kinds. Here he tells about a sports riot that occurred in Blackpool, a small holiday town on the northwest coast of England, where he and several other officers were nearly killed policing a soccer match.

One of our duties at soccer matches was to patrol the perimeter line of the field, a necessary duty since fans could, and often did, invade the pitch [the playing field]. On more than one occasion I had to rush to the assistance of cornered officers. The problem was that due to the vast amount of crowd violence at soccer games in 1980s Britain, most grounds had huge wire fences around the perimeter to keep people from invading the pitch. This also separated officers on the playing side of the fence from officers working the crowd side. Thus, help tended to be quite a few seconds away when violence erupted inside the enclosure.

On one occasion, I had to scale a fence from the pitch side to help an officer on the spectator side who was trapped against the fencing by a raging crowd. All I could do was climb up and try to fend off the thugs with my baton as they kicked and punched the officer. Fortunately, fellow officers were able to force their way through the crowd to save him, but not before he had sustained a severe beating. I felt so angry at the faceless mob and so helpless because I couldn't get to my trapped colleague and pull him to safety.

I was rotated into that same enclosure later in the same game, one of several officers in there to prevent crowd violence. One of the teams scored and the crowd erupted, shouting and leaping into the air. It feels very intimidating to be near such a powerful and angry thing; it's like a powerful sea, surging and rolling.

The crowd welled and their weight shoved toward me and my fellow officers, slamming us against the corrugated fence. I was aware of a feeling of being crushed and I could see fists and feet coming at me, but I couldn't feel any of the blows hit. I felt as if I were on my own against them and I couldn't do anything to help myself. I grabbed on to a body that was jammed into me and used it as a shield as the mass continued to press me into the corrugated fence.

Time stood still. I couldn't hear anything. I felt apart from what was going on around me. I didn't feel fear. I don't think I had time to.

Some time after, probably only a few seconds, I was aware of officers striking out at the thugs with their batons as they drug me through the mob to safety. I don't think anyone was arrested for assaulting us, as there were so many of them. It was impossible to identify any faces. Besides, we were too occupied with survival to think of anything else. The following day I tried to account for cuts and bruises I had sustained. Although they stung a bit later, I didn't feel any of them when they were being inflicted. Adrenaline is a great anesthetic.

I will say that there is nothing more terrifying than a mass of angry young yobs charging at you, when all you have is a small baton to defend yourself. Although you're one of many officers on the scene, you still feel awfully alone.

A friend of mine, Lawrence Kane, a martial arts instructor and writer, has worked stadium security for more than 20 years. Here he tells of one riotous post-game incident that happened in Seattle.

It was the Apple Cup, an intrastate rivalry at Husky Stadium, where more than 78,000 fans watched an intense, hard-fought football game. The visiting team [Washington State Cougars] ultimately won. At the end of the game, their fans stormed the field, knocking over a fence in the process. Home team fans, upset not only by the loss but also by the intrusion, followed them onto the field to protect their turf.

Police and security actively tried, but were unable, to stem the flow of students because we were so vastly outnumbered. Several fights broke out amongst home and visiting fans, both in the stadium seating area and on the field. During the mayhem, the Cougar fans attempted to knock down the goalposts by getting enough students on top of them so that their weight would topple the structures. Dozens of kids climbed onto the uprights.

After the field was taken, the police responded by macing everyone on the goalposts and many in the crowd, using huge canisters of the spray. I couldn't get out of the way fast enough and got hit with enough overspray that my clothes were drenched with the stuff, yet it wasn't horribly effective (I didn't get any directly on my face, though). It was cold, wet, and slippery. And it smelled bad too.

They hosed one guy down for several seconds before he finally fell off the upright he was clinging to. I'm kind of surprised he wasn't hurt by the fall, but I suppose that's the upside to drinking excessively. The Cougar fans ultimately got one goalpost knocked over, nearly crushing a couple people beneath it who were either too intoxicated or too inattentive to get out of the way fast enough, and carried it down to the lake, throwing it in the water. One guy was grazed on the arm as the goalpost fell . . . couple inches more and he probably would have been hit in the head and been seriously injured or even killed.

Eventually the field was cleared and order was restored. The mace response, however, was embarrassing and ineffective. The next year the school replaced the uprights with new ones that could not be broken no matter how many people climbed up on them. We also developed new procedures to clear the field when these types of things happen, no longer relying on chemical sprays to do the job.

A BRIEF HISTORY OF SPORTS RIOTS

Sports fan violence is as old as sports. The first documented case occurred in 532 BC in Constantinople when rioting fans took over a large stadium. Roman soldiers responded, retook the stadium, and restored peace, but at a cost of 30,000 lives. A few hundred years later during gladiator fights in Pompeii, fan violence in the audience exceeded the violence in the arena, eventually escalating to such an extreme that the Roman Senate banned the fights for 10 years.

I could find little in the historical record about sports-related violence in the centuries that followed, but beginning around 1850, the number of incidents began to increase, some sparked by long-standing tensions, especially when it came to matters of race. For example, in the early 1900s, black boxer Jack Johnson soundly defeated white boxer James Jeffries, a win that enraged many people, resulting in increased racial tension, violence, and killings all around the United States.

Here are just a few of the more significant incidents that have occurred in recent years. As you will see here and throughout the rest of this chapter, they cut across the entire spectrum of spectator sports.

Soccer: European Cup Final, 1985

It's likely that the deadly 1985 riot at Heysel Stadium actually began the year before when the same English and Italian soccer teams met in Rome. All bets were on Italy to win that year, but the team from Liverpool, England, defeated them in a penalty shoot-out. The English press published multiple pages covering the winning team and dozens of pictures of ecstatic English fans dancing in the Trevi fountain. This no doubt enraged the roaming Italian scooter gangs that were already hunting down Liverpool supporters, attacking dozens of people, many of whom were families returning to hotels from the game. Someone slashed a 13-year-old boy's face so badly that it took 200 stitches to repair it.

Many hoteliers refused to let their English guests back into their establishments, either because they had won the match or because they were fearful of attacks on their premises. There was little protection from the police, since they, too, were routinely attacking and robbing English supporters in revenge for their team's defeat.

Prior to the 1985 match in Brussels, Belgium, that paired the rival teams once again, there had been several incidents of fan violence throughout the city. Unfortunately, the police didn't arrest the troublemakers but rather hurried them into the stadium. Although there were ill feelings between the opposing fans because of the violence that had occurred in Rome the year before,

Hooliganism and Yobs

No one knows for certain where the word "hooliganism" originated, though it appears in a London police report written in 1898. Here are some current beliefs as to its origin:

- Hooliganism derived from a man named Patrick Hooligan, an Irish hoodlum from London.
- It came from a street gang in Islington in northern London named Hooley.
- "Hooley" is an Irish word meaning a wild, spirited party.

Today, many people think of hooliganism—commonly defined as unruly and destructive behavior—as what happens when fans riot at international soccer games. While that is still valid, the term has expanded to include riotous behavior at other sporting events, like rugby and cricket, and in general, mob behavior among street gangs.

"Yob" is a popular term in England for a form of rude, obnoxious, and sometimes violent behavior carried out mostly, though not entirely, by young people. A yob is virtually any young person who displays a disregard for proper behavior and disrespect for others. Typically, rowdy groups of teenagers and people in their early 20s spill out of pubs after a bout of hard drinking and then rampage through the streets, pushing each other and anyone else in their drunken path. Yobs and yob culture include hard-core pub drinkers, soccer hooligans, and teens who loiter about on street corners.

there was very little segregation. This would prove to be a fatal mistake, because once the violence broke out, the authorities were unable to determine what groups of fans were sympathetic to what team, and who and where the agitators were. This allowed the troublemakers to gather freely to plan their attacks.

Violence erupted even before the game began. Some versions of that day say the Italians attacked the English fans first, while others sources say it was the other way around. Scuffles turned to all-out fighting in the stands and on the grounds, and there was a report of someone firing a gun into the crowd (it turned out to be a starter pistol). At one point, the Liverpool fans charged the Italians, trapping them on three sides. The Italians tried to retreat but instead piled on top of each other. Panic set in when Liverpool fans continued to charge forward, crushing the Italians. And that's when things turned especially deadly.

Heysel Stadium was around 60 years old in May 1985. Authorities considered the stadium, especially in the aftermath of the tragedy, to have been the worst possible venue for the soccer rematch. Literally falling apart in places, years earlier it was condemned for not meeting modern requirements for structure integrity and safety, and it was in no way fit to hold the 40,000 volatile football fans that would fill it that fateful day.

In the surge of fighting fans, an old crumbling wall collapsed, trapping people against the jagged ruins. Unable to move or resist the human wave, helpless people fell screaming and pleading as the onslaught of panicking fans continued to advance and trample them. It was here that most of the 39 deaths would occur.

Police and Belgian troops restored enough order for the teams to begin playing. Yes—they went ahead and played. While neither team wanted to, it was felt that if authorities forced people in the stadium to leave at such a volatile time, there would be chaos and carnage in the streets. So the teams played on, as authorities tended to the horror in the stands.

The Italian team won, 1 to 0.

Boxing: Bowe vs. Golota Title Fight, 1996

In the mid-1990s, Riddick Bowe held the title of Heavyweight Champion of the World, which he won by beating Evander Holyfield in an incredible fight of heart and determination in 1992. Later in the decade, he faced off with Andrew Golota, an up-and-coming hard-hitter who was establishing a growing list of knocked-out opponents. However, Golota was also building a reputation for throwing low blows as well as head butts, forearm smashes, and hits after the bell. The two heavyweight champions didn't like each other even a little bit, and they brought their ill feelings into the ring. All this made for a preheated Madison Square Garden, filled to the rafters with opposing camps of fight fans.

Bowe stepped into the ring out of shape, throwing nothing more than lackluster punches. Golota started right off with heavy blows that rocked the champ, but then, for some unknown reason, the challenger began landing low blows. He received one warning; then he had a point deducted. At the end of the fifth round, a frustrated and angry Bowe angrily pushed Golota, thickening the tension in the ring and out in the crowd. In the sixth round, Golota drove another hard punch below the belt. Now the tension was palpable. Then came the seventh round.

Although Golota was far ahead on the judges' scorecards, he punched Bowe in the groin. Then again. And again after that. Now, one can always say that a single hit to the groin was an accident—but three accidents in rapid succession? The champ crumpled to the mat.

Shouting with rage, Bowe's manager and a member of his corner charged Golota's corner. Golota swung at the team member, who clearly was not intimidated and smashed Golota in the head with a walkie-talkie. Fights broke out in the ring in this corner, at that corner, in the center of the ring, and out on the floor, as fans, hundreds of them from both sides, slammed into each other with flailing fists. Chairs flew through the air. Some hard-hearted fan tipped a wheelchair, spilling the crippled occupant onto the floor.

Golota's manager staggered with sudden chest pains and had to be whisked away to the hospital.

An outnumbered Madison Square Garden security made a hurried call to the New York City Police Department for assistance. Police subsequently evacuated the giant arena and arrested 17 rioters. Bowes' people carried the injured fighter to the locker room. Officials awarded the match to him by disqualification.

It would be the last professional boxing event at the venue for years.

Basketball: NBA Championships, 2000

More than 10,000 fans gathered outside the Staples Center in Los Angeles to watch the Lakers win the 2000 NBA Championship over the Indiana Pacers on a giant outdoor screen. The viewing went peacefully, but minutes after the game ended, fans outside went on a rampage, throwing rocks and bottles at the police, setting bonfires, breaking shop windows, and vandalizing news vans, limousines, and police cars.

The 20,000 fans inside the arena, as well as the basketball teams, had to stay put for the two hours it took the fire department to extinguish the blazes and for the police, mounted on horseback and on motorcycles, to regain order. There were numerous injuries, some from fire, and at least a dozen people were arrested.

Upon seeing the live news story on television, one local man quickly grabbed his video camera and ran to where the riot was unfolding. He noted that the crowd was mostly Hispanic and about 80 percent male. He filmed people setting fires and looting businesses, and he captured the aftermath of vandalism, to include a fire-engulfed police car.

Oddly, the man didn't see anything terribly wrong with the riot, including the damage that some estimated at $750,000. He was, however, angry at local talk shows in Los Angeles that characterized the rioters, vandals, and looters as criminals, barbarians, savages, and gangsters. He argued that these were overstatements and that the participants were merely Hispanic youths. In one bit of tortured rationalization, he stated:

> OK, several people vandalized a police vehicle and set fires, but there were no gang members involved. You may even work with and know some of these people, and they are not savages or criminal deviants. It was a celebration that went out of control. To be surprised that this riot took place and that the destruction occurred would suggest to me that you are flat out naive. I was not surprised at what took place because this was the first time in 12 years that the Lakers won a championship.

Clearly, this man was not an owner of one of the looted businesses or anyone else financially affected or physically injured. He was simply a person who thought the riotous behavior was perfectly normal and acceptable given the Lakers' victory that day.

Baseball: American League Championship, 2004

After the Red Sox defeated the Yankees in Game 7 of the American League Championship Series, crowds estimated at between 60,000 and 80,000 streamed from the stadium and gathered around Fenway Park and Kenmore Square. Celebrants began overturning cars, setting them on fire, and vandalizing a number of businesses.

Police responded with 1,000 officers in full riot gear, K-9 units, batons, and rubber bullets. They made eight arrests, and 16 people received injuries, including a police officer. A stray rubber bullet struck a 21-year-old female university student in the eye during the melee; she would subsequently die from the injury.

VIOLENT SPORTS = VIOLENT FANS

While violent sports don't always mean there will be violent fans in the crowd, it's safe to say that the odds for crowd violence is greater at football, boxing, basketball, and soccer events—i.e., sports in which there is body contact—than at gymnastics, badminton, tennis, and Ping-Pong competitions. To this add a dash of national or regional rivalry; a young, adrenaline-charged fan base; pre-event hype; blaring, get-'em-psyched-up music; lots of beer and all-day drinking; and you have a recipe for potential violence.

Want it spicier? Add some incompetent or corrupt refereeing. Consider a riot that broke out at a soccer match in Xian, a city in northern China, in the spring of 2002. When a referee awarded a late penalty to the visiting team, Xian fans went berserk. When the ref awarded the penalty point, the throng began to chant, "Black whistle! Black whistle!" which apparently means something negative about the referee's obvious favoritism. They shouted this with such fevered intensity that it "shook the heavens and the earth," as noted by a reporter in *Xinhua Sports Express*. Such powerful descriptions are unusual in the government-controlled media, which commonly downplays social unrest. The mob threw bottles, lighters, and anything else they could find. When they ran out of stuff to hurl, they began setting fires to the stadium seats. They ended up torching a police van, overturning four other police cars, and slugging it out in the stands and streets.

Are Violent Sports a Catharsis for Fans?

People believed for a long time that violent sports were an outlet for fans, a way for them to purge all their inner rage and stress vicariously through the players. However, all you have to do is attend one of these sporting events to wonder where those beliefs came from.

When we were teenagers, a friend and I would go every week to "Friday nite wreslin'." It didn't take more than a few times to realize that the real entertainment was in the audience, an emotionally charged crowd that fluctuated between going berserk and stark-raving mad. The wrestler-actors added to the chaos by masterfully manipulating the throng into a frenzy that included chairs and garbage

Scoring Impact

In those team sports that involve high scores, such as basketball and Australian football, an official's decision to award a point is not always as crucial as is a single point in low-scoring games, such as soccer. A bad decision or a prejudicial one by a referee in soccer is more likely to spark a violent outburst from the fans than it would in a high-scoring game. There are exceptions to this, of course.

hurled into the ring as ecstatic fans bordered on cardiac arrest.

Although the wrestlers stirred the emotional pot, they were often victims of their own doing. It was quite common for the fans to punch the wrestlers, kick them, burn them with cigarettes, and even knife them as they made the dangerous trek from ring to locker room. Catharsis? I didn't see no stinkin' catharsis. Those fans came to the show with the deliberate intention of being part of the melee.

I recall one night when three or four wrestling fans were exchanging blows in the fifth row. The wrestlers in the ring, who were engaged in a well-hyped grudge match, stopped, leaned on the ropes next to each other, and watched and discussed the mongrel-like fighting taking place on the floor below them. Even they found the violence in the crowd more entertaining than the pretend mayhem in the ring.

A friend of mine, a hard-core sports enthusiast, recently attended a mixed martial arts event in town. This is a *mano-a-mano* sport, in which two men fight one another using full-contact martial art blows. It's a brutal sport that more and more cities and states are banning. My friend said there were at least four fights in the crowd that he could see from where he sat. He laughed when telling me about it, shaking his head in amazement. "The crowd really drew from the gene pool's bottom feeders." That part is arguable, but what can't be argued is that the violence in the ring, rather than serving as a catharsis for fan violence, instead was the potent catalyst for it.

The Study That Caused the Confusion

UCLA psychologist Seymour Feshbach gained fame in the 1960s after he released his findings that showed that watching violence is a catharsis. For example, two of his studies found that spectators' feelings of aggression become purged by doing nothing more than sprawling on the sofa and viewing others going head-to-head. His work on the effect of watching boxing showed that angered spectators displayed less aggressiveness in a word test administered after the match.

Although Feshbach's study is the only one in the last 50 years to show a positive effect from watching boxing matches, his findings have nonetheless taken on a sort of urban legend that has caused lots of confusion in the years since. Feshbach's studies are now considered quite dated, since many later ones were better administered and showed different findings. According to Dr. Thomas E. Radecki, a psychiatrist and lawyer, 30 studies since Feshbach's work have linked viewing of boxing and other types of sport fighting with increases in anger, physical violence, and even murder.

I certainly agree about boxing matches. In fact, it's been my experience attending live and closed-circuit boxing matches that fans become especially aggressive at the conclusion of a title match. Shouting, pushing, and throwing trash in the ring are common responses at the end of a big fight, especially if it was a close one. So dangerous is the environment that boxers often leave the ring under tight security. There is no better way to describe the atmosphere at some boxing matches than to use the cliché "the air is charged with electricity." Stir in the elements of a closely matched battle between two popular fighters, both of whom have loyal supporters in the crowd, and you have the recipe for violence on both sides of the ropes. There is not an ounce of catharsis going on. (A good example is what happened at Madison Square Garden in 1996 during the Bowe-Golota title fight, described above.)

Research conducted at Murray State University in Kentucky by Dr. Daniel Wann has shown that sports fans, as a group, are no more aggressive than others groups in society, including people who don't follow sports. However, Wann and others who have done similar research say that ardent, impassioned, hard-core fans can become aggressive and violent when their team appears to be losing. Dr. Wann theorizes that fans see a sports team as an extension of themselves, so that when "their" team begins to lose the game they feel personally threatened. "These highly identified people are more likely to act in an aggressive fashion when the team suffers," the doctor says. No catharsis here, either.

Nor is there catharsis at play when fans of *winning* teams turn violent. This phenomenon occurs more and more every year in major cities across the country as fans from the winning side go about breaking things in celebration. I first witnessed it when the Portland Trail Blazers won the NBA championship in 1977. So

Are there more battered women on Super Bowl Sunday?

Every year there are "experts" on news programs proclaiming that there are more cases of battered women in our nation's hospital emergency rooms on Super Bowl Sunday than any other day of the year. Many advocates of battered women quote from a study done in the early 1990s that allegedly found the increase to be as much as 40 percent.

However, when a reporter contacted Janet Katz, a professor of sociology and criminal justice at Old Dominion University and one of the authors of the study, she said that that was not what they found at all. When they looked at win days alone, they found that the number of women admitted for gunshot wounds, stabbings, assaults, falls, lacerations, and wounds from being hit by objects was slightly higher than average. But not 40 percent.

"These are interesting but very tentative findings," Katz said, "suggesting what violence there is from males after football may spring not from a feeling of defensive insecurity, which you'd associate with a loss, but from the sense of empowerment following a win. We found that significant. But it certainly doesn't support what those women are saying."

The reporter's follow-up story of his interview with Professor Katz and a few unscientific polls with domestic violence counselors in several cities prompted retractions and corrections by the media. Those didn't get the same big headlines as the original stories received.

ecstatic were Portland fans that they rioted through the streets, setting fires and overturning police cars.

How can happiness mutate to destruction? Was it not enough of an emotional rush that our team won the biggest championship in basketball? Didn't that final winning hoop release all the tension that had built throughout the game? Apparently not. People still needed to destroy cars and set things ablaze.

In the same vein, consider European soccer matches, where nationalism runs high and fan violence is as common as missed field goals. Powerful patriotic emotions quickly turn to violence as rejoicing fans from the winning side/country—their minds and bodies overdosing on gushing hormones, testosterone, and a sense of invulnerability—clash with the angry and resentful fans of the losing team/country. There is no time for catharsis when you're kicking someone's head in.

WHY FANS ACT OUT

Given the findings of these recent studies, it's not surprising that riots happen before, during, and after sporting events. What should be surprising is that they do not happen more often. Briefly, here are a few of the reasons why fans act out verbally and physically during sporting events:

- Some become so psychologically attached to a team that they believe they actually are part of it. "We won tonight," they say. Or "We were having a bad game, but we will have it back together by the next game." To them, "we" means the team players and themselves. So when a rival team or specific rival players upset them in some fashion, they take it personally and strike out.
- Some fans strive to gain control over the players and the outcome of the game. They try to anger players by pushing them as far as they can.

- Some fans are simply jerks and, though they are interested in the outcome of the game, they are more interested in harassing players with insults and thrown missiles.
- A male fan might act out to impress his buddies, or because his girlfriend has indicated that she thinks a particular player is attractive.
- Alcohol and drugs always play a significant role in judgment. When excessive intoxicants combine with crudeness, cowardice, and stupidity, it makes for an explosive combination.

Let's look at some of the contributing factors to sports fan violence in more depth.

Lack of Basic Self-Control

A high school basketball or football game draws several hundred fans, in some cases a few thousand. Professional teams draw tens of thousands. Most in attendance behave themselves even when consuming alcohol. Although they could easily swoop down from the stands and overwhelm the players, such occurrences are rare, at least in the United States. Thankfully, most people have their inner controls turned on.

Those few who don't have their inner controls activated or don't have self-control to begin with are those who make the event miserable for everyone else in the audience. Italian soccer commentator Beppe Severgnini once said:

> Soccer is our popular romance, made of dreams and feats, defeats and breathtaking joy. Certainly, soccer is also made up of rivalries . . . But I like to joke about these things in a bar. I've never thought of hitting someone. Am I a mediocre fan? I don't think so, [because] 999 out of 1,000 are just like me.

M.D. Smith, author of *Violence and Sport* (Butterworths, 1983), wrote that there are several theories on the causes of sports violence on the playing field:

- Biology—This theory suggests that humans are inherently violent and that sports offer a relatively safe and controlled way to discharge aggression.
- Psychology—Frustration leads to violence when one's efforts to reach a goal are blocked. In sports, frustration stems most often from the actions of officials, opponents, and others.
- Social learning—This is currently considered the most persuasive explanation. Through learning, violence in sports becomes an accepted method of playing the game. Violence, or fighting, might be officially condemned and penalized, but it is unofficially praised by coaches, teammates, fans, and the media. The official penalties may be insufficient to deter behavior.

Although Smith wrote about violence among players and participants, allow me to comment briefly on each as I see them relating to self-control problems in the bleachers.

Biology

A debate on whether humans are inherently violent could go on forever and no doubt lead to fistfights. However, today there are few debates about whether sports are a safe and controlled way for fans to discharge innate aggression. Earlier in the chapter, we saw that UCLA psychologist Seymour Feshbach's 1960 findings that viewing violent sports is a catharsis has since been disproved by numerous and more recent studies. We know that a hard-hitting football game isn't much of a catharsis for fans of either the losing or winning side—as brawling spectators, broken store windows, burning cars, and responding riot police can attest.

Player/Fan Violence

Violence between sports competitors—whether the game is football, basketball, or baseball—is nothing new, nor is violence between players and fans. However, the latter has never received as much attention as it did in November of 2004 when during an NBA game between the Detroit Pistons and the Indiana Pacers, a player named Ron Artest charged into the stands and punched out a fan, igniting what many observers say was the worst brawl in the history of United States sports.

It all began when Artest was deliberately pushed by a rival player. Though some of his Pacer teammates got into a shoving match with a few of the Pistons, Artest backed off to take himself out of the fray. He had no sooner sat down on the scorer's table to watch the fight play itself out when a fan doused him with a drink. The situation exploded and the rest is history. Artest punched the fan who doused him and then punched another fan who came onto the court. Some of Artest's teammates leaped into the battle that would continue for three long minutes, a long time to punch, push, chase, and throw things. When the Pacers left the court, irate fans threw beer, popcorn, and even a folding chair at them.

Film footage of the incident played repeatedly on television in the weeks that followed. To many, Ron Artest was a street hooligan symbolizing all that is wrong not only with the NBA but possibly all of professional sports. To be fair, Artest was just one part of the incident—management suspended other teammates with him, and police charged players and fans criminally—but his name remains synonymous with the riot, in part because of his bad reputation as a volatile personality.

While the Artest incident shocked most sports fans, players, referees, and sports commentators, some sick people love such violence. Certainly, some young people are going to see it as a high-five moment and feel that it gives them permission to model the same behavior. In fact, there have been similar events since, perhaps copycat events, at the high school level.

"Fan influence on players and player influence on fans suggest that players are not significantly influenced by fan behavior, but fans are influenced by the behavior of players," said Lynn Jamieson, professor and chair of the Department of Recreation and Park Administration in Indiana University Bloomington's School of Health, Physical Education and Recreation. She said that the riotous fight at the Pacers-Pistons game raises the issue of competitors crossing through the imaginary barrier between them and the fans. She said that while the breach has been going on for a while whenever players approach fans to encourage them to cheer and heap praise on them, this is the first time (in her view) that there has been such an intensely violent player-to-fan confrontation. She went on to suggest that sports tend to reflect society: "We have a violent society where people use violence to solve problems."

So if some players deem it okay to dive into the spectators and whale away at those who catcall or throw soda, and some fans think it's permissible to assault players with drinks, food, and chairs, one must wonder what will happen next. How about a fan shooting at a player? If fans can sneak a bottle of hard liquor into the stands, how hard is it to sneak in a 9mm semiautomatic? That same rage that can stir a fan— one living only in the now—to throw pop, a glass bottle, and a metal chair, just might stir him to pull a trigger.

Psychology

Anyone who has played a sport knows of the frustration of try-ing to win, of being so close, only to have the other side prevail at the last second. It's certainly maddening for the losing players, but it's also difficult for diehard fans who identify with their team, who in a weird way believe that they are right there on the field or in the ring participating. Though they might think abstractly that they are in the play, the reality is that they are not actually partici-pating, which is an underlying cause of their frustration, anger, and need to strike out.

Players on the winning side feel the exhilaration of making that winning basket at the buzzer or landing that knockout punch that made it through a small window of opportunity. Their scream-ing fans feel that emotion, too. Additionally, the fans are convinced that it was their cheers, their screams, and their very presence at the event that made the winning difference. This empowers them with victory, charges them with adrenaline, and inflicts them with a powerful need to set something ablaze.

Social Learning

This phenomenon fuels the pattern of player and fan violence.

Many adults see it happening on a regular basis, which they feel allows them to act out similarly. Then when the police nab them, the fan might cry, "Hey cop, why are you arresting me? You didn't arrest those guys last week when they were shoving people around in the stands." It's similar to when motorists ask, "Why are you stopping me? Everyone else is speeding on this street, too."

The Kids are Watching

If some adults are good social learners and easily swayed to mimic the behavior of others, how easy is it for children to do the same? The sad truth is that it's extremely easy. Some sports psychologists and psychiatrists worry that the media's habit of highlighting group brawls on the basketball court, brutal one-on-one fights during hockey games, and chaotic waves of rioters engaged in a post-game mayhem influence the young and ever more desensitized adult viewers to mimic that behavior.

Allow me to add two more theories based on what I've seen over the years. The first is tradition. "Hey, we had so much fun tearing up things after the last game, let's do it again." The other is the power of wanting to impress one's friends. "Did you guys see me throw a bottle at that cop? It was so cool."

Tradition

An out-of-town visitor thumbed through a dozen photographs taken at a riot that erupted after a game at the local university. The school's team had won and the fans had taken their destructive jubilation to the street. The man shook his head with disgust as he examined the shots. "These pictures could have been taken after last week's game in my town," he said.

Has post-game bedlam and rioting at some campuses and professional sporting events become a tradition? In some cases, yes. Whether they were actually there or not, fans well remember the excitement of past disturbances and seemingly feel the need to recreate the drama year after year. Along with the memory of past riotous moments, add a copious amount of alcohol, a powerful desire to engage in a momentous event (and possibly appear on the 5 o'clock news), and intense team and fan rivalry, and the tradition continues. And it's not a stretch to find a correlation between big sports riots of the past and what is happening today at small and large colleges as well as at Saturday peewee soccer matches.

Impressing One's Peers

It's been my experience that mob members, especially young men, want to impress their peers. Just as criminal gang members rarely act out without their buddies next to them to offer support, encouragement, and an audience, you would be hard-pressed to find one lone rioter breaking windows or setting trash can fires. An individual rioter might very well be acting out under the influence of alcohol, drugs, and all the psychological influences discussed in this book, but he is also acting out to entertain other rioters.

In the harsh light of Monday morning, a few, now embarrassed ex-rioters from the weekend scurry along the campus paths or the hallways at work hoping that no one notices them. However, there will be plenty of others who will be boisterously telling and retelling tales of their glorious and riotous exploits.

Solidarity with Other Fans

Rick Grieve, a psychology professor at Western Kentucky University in Bowling Green, says that some fans feel that their group of friends in the crowd, all of whom are rooting for the same team, provides them with a network of valued connections. He says, "I think it's a shared experience or phenomena, because we can look not only at aggressive behaviors but superstitious behaviors, rituals, the things people say and chant, all those things that are supposed to help the team win." He says that identification with a team gives a kind of social support network. It "provides a buffer from things like anxiety, loneliness, and depression. There's also evidence that people who have established social support networks have some protection against physical illness. There are a whole host of benefits."

Christian End at Xavier University in Cincinnati, Ohio, is a nationally recognized expert in sports fan behavior. He, too, talks about the need for fans to fit in with those around them. "When tens of thousands of people are chanting 'We're number one,' wearing team apparel, our group identity is strong and we want to fit in. So if we see someone throw a beer bottle and it draws cheers from our group members who we're really identifying with at the time, we might be apt to match that behavior or up it." End also notes that the environment at many sporting events permits, and even encourages, behavior that is outside of society's norm. He says, "Face painting, at the stadium, is socially acceptable. People yell things that they definitely would not be yelling in the boardroom or if their name and home phone number were available."

Media Attention

There is diverse audience reaction when television cameras show violence during a game, whether it's on the field or in the stands. But the question remains: does viewing violence during sporting events on TV instigate riotous behavior elsewhere? The clear and definitive answer is this: maybe.

There are two opposing camps on the issue. Those on the side of always showing violence to the television crowd say this:

Should Teams Play to Empty Seats?
In 2003, a 19-year-old man at the Avellino stadium in Italy fell 35 feet from the stands during a riotous fight between soccer fans. At least 20 other fans and 20 police officers were hurt during the clash.

Afterward, the Italian media talked of holding future matches behind closed doors or banning matches altogether. Government officials considered banning matches between teams whose fans frequently fight one another, closing stadiums to fans in other matches, and banning ticket sales to visiting fans on match days.

- You cannot censor it. If someone does not want to watch it, they can switch channels or turn off the TV.
- If it's not shown, events that happen afterward won't make sense to viewers.
- Violence, the kind on the field and the kind in the stands, is just part of the sporting event.
- And the number one reason: most viewers love it.

Those on the side of not showing it to the television crowd say this:

- It does harm to the game.
- It glorifies violence and desensitizes fans to it.
- Teams will act out violently because they believe that is what the television viewers want.
- Fans in the stands who have seen televised violence at games in the past will try to instigate an incident to get themselves on TV, or because they feel it is expected of them.
- And the number one reason: it perpetuates the problem at a time when it's getting worse.

The final decision is going to be made by the media, which means it's going to be influenced by the power of the almighty dollar. Which way do you think it will go?

Alcohol

Many people cite alcohol at sporting events as the primary cause of rowdy behavior that escalates to violence. For sure, you would have a hard time finding a sober kid participating in a post-game riot. But sports fan behavior expert Christian End says that while many people cite alcohol for its role in riotous behavior among sports fans, it might not be the most important factor. He says, "Alcohol plays a role, and sometimes it's pointed out as the ultimate villain, the sole contributor. But there are a lot of other things going on. They serve alcohol at church socials and in the theater, but you don't see these kinds of behaviors."

So while alcohol might serve as the gasoline that fuels the fire of fan violence, it is all the other factors discussed in this chapter that serve as the match. And let's get real: alcohol at major sporting events is not going away any time soon. Setting aside all the partying that goes on before the game, the dollars-and-cents reality is that booze is a sizable moneymaker for stadiums and arenas, especially at its inflated prices. If alcohol was banned routinely at games, it's likely that some fans would not attend. The loss of beer and ticket sales is a powerful motivator for stadiums not to turn sporting events into dry ones.

That said, there are times when a stadium bans alcohol on a temporary basis. For example, there were no alcohol sales during the Patriots-Jets football game in Boston in December of 2005. This was a temporary precautionary measure because of the violence a month earlier at a Jets-Saints game, in which people threw beer bottles, two fans were stabbed, and a police officer suffered a broken leg. There were news articles before the game in which writers warned fans of the no-booze policy. Fans still went, and the game unfolded without a newsworthy hitch.

PROTECT YOURSELF

When attending sporting events, it's important that you're not susceptible to negative social learning and that you stay aware of what is going on around you. Be alert to mood changes in the crowd, to seeing and hearing instigators, to observing the actions of intoxicated fans, and to monitoring the teams or individual players as to their actions and their influences on the crowd.

When your gut feeling tells you that the environment is becoming tense and your instinct tells you that all hell is about to break loose, make the intelligent choice to leave. Yes, you have a right to watch, but keep in mind that you place yourself at risk when you do so. A thrown bottle does not care that you're not participating in the riot, nor does a stray rubber bullet fired by a police weapon, or a dose of pepper spray, or a shove that knocks you to the ground in front of a pressing, combative throng.

A friend of mine, Dan, was in Italy during the 1990 World Cup Championships, an enormously significant soccer event that brings together 13 national teams from around the world, as well as their supporters—their passionate, obsessive, hard-drinking, combative, belligerent, and obsessively patriotic supporters. (How fanatical are soccer fans? In some countries, fans have bought coffins for themselves decorated in the colors and symbols of their favorite teams.)

Although Dan was not a fan of the game (no doubt a minority in Florence that summer), his travels took him and his two friends to the city center a few times during the weeklong championships.

> There was continuous celebration in the streets, before the games and after. Most were young people who were drinking, singing, and chanting their team's songs. I don't know if they were drunk on the experience or just plain drunk. Maybe both.

The configuration of buildings in the core of most large cities has a way of amplifying sound—the wail of sirens, exploding fireworks over a waterfront park, and the chorus of thousands of fervent soccer fans. "The closer you got to the stadium," Dan says, "the greater the roar. At times it was constant and it echoed throughout the streets."

It's difficult for a drunken crowd of hundreds, perhaps thousands, of opposing fans to stay warm and fuzzy to each other as the hours, the booze, and the outcome of each game takes its toll. There is history, too—those violent soccer games of years past that have turned into bloodbaths in the stands, on the playing field, and in the streets. Every hard-drinking fan knows about those, and the bitterness never fades.

As the booze-sopped brains transitioned from buzz to ugly, tensions grew.

> There were the vibes, for lack of a better word. Things just started to feel weird. It's difficult to verbalize what it was other than to say that there was a sense that things were starting to go badly. There were a few minor scuffles and some property damage, and it was becoming increasingly clear that the crowd was not going to stay satisfied just chanting and drinking. It was definitely frightening when it got like that. It seemed like a big machine that could just roll right over you if it headed your way. It was not as if things were terribly violent; it was the potential for violence and mayhem that was scary. That's when we decided to head back to our hotel in another city.

Dan and his friends made their way to a train station to wait for their connection. However, their relief over escaping the insanity of all that was going on in the city center was short-lived.

> At least a couple hundred drunken, celebrating fans suddenly filled the platform. These were mostly, if not all, young guys, clearly drunk and still drinking. Most were wearing clothing similar to what their teams wore, and they had towels draped around their necks. They wave them when they're sitting in the bleachers. Given the nature of the platform, there was no place for us to escape without going through their midst.
>
> They weren't actively aggressive toward us, but they had a bit of a swagger that said they knew they had us if they wanted us. It was that potential for violence that was frightening.

Dan and his friends sat motionless for a few moments trying their hardest not to look American. But it didn't work.

A couple of them came over to us and spoke. I think they were Dutch. I'm not sure what they said, but I quickly popped out with, "We're Americans. Our team sucks!"

For the record, America's soccer team that year did suck, performing poorly in international play. Dan's recognition of that fact quickly disarmed the drunks. "It worked like a charm," he says. "They laughed and repeated what I said: 'Your team sucks!'"

The drunken youths left Dan and his friends alone after that, other than to offer them some beer.

Problems at sporting events are not about to stop this week or next. Therefore, when you go to an event, assume the responsibility to protect yourself by being alert and aware of your environment. In virtually every sports riot, innocent people are hurt because they waited too long to get away or they chose to stand around and watch.

• • • • •

The good news is that there are many people addressing the issue of sports riots in an effort to reduce what appears to be a growing trend. Leaders are examining such causation factors as media coverage, officiating, and alcohol and studying ways to implement new and improved security, video surveillance, and other tools. These will help, but the bad news is that when all the negative conditions are present to riot, people just do it. They don't care about cameras, security, police, or the simple social expectation to behave properly in public.

Sources

"Sport and Deviance," *Sport in Contemporary Society*, by D.S. Eitzen (ed.), St. Martin Press, 1979.
"Don't expect Pacer's Ron Artest to change," by Nancy Armour, Yahoo! News, www.yahoo.com, October 29, 2005.

"Hillsborough jibes spark fan violence," author unknown, Edinburghnews.com, http://edinburghnews.scotsman.com/>/, October 27, 2004.

"Sports violence and fan behavior," author unknown, Indiana University, http://newsinfo.iu.edu/tips/page/normal/1736.html.

"Fan's death may prompt action in Italy," author unknown, http://sportsillustrated.cnn.com/2003/soccer/09/23/bc.eu.spt.soc.italy.violence.ap/, September 23, 2003.

"Hooliganism," Wikipedia, http://en.wikipedia.org/wiki/Hooliganism.

"Boxing and sports fighting annotated bibliography," by Thomas E. Radecki, M.D., J.D., http://www.modern-psychiatry.com/sports_violence.htm.

"Super Bull Sunday," unknown author, www.snopes.com/crime/statistics/superbowl.asp.

"Team is an extension of fan," by James C, McKinley Jr., *The New York Times* online edition, http://partners.nytimes.com/library/sports/other/081100fans-violence.html.

"Bowe vs. Golota," author unknown, www.hboppv.com/ web_exclusives/boxing_history/bowe_golota.shtml.

"Chinese football fans riot over penalty," author unknown, BBC News, http://news.bbc.co.uk/2/hi/asia-pacific/1892421.stm.

"Violence erupts after Lakers win NBA title," CNN.com, http://archives.cnn.com/2000/US/06/20/lakers.violence/

"Police devastated by Red Sox fan's death," Local6.com, www.local6.com/news/3841878/detail.html.

"Heysel tragedy," by Danilo Paparazzo, http://bianconeri.tripod.com/heysel.html.

"The Heysel Stadium tragedy, 1985," www.bbc.co.uk/dna/h2g2/alabaster/A713909.

"Heysel: the tragedy that should never have happened," by Brian Glanville, Times Online, http://www.timesonline.co.uk/tol/sport/football/article432432.ece>.

"A Psychosocial Model of Fan Violence," *International Journal of Sport Psychology,* by R. Simons and J. Taylor, 1992.

"Small riot erupts outside the Staples Center after Lakers win championship," by Alejandro A. Alonso, www.streetgangs. com, May 30, 2000.

"Sports Riots: The Psychology of Fan Mayhem," by Brian Handwerk, National Geographic News, www.news.nationalgeographic.com.

Chapter 6

Race Riots

News reporter to a fleeing looter: "Is this in response to Rodney King?"

Looter: "Who's Rodney King?"

Doesn't it seem as if racism festers just beneath the veneer of our societal graces? So many profess nonracist views, but it does not take much for the ugliness of bigotry to come boiling to the surface, scalding and violent. White supremacists and self-proclaimed racist Hispanic, Asian, and black groups are clearly and proudly open about their hatred and anger toward other skin colors. Therefore, to see them explode viciously into rioting, while not pretty, is not terribly surprising. It's what they are about and who they are. What is surprising, though, is when regular folks—people who have never openly professed any feelings about other races or ethnicities—suddenly detonate . . . or at least it seems sudden.

In my experience as a police officer, I recall many mini race riots where, for example, a drunken teen party suddenly turned violent when racism erupted after too many beers and a bad choice of words. I saw it happen on high school campuses, and I saw it happen in crowded summertime parks. I recall an episode at a local mall that erupted when a dozen or so young white people clashed with an equal number of young African Americans. A white teen nearly died from being stomped repeatedly on a cement staircase. None of the kids on either side had a reputation for racist activities, but it took only seconds for a teen fight to erupt over racial differences and for those latent feelings to rush to the surface and lash out.

THE INTENSITY OF RACIAL VIOLENCE

Many police officers will say that, in their experience, racial homicides are often brutal beyond the norm. The victim is over-killed, if you will. Are some of these cases examples of inner hate, rage, and racism bursting from within? Based on my experiences, I say yes. Three different incidents that occurred overseas illustrate different aspects of this dangerous phenomenon.

Liverpool Riot

Retired English police officer Martin Cooper tells of the horror of a massive race riot that he and his fellow officers experienced in a Liverpool borough. As you read his account about what the officers had to contend with—deadly thrown missiles, burning cars driven into their lines, hordes of attacking youths, and the absolute intensity of the attacks—keep in mind that these officers had no firearms. They were equipped only with their British bobby helmets, truncheons, and six-foot Perspex shields. The Chief Constable and the House of Commons later recognized Martin for his actions during this riot. He quickly points out that hundreds of other officers were there, too, and they made some of the same decisions under the same awful conditions. Martin's story:

The most violent civil disturbances in Britain of the twentieth century took place in the Toxteth district, a borough of Liverpool with a large black population. In the course of three days, more than 500 people went to jail, 1,000 police officers suffered injuries, and over 19 million dollars in property was looted or destroyed. For the first time in the UK outside Northern Ireland, police employed tear gas against civilians. It's not often that one UK police force asks for help from a neighboring force, but it did happen during this riot.

While I was working the afternoon shift in my department, a panic call went out from Liverpool for all officers to return to the station. We were immediately shipped in trucks and personnel carriers into the Toxteth area, leaving our entire department covered by only two female officers.

On arrival, I saw why hundreds of officers were drafted in short notice. We were waiting in a holding area at a city center police station as hundreds of local officers returned after taking a beating on the Toxteth streets. Their clothes were torn, burnt, and they smelled of burnt debris. Not knowing what we were about to face, I began feeling a mix of doubt and anticipation. I felt like a lamb led to the slaughter, which would turn out to be nearer the truth than I thought.

We were shipped to the front line of the police defense on Upper Parliament Street in Toxteth. It was nighttime by then as we moved in to take over the front line. I could see the ranks of hundreds of officers silhouetted in the flames of burning buildings and vehicles. Behind the vehicles, a ravaging mob of youths, hundreds of them illuminated by the flames. It was a sight that filled me with awe.

They were hurling Molotov cocktails at us, which were smashing on our shields and bursting into flames. They then rushed the line, hitting and kicking the shields before retreating as the next wave of Molotov cocktails launched. They were much too quick and mobile for the police lines to deal with. I will never understand how we held our line.

I'm sure we all felt the same fear and confusion. I was terrified! The mob set a car on fire and drove it at our line. In sheer panic, we split our formation and allowed it to hurtle through; it crashed into a nearby building. Then the rioters ripped wrought-iron spikes off the perimeter fencing of buildings and threw them at us like spears, many of them thudding into our police lines. On several occasions, I saw these iron spikes impale officers' helmets; how they weren't killed I don't know. When the fire department tried to get to our location to extinguish the flames, the mob turned on them, throwing their makeshift spears and Molotov cocktails at the vehicle and its men.

This vicious turmoil went on for hours. When we finally gained a few feet, they lit a car ablaze and drove it at our lines, forcing us to retreat. As we tried to take back an intersection that was occupied by the mob during the riot, they launched another burning car at us. This time I dove over a garden wall and got behind cover as the vehicle exploded about four yards away. It was a miracle nobody was killed. We were all soaked in sweat: some of it from the heat of the fires and some of it from pure fear.

We resumed our position on the front line, again taking the brunt of the attacks. A thrown house brick struck the man on my left and he collapsed without a word. I managed to grab him before he hit the ground and dragged him behind the meager protection of the front-line shields. Then another missile sailed over the shields and struck the guy on my right, collapsing him. Just as I grabbed him with my free arm, I realized that the three of us were vulnerable because we couldn't keep up with the moving shield line. So I scurried toward a building, dragging the injured officers with me. We managed to take cover in a doorway, although we were being continually pelted with missiles. I have never felt so scared in my life.

At that moment, we got information that the cinema

building immediately to the right of us on the other side of the street, which had been steadily burning for several hours, had become so compromised by fire damage that it was expected to collapse any minute.

The entire police line immediately retreated back, leaving us behind. Seeing how extremely vulnerable we were, I explained to my two groggy companions that we needed to run back behind the lines. But due to their injuries they didn't understand our dilemma. So I broke cover and bolted like a scared rabbit, dragging them with me.

Wholesale looting was the order of the day. Behind the protection of their violence, the looters smashed into all the nearby stores, stealing everything possible and laying waste to anything else. This only abated as the sun began coming up and we were able to coordinate officers better. Even at this juncture, any officer who chased a looter too far into the alleys would find himself surrounded by violent thugs.

By full daylight all the offenders had bolted, leaving in their wake something that looked like a scene out of a sci-fi movie: injured people staggering about the debris-strewn roadways and burning buildings spewing smoke. Upturned and scorched vehicles were strewn along the roads. Police officers, exhausted and needing food and water, just lay down on their six-foot-tall Perspex riot shields. Some fell into an exhausted sleep.

Venting Rage in Paris

"Because we hate," said one young Arab immigrant during the fall 2005 riots that rocked France. "Because we're mad, because we've had it up to here. Look around you. This place is shit, a dump. We have nothing here. There's nothing for us."

The violence, which in the beginning of the riot was concentrated in neighborhoods with large African and Muslim populations, later spread to other parts of the country. Suddenly, France had to address the burning rage in its suburbs, where immigrants and their French-born children live on the margins of society.

Another rioter complained about the police, 9,500 of whom were on riot duty:

> They harass you, they hassle you, and they insult you the whole time. ID checks now, scooter checks next. They call you nigger names. I got caught the other week smoking on the train. OK, you shouldn't smoke on the train. But when we get to Aulnay station, there are six cops waiting for us, three cars. They did the whole body search; they had me with my hands on the roof of the car. One said, "Go back home, Arab. Screw your race."

"It's so easy," a 16-year-old said, discussing the best way to make and employ homemade incendiaries. "You need a beer bottle, a bit of petrol or white spirit, a strip of rag, and a lighter. Cars are better, though, when the tank goes. One of you smashes a window, the other lobs the bottle."

"We hate France and France hates us," another Arab teen said, continuing:

> I don't know what I am. Here's not home; my grandmother is in Algeria. But in any case, France is just fucking with us. We're like mad dogs, you know. We have to do this. Our parents, they should understand. They did nothing; they suffered in silence. We don't have a choice. We're sinking in shit, and France is standing on our heads. One way or another we're heading for prison. It might as well be for actually doing something.

"The anger displayed, and the intensity with which it has spread, is alarming," said one political analyst.

Racial Fighting in Australia

In Sydney, Australia, in 2005, news reports said that 5,000 white youths attacked people believed to be of Arab and Middle Eastern descent after rumors spread that Lebanese youths had assaulted two white lifeguards. People on the beach began circulating mobile phone text messages, heavy with racial slurs, encouraging others to return to the beach the following Sunday and retaliate.

A week later, carloads of people from other parts of Sydney roared onto the beach and began what one reporter described as "scenes of chaos." Thousands of young white men, many fueled with alcohol, commenced attacking people who appeared to be Arabic or of Mediterranean descent. When there were no human targets left, the mobs struck out at businesses, parked cars, and passing motorists. Even police cars and ambulances came under fire of bricks and bottles. By the second night, many of the rioters were in jail and dozens had suffered injuries, including police officers.

The majority of these youths were probably not hard-core white supremacists—though many were encouraged by neo-Nazi groups—but rather young people harboring resentment toward Muslim immigrants fueled by the September 11, 2001, attack in the United States as well as the 2002 bombings in Bali that killed 202 people, including 88 Australians. Fanning the flames were memories of a gang rape in 2002 in which Lebanese suspects shouted racial abuse at their white victims during the course of the assault. One suspect in that crime received a 55-year sentence, a severe punishment by Australian standards.

According to a 2001 census, 300,000 Muslims live in Australia, most in lower-income suburbs. They look different, speak a different language, and follow customs different from those of native-born Australians. This makes them easy targets for people to blame and to hate, and it makes them especially easy targets in light of such extraordinary events as 9/11 and Bali. It's a hate that builds and builds.

Then, when an incident occurs that has racial implications—in this case, an assault on the beach by suspects described as Arab or Mediterranean—all that hate ignites. It's quite possible there had been other incidents committed by Arab-looking suspects, but in this case the timing was such that someone or several people heard about it right afterwards and made calls, sent messages, contacted white supremacists, and so on. Everything fell into place for thousands of people, many of whom had a festering hatred for Middle Easterners, to gather and erupt.

RACE RIOTS IN THE 1960s

Let's now consider the American experience and take a brief look at a few race riots that occurred during the 1960s. These and others like them are most salient in the minds of those readers of the baby boom generation who survived that turbulent decade. Then we will finish our glance at history with a look at the riots that took place after the Rodney King trial verdict in 1992, followed by an illuminating interview with a Los Angeles police officer who served in the thick of the chaos following the verdict and who has strong opinions and insights into the event.

Watts, California, 1965

It was a small incident in 1965 that would spark the inferno known as the Watts riot. It began when a white police officer was informed by a black citizen that he had just witnessed an intoxicated driver swerving all over the road. The officer caught up to the car, driven by two black brothers, and pulled it over two blocks from their home. The driver failed the field sobriety test and the officer arrested him.

When the officer told the driver's brother that he could not take the car—perhaps he was underage or he was also intoxicated—the brother ran to get their mother so that she could take possession. Meanwhile, a crowd of 25 to 50 African-American people from the neighborhood had gathered to watch. It would soon grow to 300, and by the time the police left the scene 20 minutes later, there would be 1,000 people growing ever more agitated.

When the passenger returned with the mother, the driver, who had been cooperative, suddenly became emboldened by her presence. He moved into the crowd, shouting that the police would have to kill him to take him to jail. When he resisted attempts to get him into handcuffs, his mother jumped into the fray. As more officers rushed to the scene, the situation rapidly deteriorated as the mother attacked an officer and officers beat her combative son with batons.

The police decided that it was best to leave the area before things worsened. As they struggled back to their cars, someone in the growing crowd spat on them. Two of the officers charged back into the mass and arrested a man and a woman who had been the primary agitators, though it's unknown if they were the spitters. This enraged the already volatile crowd to a point where several of them picked up whatever was lying about and threw it at the police cars as they drove away.

Rumors spread quickly up and down the streets, first stirring anger and then igniting a rage, a rage that needed venting. The agitated and expanding crowd threw rocks at passing cars, dragged white motorists from their vehicles and beat them, and even threatened a police command post.

Over the next few days, National Guard troops would help the police restore some semblance of peace. Thirty-four people died violently, including a sheriff's deputy and a firefighter. More than 1,000 people received injuries (118 from gunshots), including firefighters, police officers, and National Guardsmen. More than 600 buildings were heavily damaged by fire and looting, total property damage topped $40 million, and 3,438 people went to jail.

Newark, New Jersey, 1967

In the summer of 1967, an African-American cab driver named John Smith drove around a double-parked police car, an action that for some reason offended the officers. Smith's and the officers'

versions differ as to why he was subsequently stopped and what
led to his arrest. However, what is known is that when a small
group of civil rights leaders from the crowd that had gathered outside the police station was allowed inside to examine Smith, they
found that he had sustained injuries to the extent that they
demanded he be taken to a hospital.

Multiple Causes

Between 1964 and 1971, an unprecedented number of race-related
riots in the United States—more than 700 by some counts—resulted in
countless number of injuries, deaths, arrests, and millions of dollars in
property damage.

Library bookshelves are jammed with volumes written on the cause
of race riots during the turbulent 1960s. While most were ignited by a
singular incident—an arrest by police, the assassination of Martin
Luther King—larger issues certainly played a part: ongoing police inter-
actions, poor housing, extreme poverty, unemployment, discrimination,
and segregation, to name a few. In addition, some scholars believe that
many riots were the result of the contagion factor. That is, the media's
coverage of a race-related riot in one area influenced the outbreak of a
riot in another.

As officers whisked the man out a back door and drove him to a
hospital, the civil rights leaders tried to calm the crowd in front of the
building, but the people shouted them down. A quickly spreading
rumor that Smith had died at the hands of the police turned the crowd
into a mob that bombarded the police station with bottles, bricks, and
a Molotov cocktail. The police poured from the station and, while they
did manage to disperse the mob, it actually made matters worse
because the maddened crowd began looting stores as they moved
down the streets. Within hours, widespread violence had progressed
from the predominately black community to Newark city proper.

The New Jersey State Police mobilized and, within two days,
the National Guard joined the battle. The rioting lasted six days,
killed 23 people, and injured 725. Nearly 1,500 people went to jail,
and property damage skyrocketed to $10 million.

Detroit, Michigan, 1967

On July 23, 1967, the Detroit Police Department's vice squad conducted a raid on an illegal after-hours bar on 12th Street, a typical night's work for law enforcement. This time, however, it would set off the infamous "12th Street Riot."

Officers expected just a few people when they charged into the club, but to their surprise, they found more than 80, all of them celebrating the return of two soldiers from Vietnam. Officers decided to arrest everyone, which would prove not to be their best decision that day.

A crowd gathered to protest as officers led the 80 prisoners outside to waiting police vehicles. Sensing the bad vibes in the air, the police hurriedly stuffed everyone into their vehicles and roared off just seconds before the crowd evolved into a window-breaking mob. It was not long before an all-out riot exploded. First they set fires and looted the neighborhood, but soon the violence spread to other parts of the city.

As the fires colored the skyline red, the National Guard mobilized along with regular army troops. Even with help from the military, the police would be unable to regain control of the city for five days. In the end, 43 people died, nearly 1,200 received injuries, some 7,000 went to jail, and fire damaged or destroyed more than 1,400 buildings.

Washington, D.C., 1968

On April 4, 1968, a rifle bullet fatally struck Martin Luther King as he stood on a balcony outside a Memphis, Tennessee, motel, and while his earlier speech might have prophesied his early demise—"I've seen the promised land. I may not get there with you. But I want you to know tonight, that we, as a people, will get to the Promised Land"—he would have been deeply saddened at the events that followed.

That evening, in the heavily populated African-American neighborhoods of Washington D.C., Stokely Carmichael, an activist who had formerly worked with King, led followers of the Student Nonviolent Coordinating Committee to neighbor-hood businesses and demanded that they close their doors in honor of King's death. Near midnight, however, the quiet crowd turned riotous and began breaking windows and loot-ing. (Nearly three dozen other American cities experienced similar violence.)

The next day, Carmichael warned students attending a rally at Howard University of the potential for violence in the aftermath of King's assasination. Sure enough, when the rally ended, the crowd smashed head on with the police. By noon, buildings burned as rock- and bottle-throwing rioters held firemen at bay.

When the D.C. police department found itself outnumbered by crowds of 20,000 strong, President Lyndon Johnson sent in nearly 14,000 federal troops and another 1,700 National Guardsmen. (I was an army military policeman serving in the Florida Keys at the time, and my unit was put on alert in anticipation of being dis-patched to D.C. to assist. The alert was canceled a few days later.) Machine guns pointed outward from the steps of the Capitol, and squads of troops stood guard around the White House in what was the largest military occupation of Washington D.C. or any American city since the Civil War. On the second day of rioting, mobs came within just two blocks of the White House before being forced to retreat.

It would take four days before some semblance of peace set-tled on the capital. In the end, 12 people lay dead, 1,100 injured, and more than 6,000 arrested. Property damage exceeded $27 mil-lion, which included 1,200 burned buildings, three quarters of them businesses.

Saigon, Vietnam, 1969

I was a military policeman in Saigon during a time when racial strife in the military burned red hot. The racial tension and vio-lence in the United States in the 1960s had spread to the military, to the extent that in many American units in Vietnam, there was a clear separation among the troops into black and whites—more accurately, blacks vs. whites. Many black GIs grew their hair into large Afros, and some added sunglasses, black power fists painted on hats, black wristbands made from boot laces, green army towels draped around necks, and the ritual of "dapping," an elaborate handshake done upon greeting one another. All this paraphernalia, dress style, and ritual was a way for black GIs to separate themselves while at the same time alienating and even frightening white soldiers. Many whites wondered on which side blacks soldiers were fighting, not an overreaction considering some blacks were vocal in their solidarity with the Vietnamese. One black GI wrote years later:

> Ho Chi Minh [president of North Vietnam] made a point that stuck in many of our minds. He said, "It's a civil war. The war is between the Vietnamese, between the North and the South." Old Ho Chi made sense to most of us. This kinda idea especially made sense to me, because we had too many Americans dying. And it was obvious that we were the aggressors because we were fourteen thousand miles from home rather than vice versa. We were fighting Charlie in his own backyard. We didn't really feel that we were fighting for our country; half the brothers felt it wasn't even our war and were sympathetic with Ho Chi Minh.

The North Vietnamese were not ignorant of these issues, and they responded by appealing to black troops to abandon the military and depart their country. The North scattered leaflets in the jungle encouraging them to leave since, after all, the war was not their fight. All this worked to some extent, as many blacks came to believe the message in the leaflets and Ho's comments. In addition, black GIs had a hero in heavyweight boxing champion Muhammad Ali. The champ relinquished his title in 1967 by refusing induction into the military. "I ain't got no quarrel with those Viet Cong, anyway. They never called me nigger," Ali was quoted as saying.

MPs labeled several alleys and bars in Saigon as "black areas," places where black GIs congregated to drink beer, listen to music, and socialize. Many blacks wanted for crimes or for going AWOL hung out in these places, which made them hotspots for patrolling MPs. During my tour, I saw some of my colleagues charge into the black-dominated locations using more force than necessary, and I saw incidents where some black soldiers deliberately created con-frontations with the MPs where problems need not have happened. Both wrongs created tension and mistrust that frequently erupted into mini riots—brawls between a dozen blacks and a dozen MPs—as well as clashes involving scores more on both sides.

I cannot listen to Sly and the Family Stone's 1968 hit "Dance to the Music" without reminiscing about a riotous brawl a half-dozen or more of my fellow MPs and I got into in Saigon's USO. Besides the regular GIs who frequented the place throughout the day to eat, read, and listen to music blaring from oversized speak-ers mounted on the walls, there were always several MPs inside getting a cold soda and using the restroom facilities.

One day my two partners and I stopped in to grab lunch. The sound system was especially loud, with Sly and the Family Stone thumping the skull-rattling bass throughout the cavernous and crowded room. As was always the case, every eye in the place focused on us the moment we entered and stayed on us as we made our way along one wall to the eatery at the back.

One of my partners spotted a black soldier who had run from him a couple days prior. My first partner, a little too gung-ho for his own good, scurried through the crowded tables and grabbed the man by his neck. It was not good police procedure, especially since there were about 40 people in the dining area, more than half of whom were black. All the blacks sprang to their feet as one body and charged toward the MP as my second partner and I rushed to back him up. Other MPs in the back of the room joined the fray.

As Sly screamed "Daaaaance to the music," several dozen of us crashed about the dining area, knocking over chairs, rolling over tables, and sending plates of burgers and fries onto the floor. More MPs arrived and more black GIs from outside ran in to join the mayhem.

When it was over, several on both sides of the fight were injured, and a dozen soldiers were in handcuffs. Sly had moved on to something else.

Incidentally, I still like "Dance to the Music." It never fails to ignite my juices.

Los Angeles, California, 1992

On March 3, 1991, Los Angeles police stopped motorist Rodney King for driving recklessly. When King charged officers and knocked them to the pavement, they fought back by shooting 50,000 volts of electricity into his body, which went unnoticed by the massive man. Believing that King might be under the influence of mind-numbing drugs, officers struck him repeatedly with their batons as he continued to disobey their commands to lie down and stay down. When it was over, King had been kicked and struck 56 times.

A citizen across the street videotaped most of the incident, which news programs showed for weeks afterwards. While many viewers were shocked, the tape nonetheless divided people as to the necessity of such force by police officers. The ensuing court proceedings would rivet the nation.

Three officers and a sergeant received indictments for assault later that month. A year later, on April 29, 1992, three of the officers were acquitted by a jury of 10 non-Hispanic whites, one Hispanic, and one Asian. The verdict shocked much of the United States. Even President George H. W. Bush stated that the verdict "has left us all with a deep sense of personal frustration and anguish." California State Senator Ed Smith was quoted as saying, "It's hard to believe that there was no sustaining of the charges at all . . . the world saw the videotape, and if that conduct is sanc-

Perception
The Rodney King incident is a prime example of differences in perception. Many police officers with similar resist-arrest experiences saw the beating as necessary to control a giant man who seemed impervious to pain and the effects of the TASER. Others saw the beating as racially motivated, and the exoneration of the officers supported their belief that America is still a racist country

tioned by law in California, then we have to rewrite the law."

People living in Southeast and South Central Los Angeles, however, were not about to wait for changes in the law. For the next three days, Los Angeles turned into a war zone. It began on the same day as the verdict, at such locales as the Los Angeles Police Headquarters in Parker Center and in South Central Park neighborhoods. Rioters vented their rage on businesses with bricks and Molotov cocktails. When ambulances and firetrucks raced to scenes of fire and injury, sniper rounds punched holes in their rigs and forced the drivers to turn around.

Burning cars jammed intersections, and motorists were carjacked or ripped out of their vehicles and beaten to the pavement. The most infamous beating incident, which was broadcast on live television, happened to a white truck driver named Reginald Denny. Dragged from his vehicle after he had stopped at a red light, a mob of black youths beat Denny to the pavement as news helicopters hovered above, recording every stomping kick. Even after the man appeared unconscious, a teenager, fully aware that a news helicopter was right over him, dropped a heavy cinder block onto Denny's head. Then the teen danced in jubilation for the cameras. Black neighbors who witnessed the beating and cinder block assault live on their television sets ran to the intersection and saved Denny from further injury, ultimately saving his life.

By nightfall of the first day, hundreds of stores were openly looted by thieves. The fire department couldn't respond to the many burning buildings due to heavy sniper fire, and the Los Angeles Police Departnment, which would subsequently be severely criticized for its poor response, were not to be seen in many sections of the city.

As the California sun rose the second day, the riot had become even more widespread. Live television showed Korean storeowners engaged in open gun battles with looters, while the LAPD remained mostly unresponsive. Not until later in the day was there an organized response by firefighters with police escorts. Airlifted California Highway Patrol reinforcements were flown to the area, LA Mayor Tom Bradley declared a state of emergency, and the National Guard sent in 2,000 soldiers, increasing the number to 4,000 the next day.

Day three saw the troops move into the riot-torn areas in Humvees. An additional 1,700 federal law-enforcement officers arrived in the city to protect federal facilities and help the LAPD and state police. Soon a feeling of normalcy began to descend.

By day four, an additional 4,000 regular army soldiers and Marines were ready to deploy, but the presence of the federal officers helped the LAPD establish calm in the streets. A scattering of parties that night required police attention, but mostly people left the city or just holed up in their homes to watch the news on television.

Although Mayor Bradley lifted the curfew on the sixth day, there were still sporadic acts of violence and crime.

The military would stay on the job for another month.

When it was over, 53 people lay dead, 2,300 injured, and 10,000 arrested. More than 1,000 buildings were lost to fire, thousands of people were put out of work, and damage to the city added up to $1 billion.

Rodney King Riot: One Cop's Experience

With a B.S. degree in Criminal Justice Studies, Mark Mireles has worked as a Los Angeles police officer since 1990. He has served in a variety of assignments, including patrol, narcotics, gangs, and career criminal apprehension. His current assignment is uniform patrol, where he works a drug enforcement detail. In addition to his field duties, Mark teaches police defensive tactics, officer safety, use-of-force policy, and interrogation/interview techniques to patrol officers.

Mark is a two-time recipient of the Medal of Valor, the highest award for bravery given by the LAPD, and he was nominated for the Carnegie Medal, a prestigious award that honors extreme heroism to recipients in the United States and Canada. He has received more than 200 letters of commendation, to include citations from the U.S. Congress and Senate.

Mark owns Mireles & Associates, an investigative, security, and law-enforcement consulting firm. In his spare time, the former United States Marine studies and teaches martial arts. He writes regularly for *Black Belt* magazine.

I first met Mark through an exchange of e-mails regarding our mutual life-long study of the martial arts. During the course of our conversations, I learned that he had been on the front lines of the Rodney King riots. When I interviewed Mark about the episode, I found him to be open, honest, and not one to sugarcoat things.

Loren Christensen (LWC): As a veteran martial artist, how do you feel about the physical aspects of the so-called Rodney King beating?

Mark Mireles (MM): I had just completed 10 years of competitive wrestling and 13 years of judo when this happened. I had boxed and studied other forms of martial arts, too. I had finished serving my tour in the Marines and though I was a kid of 23, I had grown up in a tough part of San Francisco and had more than a few street fights under my belt.

Based on my street experience and my martial arts background, I understood that the police academy defensive tactics training was not the totality of what goes on in a fight. Clinches and ground fighting are common, but the academy's school of thought was never to go to the ground. I knew that the training, while good, wasn't totally realistic. But I did not know that it would soon be an aspect of an incident that would receive international attention.

I learned later that in the early 1980s, the LAPD had done away with the neck restraint hold, commonly known as the "choke hold." The hold constricts the blood supply from a person's brain, thus rendering him unconscious. It was widely used prior to the '80s in the LAPD, but after a man who was intoxicated on PCP or cocaine died after being choked out, the technique became a political hot potato. So the hold was moved to the level of deadly force, on a par with using a firearm.

There was a total shift in LAPD's methods to gain compliance over a combative suspect when a situation required less than deadly force. Training in the academy moved away from significant reliance on the neck hold and replaced it with the PR-24, the side-handled baton. We also learned a basic curriculum called pugilism, which consisted of low-line methods of kicking and linear punching. We even did simulated foot pursuit that ended in a full-contact boxing match, gloves and all.

But the curriculum didn't totally prepare us for what we were going to experience on the street. A cop should always attempt to talk someone down, which works almost all the time. There are other times when a person isn't going to submit no matter what you say. That's when an officer needs the right tool for the job, one that lets him use the minimal amount of force to affect an arrest.

The goal is to get handcuffs on the suspect, something that requires a hands-on approach. If he resists, his resistance has to be overcome with force. The police academy must teach recruits a wide variety of arrest and control techniques: pummeling, standing wrestling, ways to attack and defend, and offense and defense techniques on the ground. But when I was in the academy, we didn't do enough of this type of training. I think we had one two-hour block of ground fighting in the entire six-month academy. In contrast, we spent hour after hour drilling with the PR-24 baton. In my opinion, that was a problem.

Let me explain something that needs explanation, because it sheds a tremendous light on what happened the night those officers stopped Rodney King. I was classmates with Timothy Wind, one of the officers on the scene of King's traffic stop, and as such, I was present through all of his training. As I said, I know from my wrestling and judo background the effectiveness of ground grappling, and I know that sometimes it cannot be avoided. You might not want to go down, but suddenly there you are on the ground, so you need to be able to deal with it. However, the department's school of thought and curriculum in the police academy strongly discouraged grappling of any sort. Maybe this was a clear step away from the neck restraint.

Today, as a defensive tactics instructor, I might not advocate grappling as a primary system of defensive tactics, but it's still a reality on the street. Many combative suspects are taken to the ground, just as Rodney King was. Then the suspect has to be handcuffed. The officer needs to learn grappling. To reiterate, that was not the school of thought in the LAPD academy in the 1980s and through 1991. Then it was all about the side-handled baton.

LWC: What was your assignment at the time of the riot?

MM: I was assigned to the Foothill area at the time, which is where the King beating occurred (the intersection of Osborne Street and Foothill Boulevard) and where the biker bar that was featured in the movie *Terminator 2* is located. I had been assigned to the Hollenbeck area in East Los Angeles during my probationary period and was transferred to Foothill in February of 1992, about two and a half months prior to the riots.

Working in a big city like LA was overwhelming and demanding at first, like being dropped into the middle of a busy intersection. From day one, I was out there on the street dealing with all sorts of situations, including violent criminals. It's a lot like former LA detective turned famous author Joseph Wambaugh explained it in his books, particularly in *The New Centurions*, which by the way, ends with a depiction of the Watts riots. Street work was starting to come together for me. I was seeing things on the street that I hadn't seen a year before, and I was learning and interacting well with other coppers.

LWC: Where were you when the riot started? What were your first thoughts?

MM: I was at home in Pasadena watching television, along with everyone, to see what would be the verdict of the four officers. Once the verdict was read and we learned that all four officers were found not guilty, it was only 30 minutes before Reginald Denny, a white man driving a truck through the intersection of Florence and Normandy in South Central, was dragged from his rig and beaten by a group of rioting gangsters.

At first it seemed like an isolated incident, especially since that is a rough part of town where incidents of violent crime and homicide are high. But as I watched a little longer, I saw others being attacked, and I began to see a common thread: the victims were white and Asian. [Now] its clicking in my mind that people are being attacked and that a riot is starting. I drove into the Foothill Division Station knowing that the department would be calling people in from home and, at some point, we would be going into full mobilization.

Let me digress for a moment and say that the cops, especially those working the Foothill area, knew all the officers involved in the beating. They had all been watching the trial, and they all understood evidence. They knew that the prosecutors, the district attorney's office, were relying solely on the video as opposed to what led up to the incident. It was clear to us that the case was not going well for the prosecution, and we figured the verdict was going to be a "not guilty. "

The rest of the world was tainted from watching the emotionally charged television news that had the four officers guilty from day one. The media played that tape every night for a year, and they did all sorts of shit to it, too. For example, they broke it down into slow motion, counted every baton strike, and they noted how many times specific targets were struck. This fueled the story and fueled the city. My point is this: it was a major shock to the public when the officers were found not guilty because they had been told for a year that they were guilty.

The press was outside the courthouse interviewing African Americans who were upset that all the officers on all the counts had been found not guilty. They blamed the verdict on racism by the jury, not the fact that Rodney King was a felon in the commission of a felony and resisting arrest.

LWC: What were the first few hours like for you and the other officers?

MM: Today the LAPD has an organized and direct response to riots, but that was not the case in 1992. At that time, South Central was in mass confusion. LAPD's command staff made some very poor decisions, as cited in the Christopher Commission, the after-action report on the LAPD and the riots. For example, in one section of the riot-infected area, groups of officers were taking deliberate action, while at the same time in the south end, central command was only staging officers in stand-by-and-wait mode.

It was very different at Foothill Division in the San Fernando Valley, where angry demonstrators had surrounded the front of the station and were hurling rocks and bottles. When the watch commander finally realized that the situation was going to get a lot worse if we didn't take action, 30 of us were ordered to put on helmets, grab batons (known as "get your hats and bats" in police vernacular), and went out front to disperse the crowd.

We were immediately confronted by a mob of blacks and Hispanics to our front. Across the street, fires burned in a parking lot. Off to our side, a mob turned on a news cameraman. You could see hate brewing in their faces as we formed a skirmish line in front of the station. There was an order given to them to disperse because they were an unlawful assembly. When several people chucked rocks and bottles at us, and we could see more rioters coming from a parking lot behind a nearby burger stand, it was time to act. The watch commander gave the order to move forward in a line formation.

The mob slammed into us. As the clash ensued, someone behind the burger stand, maybe more than one, fired gunshots into the air. We were afraid that the station might be overrun or burned if we did not take action. It was over in 10 minutes; the rioters were running in every direction. One moment they had been an angry mob and the next they were an unorganized group and fleeing. It was like the troops clashing in the movies *Braveheart* and *Troy*.

Since 1992, I've heard people say that the LAPD didn't take enforcement action but just stood by. This is true, but not at Foothill.

LWC: Did you work with a partner or in teams?

MM: After the first day, there wasn't a lot of shooting or motorists being dragged out of their cars and beaten. From the second day on, it was mostly about looting.

This was what our workday was like. We worked in four-man teams, four officers to a car, with hats and bats. When we saw people looting, we would make them put the stuff back or just drop it where they stood. It was as if we were saying: you cannot do that, but due to the overwhelming riot, we aren't going to do much more . . . see you at the next store.

There were thousands of people looting. I saw a news crew running after a guy who had just ripped off a TV from a store. As he was running the newsman asked, "Is this in response to Rodney King?"

The man says in broken English, "Who's Rodney King?"

LWC: Was it tough to be neutral in your opinion and actions since one of the officers charged was an academy classmate of yours?

MM: I have always been the kind of officer and person who doesn't take things personally. I recognize that assholes come with the job. If you were to give everyone a beating who deserved it, you would be one tired son-of-a-bitch at the end of each day. I approached the '92 riots professionally. Having to use force as an extension of tactics was nothing personal; I was just relying on my training to get an ugly job done, a job no one else wanted to deal with.

The riot was a dangerous situation and when it kicked off, your average citizen ran in the other direction (an intelligent move, I might add). Even with only two years on the job, it was just business for me. Tim Wind, one of the officers charged, was my classmate. As a co-worker, I felt bad that he had to go through all that hell, but that never made the riots personal—just business. After one week of the rioting and one week of curfew and security, I was glad when it was all over.

That said, the gang members had a "let's take the gloves off" approach to their criminal acts during the riots. They first attacked ethnic groups, whites and Koreans. The cops were on that list, too. When we encountered resistance or were deliberately attacked or surprised by ambush, we met them with great force and took them to jail. There were lots of gangsters sniping in the projects, but they were dealt with quickly by our SWAT teams. Gunmen would also take potshots at us, then disappear into the blocks, and roving gangs attacked firefighters. Remember, the city was on fire. When a firefighter got shot by a gang member, all bets were off. Gangsters and all the others who were running amok were taken to jail.

We were dealing with extremely violent acts committed by extremely dangerous people, most of whom had extensive criminal histories. There wasn't room in the jail to lodge nonviolent types. It was only the violent offenders, most of whom were gang members, who got locked up. Some, as documented in use-of-force reports, were shot in gun battles with the police.

I never had to fire my weapon during the riots, but other officers had violent encounters with heavily armed and barricaded suspects who were actively shooting. I wasn't at any of these incidents, but I did have my hands full dealing with looters.

Most of the cops had military training, thankfully, since the first two days we were really in a war zone. There were many officer-involved shootings and hand-to-hand combat situations.

LWC: You said you thought the press, police officials, DA, and public treated the charged officers poorly. Did that affect how you conducted yourself during the riot?

MM: The police department distanced itself from the officers after the incident, and the press was not fair at all. In fact, the press fueled the riots. They presented only one side, which was that four white cops beat a black motorist.

One often overlooked fact is that those officers were not the kind of people who were out looking for fights on their own time. They were not criminals out capering. They were cast into that situation by the nature of their job.

Earlier, I mentioned that the police department didn't want cops going to the ground with suspects; trainers and management were concerned about officers losing their weapons. Instead, they were taught to use their side-handled baton to strike a violent attacker on the torso or extremities to gain his compliance. The officers at the Rodney King traffic stop were doing what they were trained to do. Again, this was in reaction to the department eliminating the neck restraint hold against a suspect assuming a fighting stance or physically attacking an officer.

I agree that the videotaped incident was not a pretty one to watch. Now, if the officers' actions were not appropriate, perhaps even criminal, then the officers should definitely be held accountable, not the leaders and trainers. However, if the problems that stemmed from the so-called beating were a result of the officers' department-sanctioned training, then management should have addressed those prior to eliminating the neck restraint hold and implementing the PR-24 baton.

I'm not attacking the department's leaders or the officers but rather approaching this interview with a historical review of what was going on with the cops, the training, and the department at the time. As police leaders and trainers look back on those years, they can learn important lessons: officers must receive proficient training in defensive tactics from the department, and it's the officers' responsibility to stay in shape and remain proficient in their skills. I will say that officers today receive a higher degree of training in arrest and control and in defense tactics than we did in 1992.

I remember a command staff officer, who was in charge of the way in which the department used and trained with the PR-24, testifying at the King trial about the department's use of force. He actually said that officers weren't trained to do a group takedown of a suspect, a procedure known as the "swarm technique" where two or more officers coordinate to tackle a suspect and take him to the ground. Once down, the officers use their combined body weight to control him until he is handcuffed. Shockingly, the command staff officer testified that this was something officers learned on the playground as children!

After everything was over, the department took appropriate steps to ensure officers had the right tools for the right job. Sadly, the four officers involved in the King incident never had that type of training, but still the press, police officials, DA, and the U.S. Attorney's office all condemned the force they were trained to use.

My conduct was always professional. I believe that this job has never been about me but rather the people who live in the neighborhoods where I work. Even the bad guys have mothers, fathers, sisters, and brothers. It's important to keep straight in your head that not everyone out there wants to kill you.

The riots were hectic: buildings were burning, thousands were looting, and gang members were shooting and throwing Molotov cocktail bombs. Still, even in an all-out riot, every officer's response is gauged to what the suspect does. This is how I view my personal conduct and my professional standards.

LWC: Were there officers who had problems working because they felt the rioters were justified to do what they were doing? Were these officers black, white, or both?

MM: Outside of a few incidents, officers of the LAPD see one color—blue. Nobody I knew sympathized with looters, murderers, and arsonists, which was what these people were who engaged in the criminal aspects of a riot. They were criminals, period. There were plenty of people living in South Central who did not engage in the riots; in fact, these exceptions condemned the rioters' actions.

Allow me to make one thing crystal clear: apart from what all the sociologists and academicians say, the LA riots were due to a group-mob mentality. After the first day, it was about getting loot. Few cared about Rodney King. They wanted appliances and TVs—they wanted stuff. They were even driving in from all the suburbs to loot. It was sad. It would have been better if there was really a social cause behind it all, but there wasn't. For the great majority it was plain greed. I was there and saw it with my own two eyes.

LWC: What was your mind-set during the riot? Did it change at any point?

MM: It was an all-out riot that first day or two, with gang members attacking people, shooting at the police, and burning down buildings. It was life and death if someone got in over their head. It was critical to stay cool. I had a training officer once who used to say, "Kid, no matter what happens out here, never let your pulse get over 60." That comes down to mind-set. There is a job to do, and there is no backing away from it.

When the mob attacked us at Foothill Station that first night, I didn't want to lose control. Just because someone was shooting a gun behind the burger stand didn't mean I could use deadly force on a person standing in front of me. A police officer in that situation had to do the exact opposite of what the mob was doing. My mind-set was on taking care of the problem in front of me in a coordinated effort with other officers and at the direction of the supervisor. Teamwork and discipline is how the police make it through a riot when they are outnumbered.

My mind-set never changed. As the riot turned from acts of violence to property crimes such as looting, it was a matter of getting the resources to assist. At that point, we needed more people; the National Guard and Marines greatly assisted. It's crazy to see machine guns in fortified positions and military checkpoints in the middle of a large metropolitan city. You see that in the news, but I guess that was the news, and we were all in the middle of it.

LWC: Were you ever in a position where it was just you vs. one or more rioters? If so, were you frightened? Anxious? Hyped?

MM: I was attacked by a guy the first night at Foothill Station. He tried to tackle me, but I hit him with a power-stroke blow in the thigh with my PR-24 baton and he fell to the ground. His fellow rioters saw that and decided to redirect their efforts elsewhere.

Clashing with rioters can get your blood pressure up, but I was never out of control. I think I have had good training in the PD since 1992, and I had good training in the military. I believe that if you're truly confident and have had excellent training, you will react appropriately. With a lack of confidence and training, the opposite happens.

I would have to say that my martial arts training is a significant fac-

tor in my ability to use the right tools for the job and in remaining calm
in such situations. I know what I can do and I know what I cannot, which
prevents me from getting in over my head. I've been lucky maybe, but I
always try to look at police work like a game of chess: I need to stay a
couple of moves ahead of the bad guys. That's what I did during the riots,
and it worked out good for me.

**LWC: How did it feel to have rioters look at you with hatred
because of your race and your role as a police officer? Did that influence your actions?**

MM: The first thing they saw in the riot was our uniform. Then they
might have seen that the officer wearing it was white, black, Mexican, or
Asian. There were race tensions because the Rodney King beating
involved four white cops and a black suspect. The media fueled the incident, and then when the verdict was read, they played up the fact that a
white jury had let them off.

Although I could care less about the color of a man's skin, I was
called many racial epithets by blacks. Sticks and stones may break my
bone but names . . . you know the saying. I'm a professional, and I don't
come down to that level—not ever. Being a racist is never tolerated by the
LAPD. As I said before, it's all business.

**LWC: Would you elaborate a little more about what it's like to be
called a racial name when you're just doing your job.**

MM: Anyone who has been a police officer for a while knows that
that goes with the territory. There's a saying in law enforcement: "We don't
catch the smart ones." Street cops catch people committing street crimes,
and street crimes always catch up with a crook. Knowing this, a person has
to be playing with one beer short of a six-pack to get involved in street
crime. Small-minded people have small-mind philosophies and ideologies.
When someone says something stupid to me, I just think, who cares? I'm
not going to get wrapped up in their problems. I consider the source.

I was once working with a black officer when a white suspect we
were arresting called him a "fucking nigger." I was pissed that the guy

had said it, and I thought my partner would hit the roof. But he just put the man in the backseat of the police car like nothing happened. He didn't even mention it. Later, when we were doing paperwork, I asked if that made him mad.

He looked at me with surprise and then laughed, saying, "Mark, when I leave here tonight, I'm going to a new house, and I own two. I'm going in my new car, and my fine-ass girlfriend will be waiting for me. That fool is going to jail. Then he will get out in a couple days, but in a week, he will be back in, only to get out again in two weeks. For him, that cycle will never stop. It will be like his own little life sentence as he serves two to three days at time for the rest of his life. What do I care what he calls me." He went back to the paperwork and never said another word about it.

LWC: Were there periods where you felt everything was so out of control—poor supervision, cops spread too thin, continuous violence, an overwhelming sense of unreality—that you were functioning in anarchy?

MM: The riots were anarchy, absolute bedlam. Coppers and the line supervision were doing the best they could the first and second day. The fact that the initial actions that kicked off the riots weren't dealt with immediately caused it to get out of control and spread all over the city. Again, at that time there wasn't really a "riot plan." The PD's reaction then was the same as it was 25 years earlier in the Watts riots: reactive only. I have done some reading on the Watts riots, and I've talked with cops who were there. They worked the same then as we did in 1992: small groups of officers and line supervisors driving around their assigned sectors with no particular plan other than to react.

That isn't the way LAPD works today. The Democratic National Convention [in 2000] could have easily become a riot situation, as there were many agitators who were trying to make one happen. The department's new training and methods prevented it. They learned from the 1992 riots.

The troops were spread thin at the Rodney King riots, and it was the good cops who toed the line. Things were totally out of control the first 30 hours of the riots, and management had fallen apart. We were able to get the National Guard and Marines, who helped us tremendously. The fact that the military troops were carrying assault rifles scared the gang members back into their holes.

LWC: Were there times when you felt anonymous, just another cop in the mass of cops? Did it alter your actions? Did it make you feel freer to administer a little payback? Maybe hit a little harder than necessary?

MM: I felt anonymous during the whole riot, like a police officer in the masses of other cops. During the first week, it was just cops and bad guys out on the street because all the law-abiding citizens were in their homes or had left the city. That fact made it clear who was standing in front of me.

I don't believe in paybacks or street justice. But that's not to say that force wasn't used, as it was a dangerous riot. It was about using the right tools for the right job. The goal was either to disperse a group or affect arrests. I did it the right way, nothing more or less. I'm a professional, doing a job, and that's what separates me from the bad guys.

LWC: In a race riot there is a phenomenon called "impersonality." This means that a person sees all members of a certain race or group as being all good or all bad. Did you see anything like that, on either the cops' side or the rioters' side?

MM: Yes, on the first day, there were many attacks on white motorists by blacks, most of whom were gang members. These victims were attacked only because they were white. The cops were seen by the rioters only as blue uniforms and as an authority they didn't like. This was the case even before the riots.

LWC: In a mob, there is a powerful instinct to follow the actions of others? Did you see any of this on either side? Maybe a cop broke formation to go after someone, which caused others to follow him?

Maybe one rioter threw a missile, then others did the same?

MM: The mobs didn't have leaders, but they were somewhat organized without being totally unorganized. If that sounds crazy—it was. A group would be looting a store; then five minutes later it would be burning a building. No one had a game plan in the mob; they were just playing follow the leader. Leadership changed constantly. Groups formed and disintegrated continuously for a week.

Though the police were outnumbered and had problems, we were much more organized than the mobs. That factor alone helped us prevent the entire city from being burned down. And believe me, the mob would have done it, if allowed.

LWC: Did you see rioters act out in a way that appeared as if their actions were more about having fun than rioting for a cause?

MM: As I said—and everyone I have ever talked to who was there shares this opinion—the riot wasn't so much about Rodney King as it was about getting free stuff, about looting. It was just plain greed.

LWC: What were some of the erroneous perceptions the public got from the riot? On the part of the rioters? On the part of the cops?

MM: I think some people believed that it was somehow healthy to have a riot and that healing could begin. But for the rioters, it was about breaking things, burning things, and stealing. Was that supposed to teach someone a lesson? If so, who?

Here is the real deal. Many good people lost their lives as a result of the riot. Others lost their property. Some lost their freedom because of their criminal acts. I don't know if all that has to happen so that someone could say, "Let's let the healing begin." That doesn't make any sense to me. The rioting was just plain wrong.

I think it shocked many cops that the riot was so large in scale. If different controls and decisions had been made, it might not have gone that way.

LWC: What was your mental process as you worked, knowing that so many rioters viewed you with intense hatred?

MM: My mental focus relied on two factors: objectives and objectiveness. First, we had objectives: secure a block, and enforce the curfew. Secondly, to get the job done I had to remain objective. There was hate, yes, but there was something else. To hate, you have to care. I think most of the violent rioters were in a sociopath mode. They burned down the neighborhoods where they lived. That's beyond hate; that is just crazy.

My mental process was to get the job done—one minute at a time, one hour at a time, and one day at time—which is the only to make it in a riot that was as large as this one. Schools, stores, and restaurants were closed. Life as we knew it stopped. As a cop, I knew it wasn't going to be like that forever, but at the moment I was part of the process to get things back to normal.

I've seen terrible things happen to police officers in the line of duty, and I've been to many of their funerals. I learned of the cold realities early in my career. No one makes me do the job. If an officer doesn't like it or cannot take it, they can always get out.

There are bad people out there and bad things that can happen. But I train hard to offset the chance of it happening to me. I know that in many areas I'm much stronger than a lot of other people, so I use my strengths and abilities to help those who need it.

That's all I can do.

RACE RIOT PRECURSORS

As we have discussed earlier, riots—race riots in this case—are often preceded by a common set of conditions before a final flashpoint ignites the violence. To put it another way, a race riot begins long before someone throws the first stone or loots the first store. Here are a few:

Residential Segregation

Community segregation can increase the likelihood of rioting (when other elements listed here have been met), because of the concentration of people experiencing similar triggers. Since all are in one central place, meaning they don't have to travel to a particular location at a particular time to riot, there is a greater chance of a spontaneous eruption.

Unemployment

When there is high unemployment in a community, it's likely there will be increased poverty, a higher crime rate, lack of self-esteem, loss of hope, increased fear and anxiety, political instability, and a growing, seething anger.

Youth

Young people carry out most riots. They are more likely to act out violently than baby boomers, and have fewer qualms about taking risks, physical and criminal. They are also more likely to be overtly angry about unemployment and other injustices and inequities.

Rumors

I patrolled a largely black community off and on for most of my police career. Rumors passed around and accepted as the truth never failed to amaze me. Some were total fabrications that I firmly believed were set in motion to discredit the police, some were distortions of the truth for the same reason, and some were misunderstandings based on the many fabrications and distortions.

Media

Sometimes the media sets the stage with deliberate sensationalism in their oversized, bold print headlines, or when a TV anchorperson teases early in the evening news, with a desperate tone and worried expression, "Racial tension in the city. Details at 11."

Police Action

Based on my experience as a military policeman working in

racially volatile locations and as a street cop working in black communities, this is a big precursor. As noted in the examples of race riots in recent history, police-involved events such as traffic stops, street arrests, shootings, and jury verdicts have often been the spark that sets off the inferno.

Now, there isn't a riot every time a police officer takes action in the black community. In fact, it's rare. In my years working in the black community, I made dozens of arrests, perhaps hundreds. Some were quite physical because of the suspect's violent resistance, but only a few set off what could technically be termed a riot.

Hot Day

The memory I have of those few incidents that did explode into rioting was that they happened on hot, sultry summer evenings. Of the many riots I have been in, I can only remember one in which people were wearing coats. All the others were on hot days, some blisteringly hot. Hot weather, especially hot and humid weather, the kind that makes even the kindest, sweetest person cranky, is a powerful trigger.

Cincinnati, Ohio, 2001

As we look at what happened in Cincinnati, take note of the aforementioned precursors: police action, youth, residential segregation, rumors, and media hype.

It began around 2 A.M. when a 19-year-old black male alerted on two police officers and burst into a sprint in the opposite direction, running especially fast because he had 14 warrants for traffic offenses and evading arrest. The officers pursued, chasing him through the most violent and drug-infested alleyways in the city, an area called Over-the-Rhine. Another police officer, who had heard the chase on his radio, joined in and quickly found the suspect. When the wanted man reached for his waistband, the most common location to secrete a weapon, the officer fired his. One round punctured the boy's chest and he fell dead.

At a council meeting, black politicians and activists shouted before the media and crowds that Cincinnati police officers had killed 15 black men in the last six years (see below, "15 Shootings: What the Media Left Out"). As a salivating media scribbled furiously on their steno pads, the leaders' accusations electrified the gathering with rage and a burning desire for revenge.

By the time the crowd left city hall, it was a thousand strong—a thousand vocal, angry, and revenge-seeking people. They marched to the police station, where they shouted at officers protecting the building and threatened them with deadly retaliation for the 15 slain men.

Then someone threw a rock through the PD's front door win-

15 Shootings: What the Media Left Out

The truth is that only three of the shootings in Cincinnati raised questions about police misjudgment. The others involved suspects who had committed despicable crimes, had resisted arrest, had attempted to stab police officers, or had shot them. Here are two of the more glaring examples.

One case involved a female officer whose police car was carjacked when the suspect jumped in, shot her in the stomach and legs, and then took control of the wheel. Although she was able to shoot and kill the suspect and survive the ordeal, she emerged from the incident seriously disabled. Mayor Luken commented on this case in one of his TV interviews, but when the station broadcasted his description of the incident, the transmission was somehow garbled.

In another case, a black officer approached a 12-year-old boy who was about to drive off in a car. When the officer reached in to grab the keys, the boy jammed the lever into drive and stomped the throttle. The young suspect dragged the officer 800 feet before the man could reach his gun with his free hand and shoot the boy in the chest. The officer fell free and died in the street. The boy drove the rest of the way home, where he died.

Can these be called "racially motivated" police shootings?

dow. That was the start of it. The crowd, now turned mob, pulled down the flag and hung it upside down. They threw missiles at police horses and broke more station windows, the glass shards injuring officers inside. Someone in the PD put out an order to "let them vent." It was a psychology that didn't work.

After midnight, the cops finally started making arrests, but the violence was in full swing by then. For the next three days, rioters, mostly young black males and females, would break hundreds of store windows, beat white motorists, set fires, loot businesses, and shoot guns. One estimate was that there were thousands of rounds fired, some at police officers.

On the third night of the riots, Mayor Charlie Luken issued a citywide curfew, which went into effect about the same time it began raining. One or both of these things stopped the violence.

The Cincinnati riots, which cost the city some $3.6 million in damages, is a classic case of how not one but several precursors came together to create three days and nights of madness.

Portland, Oregon, 1973

In this situation in which I was involved, you will find most of the aforementioned precursors, including:

- Residential segregation: The neighborhood was 95 percent black, as was the high school at which the incident occurred.
- Police action: The incident kicked off when we had a vehicle towed.
- Rumors: Any information the mob had as to why we were towing the car was based on conjecture and rumor.
- Youth: Not one of the 200 people was over 18 years of age.
- Hot: The incident occurred on an unseasonably hot day in late May.

I was still a rookie with less than a year on the police job when I began working with a cop named Jim, an aggressive, hard-working man whose enthusiasm for making busy work often got him and his trainee into jams.

It was nearly noon on a soon-to-be blisteringly hot day in late May when Jim spotted a brown Chevrolet parked in front of Washington High, a school with a predominately black student body and a reputation for large-scale disturbances, shootings, and a strong dislike for the police. Jim gave the license plate info to dispatch and then told me that the car belonged to a known pimp, not a student, and he thought that it might have a number of unpaid parking tags.

He rogered dispatch and replaced the mike. "Hear that?" he asked rhetorically. "It's got $235 in unpaid tags. Dispatch said to tow it."

I looked at my watch and asked if noon was the best time to tow since the students would be getting out for lunch. He reminded me that we were the police and we could do anything. I nodded like a good rookie, but secretly I thought it was a bad idea. The next few minutes would validate my concern.

The tow truck showed up 10 minutes later, complete with flashing lights and a loud, beeping backup warning system, attention-grabbing devices that brought a flood of students out the door and around our car.

There was not a single white face in the growing crowd of hostile black ones, a crowd that was getting braver as its number swelled to 100, then 150.

"What are you white muthafuckers doing with this car?"

"You aren't towing this ride, peckerwood."

"The white police always messin' with us. This is gonna stop. Now!"

Jim waved for the tow truck driver to take off with the car, but about 50 students quickly blocked its way. Their attempt lasted only a few seconds because the bruiser of a driver pushed his bruiser of a truck through the crowd, forcing it to part. In a moment, he was on his way, leaving the riled swarm, now near

200, to focus all of its attention on little ol' us.

Jim was on the driver's side of our police car and I was on the passenger's side as the crowd pressed in so tightly that we could not open the doors to enter the vehicle. One tall kid stepped deliberately on my foot as he leaned his chest against me, his face inches from mine. Others moved in behind him. I pushed against the tall kid's chest with my forearm, causing him to fall back against several of his snarling buddies. That was my window of opportunity to jerk my door open and scramble in. Jim had managed to get in a moment earlier.

"Lock the doors," he shouted, tapping the siren a couple of times to scatter the mob. But the mob stood fast. Then it began a storm of pounding fists on our trunk, roof, hood, and windows. When they tired of that, they began to rock the car, a little at first, then so much that we feared it was going to roll over onto its side.

"Hit the siren, hit the horn, hit the throttle, and let's get out of here," I shouted. This time the veteran listened to the rookie.

We inched forward through a hailstorm of rocks, bottles, kicks, and lunch bags. Several of the students cried out that the car hit them, but then they either laughed or kicked our doors. It took a long five minutes, but we eventually freed ourselves and roared off to the precinct to settle our nerves.

My jaw didn't stop trembling for 20 minutes.

RACISM AND THE NEWS MEDIA

It's not easy being the news media. People complain that they underreport the news, and some complain they sensationalize it. Sometimes both criticisms are leveled at the same news piece. Some whites complain that the newspapers underplay stories in which the suspect is black, while some blacks complain that there are too many dark suspect faces splashed in the newspapers and on television news. In my city, police charged a 30-year-old Chinese man with possessing thousands of images of child pornography on his computer and for stealing tens of thousands of girls' underwear from local college dorms. After an investigation that took months, the man admitted to everything. Still, people continued to make accusations that the police and the media targeted the man because he was Chinese.

While writing this chapter, an Associated Press news story appeared on the *CBS 3* Web site out of Philadelphia titled, "Settlement in 1969 race riot death." It tells about a settlement reached in York, Pennsylvania, that awarded $2 million to two sisters and two children of the late Lillie Belle Allen, a black woman. Allen, who was 27 years old in 1969, died of a gunshot wound after she and other family members had driven into a white neighborhood, a section of York that at the time was a hotbed of racial tension. Within minutes of realizing where they were, shots rang out and the woman died. The settlement would end a federal lawsuit against the city, four former city police officers, and the estate of a fifth former city officer. The case had gone unsolved for 30 years until prosecutors convened a grand jury and discovered new evidence.

At the bottom of the page on which the article appears, there was a one-sentence paragraph about another case involving an incident that happened during the same riot. In that case, the court convicted two black men for murdering two white police officers.

I had two quick thoughts after reading this news story. First, here is a clear example how racial violence, in this case incidents that occurred nearly four decades ago, still haunt and affect peoples' lives. My other thought concerned the single sentence allocated to the conviction of two men responsible for the deaths of two police officers. Why didn't that case deserve at least as much print as the lawsuit? Other news reports noted how relieved Allen's family was to have the case settled, but what about the families of the two police officers? I'm guessing that they, too, were relieved about the killers' convictions after so many years. This is only a guess since the one-sentence paragraph at the bottom of the page didn't say. Was this done out of racism, one might wonder? Yes? No? Maybe?

See? It never ends. Here are some other examples . . .

Hurricane Katrina: Looters?

During the chaos that followed Hurricane Katrina in August of 2005, two photos shown on the Internet site Yahoo! News caused considerable controversy and accusations. One pic showed a young African-American man wading through floodwater and carrying a large bag of unknown contents. The caption read, "A young man walks through chest-deep water after looting a grocery store in New Orleans on Tuesday, Aug. 30, 2005." Another photo depicting two young white people wading through water read, "Two residents wade through chest-deep water after finding bread and soda from a local grocery store."

A clear case of racism? Many writers on Internet blogs certainly thought so, as they were quick to blame the media for captioning one photo with such glaring racist undertones (black man loots) and the other with a seemingly innocent explanation (white men find). Not one of the blog writers questioned whether the authors of the articles might have witnessed the people in question finding or stealing the goods, and perhaps that important information was not included because of limited print space. Instead, all were quick to cry racism, which might very well have been the case. The point is this: those shouting the loudest about bias writing were being biased by making accusations without knowing all the facts.

All of this pours fuel on the ongoing fire of racial tension. In this case, the media contributed to the fire by 1) deliberately assuming the motivations of the subjects in the photos, 2) thoughtlessly assuming their motivations, or 3) practicing shoddy journalism by not including the evidence behind their captions. The blog writers were guilty of immediately assuming that the journalists were racists rather than questioning whether there were other extenuating circumstances.

Seattle Mardi Gras Riot

In March of 2001, the press in Seattle, Washington, reported on a riot that occurred at a Mardi Gras celebration, a weekend-long event that mimics the one in New Orleans, complete with drunken debauchery and street brawls. The one in Seattle in 2001 included the beating death of a 20-year-old man by a 17-year old.

The *Seattle Post-Intelligencer* ran multiple photos with the story depicting whites and blacks scuffling and vandalizing a car. A few days later, black leaders in the community thrashed the media for publishing photos of black youths on the attack. They also complained that one of the photos depicting black aggressors was larger than two photos depicting white aggressors.

While the police department's official statement was that there were more whites acting out in the riot, officers (including black officers) and newspaper reporters at the scene reported more incidents of blacks attacking whites. Black leaders, however, wanted to play down the racial aspects of the riot while others refused to sweep it under the rug. Callers to a local conservative talk show complained that if the riot had consisted of bands of white skinheads beating up blacks, the police would have closed all the streets around the event. "It's a double standard," many of them complained.

New York Police Chief Makes Racial Slur

A racial slur made by anyone is an ugly thing, but it's especially ugly when it's uttered by a high-ranking police chief, a man representing civic authorities, who we want to believe will treat everyone the same, regardless of race, ethnicity, sex, sexual orientation, or religious affiliation.

According to an April 2006 story in the *New York Post*, the chief of the police department's uniform division stood outside a Brooklyn station house watching a riot involving young Hasids rampaging through the Borough Park neighborhood, setting fires and smashing windows. As the NYPD riot squad moved against hundreds of rioters, the chief screamed, "Get the fucking Jews out of here! I want heads to roll!"

A city council member standing nearby heard the chief's racial slur and later filed a complaint. At one point, according to the council member, the chief turned toward him and said, "If you don't want to help me, get the fuck out of here."

If the accusation is valid, the chief was clearly wrong and unprofessional; he had allowed his adrenaline to get the best of him. What was interesting and revealing, however, was the way in which the *New York Post* chose to tell the story.

The violence began when officers pulled over a man who was blocking traffic as he talked on his cell phone. The driver turned out to be an elderly Jewish man. After the officers handed his license back to him, the man climbed out of his car and began to berate them, drawing a crowd in his support. When the officers commenced to take the man into custody, several young men in the crowd interfered physically, and within seconds, all was chaos. Soon, hundreds rioted, burned, and broke things.

The piece in the *New York Post* ran a 1,000-word story, containing 36 paragraphs. The first 21 discussed the chief's inappropriate language. The last 15 talked about the riot.

That does not make for balanced reporting.

ARE WE HEADED TOWARD MORE MAJOR RACE RIOTS?

It would certainly appear so judging by what is going on around the globe. Racial tensions are running high from Cincinnati to Seattle to Buffalo to northern England to Sydney to South Africa to Asia and seemingly every place in between. Has it always been so? Yes. Does it appear to be getting worse? Some think so.

Consider political scientist Carol M. Swain's book *The New White Nationalism in America: Its Challenge to Integration*. The author, who is black, contends that the United States is on the brink of an explosion of white "tribalism" that could trigger unprecedented levels of racial antagonism and an epidemic of violence. Swain says that the underlying cause is a swelling "white nationalist" movement fueled by simmering resentment of affirmative action problems. She says, "The book is a wake-up call to warn people that we're following a dangerous course by pushing identity politics and multiculturalism. There's nothing special about the U.S. that says we couldn't have ethnic cleansing and violence here like in Bosnia or Rwanda."

Swain believes that the way to steer away from this course is to understand that whites have legitimate complaints about race, and that politicians and scholars should openly debate these issues. She further believes that we should abolish racial preferences in university admissions, hiring, and government contracts that fuel resentment among whites and send a message to blacks that they cannot meet the same standards as everyone else.

Offering a different take on the issue is *San Jose Mercury News* journalist Sylvester Monroe, who writes in an article titled "Race problems go unsolved when they go unadmitted" that we fail to learn from history, even recent history. In particular, he discusses the surprise and disbelief over racial rioting in Cincinnati following the fatal shooting of a black man by a white police officer. He says that instead of asking why it happened, the real question should be "why, more than a quarter century after the Kerner Commission studied violent racial protests in eight U.S. cities, including Cincinnati, do black men continue to be brutalized and killed by police officers at much higher rates than any other group in the country?"

He says that the police shooting of an unarmed black man in Cincinnati and similar shootings in other cities that have also sparked street riots were, while ignited by the action of the police, "fueled by years of perceived neglect and indifference." According to Monroe, many Americans, especially whites, deny that race was a motive in almost any negative act against a black unless the perpetrator was wearing a white sheet. He says that police brutality cases are a symptom of the illness, while the denial that there is anything wrong is the affliction. His accusations are important when you consider that several recent race riots have been the result of perceived racially motivated acts by the police. He makes a valuable point (similar to one that Swain makes) when he says that "to deny the existence of perhaps the one thing that still consistently frays the fabric of our society is to threaten the future of this country." Monroe ultimately argues that by turning away from race issues and ignoring what has occurred before, we make this country's race problem even more difficult to solve.

There is no doubt that racial incidents happen in the boardrooms of high-rise office buildings, on the loading docks of factories, and in dark alleys where a white cop and a black suspect meet in deadly conflict. Sometimes the action is subtle, sometimes it's glaring, and sometimes it's not racial at all but only perceived to be. Either way it's a problem. It's one we can no longer deny or pretend doesn't exist. Doing so keeps the embers of hate, distrust, and misunderstanding red hot and ever ready to ignite into an inferno.

Sources

"Fanning the Flames of Oppression," by Stephanie Elizondo Griest, www.ustrek.org/odyssey/semester2/031701/031701stephwatts .html, 2001.

"Watts in Perspective," author unknown, The College of New Jersey, www.tcnj.edu/~blohm3/essay.htm.

"144 Hours in August 1965: A Report by the Governor's Commission on the Los Angeles Riots, 1965," author unknown, www.usc.edu/isd/archives/cityinstress/mccone/part4.html.

"How the 1960s riots hurt African-Americans," by the National Bureau of Economic Research, www.nber.org/digest/sep04/w10243.html.

"Newark Riots—1967," by Max A. Herman, Ph.D., The State University of New Jersey, www.67riots.rutgers.edu/n_index.htm.

"Detroit Riots—1967 by Max A. Herman, Ph.D., The State University of New Jersey, www.67riots.rutgers.edu/d_index.htm.

"D.C. Riots of 1968," by Ben W. Bilbert and the staff of the *Washington Post*, www.carolmoore.net/sfm/dc-riots1968.html, 1968.

"Nation's capital still recovering from 1968 riots," CNN Interactive, www.cnn.com/US/9804/04/mlk.dc.riots/

"Rodney King and the Los Angeles Riots," by Stan Chambers, www.citivu.com/ktla/sc-ch1.html, 2005.

"L.A.'s Darkest Days," by Daniel B. Wood, *The Christian Science Monitor*, http://csmonitor.com/2002/0429/p01s07-ussc.html, 2002.

"Settlement in 1969 race riot death," author unknown, http://kyw.com/topstories/local_story_334155418.html, November 30, 2005.

"Religion, alcohol and race," by Chip Johnson, *San Francisco Chronicle*, December 2, 2005.

"The Vietnam War and the revolt of black GIs," author unknown, Vietnam Veterans Against the War Anti-Imperialist, www.oz.net/~vvawai/index.html.

"Whites and the next racial clash in America," by Jack E. White, Free Republic, www.freerepublic.com/focus/f-news/1034930/posts.

"Race problems go unsolved when they go unadmitted," by Sylvester Monroe, *San Jose Mercury News*, April 22, 2001.

"What really happened in Cincinnati," by Heather Mac Donald, City Journal, www.city-journal.org, Summer 2001.

"The media's role in the race riots," author unknown, Aim Report, www.aim.org, 2001.

"NYPD chief in Jew 'slur,'" by John Doyle, *New York Post* online edition, April 6, 2006.

Chapter 7

Prison Riots

"Prison riots are common in Brazil, but this one was unusually shocking as rebel inmates threw the mutilated corpses of rivals from the prison walls. They decapitated two of the dead men and hung their heads from the wall."

China Daily, reporting on five-day riot at a Brazilian prison

Having served 29 years as a law-enforcement officer, I'm no stranger to jails and prisons. However, the first time I saw the gray walls and steel bars was when a cop pushed me into a cell and slammed the door. I was 19 years old, in the slammer for fighting with a man who had jumped me in the parking lot of a burger joint. Since the fight scene was somewhat chaotic, the police lodged both of us until they could sort things out. Once they determined that I was the good guy, they released me.

I didn't get a striped prison uniform or a tin cup to rake across the bars. Not even a harmonica to moan out some heavy blues. I just did my 60 minutes sitting on a steel bunk thinking about how my mom was going to kill me. I also thought about how horrible jail was, how terrifying, how final that steel door sounded—*kuh-klunk*—when it slammed shut behind me.

Three years later I was in Vietnam patrolling the mean streets of Saigon as a military policeman. Although we used two jail facilities in the city to hold American GI prisoners, there were occasions when we had to transport a hard-core criminal to the infamous Long Binh Prison, or LBJ as the troops called it, which coincidentally was the nickname and initials of President Lyndon B. Johnson. It was a typical prison, with high walls, guard towers, and lots of barbed wire. It sat ominously on a hill overlooking a sprawling valley of rice paddies, though few inside could see the view.

It was an intensely oppressive place: drab, dusty, and wilting hot. There was also a heavy quiet within the walls, apart from when someone screamed or the rumble of distant artillery echoed through the facility. Except for the defiant, most of the prisoners, stripped of their rank insignia and unit patches, moved silently from one place to another, marching in columns of half a dozen, their heads down, shoulders stooped as if carrying an invisible heavy weight, which in a way they were considering their destroyed futures. The defiant ones were not defiant for long as they were whisked away quickly to . . . somewhere special.

INSIDE

The powerful sense of place that was LBJ Prison was the same that I would experience during my civilian police career when doing business in the local jail and on the few occasions I was inside the Oregon State Prison in Salem. Other than the long, hard 60 minutes I served in the slammer as a 19-year-old, all my other experiences behind bars was as a cop: booking a prisoner, taking a report from one, or interviewing incarcerated gangbangers to gather intelligence information. As brief as these moments were, they always gave me the shivers and confirmed my belief that prison is not a good place to be.

Jim Hogshire, author of *You are Going to Prison*
(Loompanics Unlimited, 1994), doesn't mince words in his
description of prison life:

> A half dozen people die each day in U.S. prisons.
> Another one hundred are seriously injured. Savagery and
> viciousness rule our prisons . . . Fucked up the ass, locked in
> a cell and eating fatback with hair growing out of it. Your
> friends will forget you, your wife will leave you, your mama
> cannot help you, and you will live by the law of the jungle
> whether you like it or not. That's prison. Hell on Earth . . .
> You will be there for years. And prison will be in you for the
> rest of your life.

Believe this: you never want to go to prison, and if you do,
you want to escape from it in whatever way you want to define
"escape." It's a horrific subculture of extremes: fear, violence,
racism, victimization, retribution, punishment, anxiety, mental illness, perversion, rage—and the gnawing knowledge that you have
no free will. To kick up the misery a notch, let's stir into this
witch's cauldron additional ingredients, real or perceived: bad
food, abusive corrections officers, unfair rules and punishment,
and uncomfortable and unhealthy living conditions. To bring this
mix to a boil, simply add a fight, a knifing, a reprimand, or a violent apprehension of an inmate by officers.

All this makes a not-so-delicious recipe for a big serving of
prison riot.

A GLANCE AT HISTORY

While prison riots are a favorite on the 5 o'clock news and the
stuff of exciting movies, there has not been a great deal of research
done on them. Most commonly, prison uprisings are blamed on
racial tensions, gang violence, bad food, brutal guards, unreason-

able incarceration periods, and overcrowding. These elements are often already in place and causing misery, so all that is needed is an incident to set off the bomb. Let's see how this has played out by examining a few significant prison riots of the past.

Alcatraz, 1946

Called the "Battle of Alcatraz," what this riot lacked in participants it made up for with the intensity of its violence. It began with an escape attempt by six prisoners, all of whom had long histories of violence. First they overpowered a guard in the West Gun Gallery, which gave them access to firearms and riot clubs. Then they captured and locked up several guards in a cell, obtaining from one of them keys to the recreation yard. Unbeknownst to them, however, a clever guard had hidden the most critical key, thus making it impossible to get through the door to the yard. When the distress sirens sounded, the Coast Guard, Marines, and off-duty corrections officers immediately mobilized to help take back the cell house.

It didn't take long for the prisoners to realize that freedom in a prison setting comes in segments. When they lose one section to the corrections officers, they must then defeat the next section's security, and when they subsequently lose that one, they must move on to the next. The rioters on this day discovered that fact too late when they found themselves trapped.

One of them, frustrated and enraged, took a revolver, leaned against the cell in which they had imprisoned the guards, and fired wildly into it until the gun emptied. Inside the cramped cell, the critically wounded moaned and cried in agony as their blood spread across the floor.

The first rescue team came under heavy rifle fire as they tried to help a downed guard. Several team members fired suppression rounds as other corrections officers tended to the injured man. One rescuer fell, then another, and another. Those three would survive, but a fourth officer didn't make it. Two inmates attempted to get more weapons, but a storm of bullets stopped them—one, fatally.

At the same time, a steady stream of gunfire by inmates positioned on top of C Block pinned down another rescue team. One officer fell wounded before they could secure the door and trap the inmates inside.

In all the confusion—the deafening roar of gunfire and its reverberation throughout the concrete and steel structure, the screams of the wounded and dying, the blood, the choking gun smoke—the Marines erroneously thought the problem was happening in D Block; thus, their commanders ordered them to take even more extreme measures.

They drilled holes in the ceiling and lowered hand grenades attached to wires. A moment later, the grenades detonated in a series of thunderous explosions and concussions that shook the mighty structure and deafened all those who cowered and trembled behind mattresses. Water from broken pipes began flooding the block as the barrage of continuous explosions, gusts of blinding tear gas, and the cacophony of gunfire went on forever; at least seemingly so for all those engaged.

In reality, the shooting continued for nearly 48 hours. In the end, two guards lay dead and several others were wounded. Three of the escapees died in the gun battles and two others died together in the gas chamber. One other prisoner received an additional 99 years.

The cell blocks would not return to normal for several months. The marring on the cement walls from bullets and explosions would remain.

Attica, 1971

Counting the Indian massacres in the latter part of the 19th century, the retaking of Attica State Prison in 1971 was the second most bloody one-day fight between Americans since the Civil War in the 1860s.

There are many versions of that September rebellion at Attica in books, documentaries, movies, and Web sites. The story has been rewritten, distorted, selectively edited, and censored, most likely to protect the guilty. What is known is that on September 9, 1971, 1,300 prisoners overpowered their guards, taking 40 of them hostage, and seized control of the prison. They were enraged over living conditions in the facility: they wanted minimum-wage salary for the work they performed, improved education, better food, and a greater number of Spanish-speaking and black guards.

The late 1960s and early 1970s were years of tremendous racial strain in the United States. Terms like "black awareness" and "black militancy" were used as positive and negative descriptors of what was going on in some parts of the African-American community, to include the prisons. When black militancy became too intense for some prisons in the early 1970s, their administrations transferred the "troublemakers" to Attica. If things were not tense enough, a reknowned Black Panther named George Jackson died while in the custody of white prison guards at San Quentin in California. Though the arrival of e-mail was 25 years away, Attica prisoners in New York knew of the death within minutes of it happening. Conditions were ripe for violence when the uprising took place.

The rioters were in control for four days as they negotiated with officials and relayed their demands to the press. When the prisoners asked to speak to Governor Nelson Rockefeller, he refused and sent in the state police—some sources say as many as a 1,000 officers—with orders to retake the prison.

It was pouring rain as officers positioned themselves on the prison's roofs, their handguns and shotguns at the ready. Helicopters swooped about overhead and bullhorns ordered inmates to lie down and give up. Then began the bullets and tear gas. For six minutes the officers fired, more than 2,000 rounds in all, killing 29 inmates and 10 hostages. When it was over, the final death count was 43, including three prisoners killed by fellow inmates.

The first reports were that several hostages had had their throats slit. However, 24 hours later the autopsies disclosed that that had not happened at all. The rescuing officers had in fact shot them.

The Attica riots brought national media attention to what was going on in American prisons at the time, especially in regard to matters of race. While more than three-quarters of the inmates at Attica were Puerto Rican and black, the entire corrections staff, over 380, was white. The guards were seen as bigots because of how they treated inmates of color. Case in point: there were complaints that many guards called their truncheons their "nigger sticks."

In 2004, 33 years after the riot, the State of New York settled a $12 million wrongful-death lawsuit with the families of inmates who were killed during the Attica riot.

Why Prisoners Riot

Few prison riots result in inmates freeing themselves from behind the high walls. They might move from one area of the prison structure to another, but they remain incarcerated. Therefore, the reasons behind a prison riot are not about getting out but rather trying to force someone in authority to hear their grievances, creating chaos so they can administer revenge on a guard or another prisoner, and showing everyone that inmates still possess power. Sometimes, as we have seen in other riots discussed throughout this book, it's also about having a little violent fun.

Penitentiary of New Mexico, 1980

One Associated Press reporter wrote that the 36-hour riot at the Penitentiary of New Mexico was a "merry-go-round gone crazy." Those who lived it—guards and prisoners—would no doubt say that if the leaderless and goalless horror was indeed a merry-go-round, it was one from hell.

The riot began on February 2, 1989, when corrections officers entered dormitory E-2 on the south side of the sprawling structure. Prisoners took four guards hostage, four out of the 15 on duty that night who had the daunting task of monitoring more than 1,100 prisoners.

Inmates ran along the main corridor and smashed out what was supposed to be shatterproof glass encasing the control center. The on-duty guard wisely fled, but he left in his wake a cluster of keys that opened virtually all the doors and gates throughout the prison. With instant access to just about any place the prisoners wanted to go, their first choice was to demolish the structure before administering some deadly payback.

They set fires, destroyed plumbing fixtures, and broke into the infirmary and took drugs, lots and lots of drugs. The frenzied mob then proceeded to Cellblock 4, a special unit for prisoners who had snitched and who were segregated for their protection because of issues they had had with other prisoners. They immediately found two they were looking for; they hung one and removed the head of the other.

Author G. Hirliman wrote a book about the riot, titled *The Hate Factory* (Dell Publishing Co., 1985; iUniverse, 2005). Hirliman writes this about the hanging incident:

> Tying the rope under his arms and around his chest, they strung him up on the basketball hoop for all to see. There he would hang for the rest of the riot . . . During those hours of madness that were to follow, inmates would come in and hack at his dangling corpse with knives, beat it with pipes, mutilating it so totally that it was beyond recognition, a raw, bloody mass of flesh, by the time the uprising was over.

Of the 33 prisoners found dead at the riot's end, most were from Cellblock 4.

Though it was apparent that neither the state nor the inmates had a spokesperson to represent them, there was an attempt the next day to negotiate. The prisoners had the usual concerns: overcrowding, harsh discipline, lousy food, and the need to talk with federal officials and the news media. Though negotiations would go on for hours, they eventually broke off with no concessions made.

Meanwhile, ambulances stayed busy transporting the injured and dead to an area hospital as smoke poured from one part of the prison. Prisoners allowed a few guard hostages to leave, some of whom the inmates had protected throughout the ordeal, and others they had injured during the riot. One hostage sat tied to a chair for hours and another had lain naked and wounded on a stretcher.

When the negotiations failed, many of the prisoners considered the uprising over. They began to exit the facility and cross over to a fence where National Guardsmen stood armed with M16s. The local hospital treated more than 100 injured or overdosed inmates as well as the 12 guards who were held hostage.

Hirliman summarizes the incident in *The Hate Factory*:

> Overcrowded conditions, young and unskilled guards,
> and a no-care attitude of prison administrators all contributed
> to the anger, despair, and bitter fury that erupted with mind-
> searing violence. Fortified with liquor and homemade knives,
> 62 inmates… [took] control of the prison. Though 14 guards
> were held hostage, beaten, and sodomized, none were killed;
> the inmates saved the brunt of their rage for fellow convicts.

Decapitated Hostages

In the spring of 2005, prisoners of Sao Paulo penitentiary in Brazil held 11 guards hostage and terrorized an unknown number of other prisoners during a riot over better living conditions. The prison's capacity is 680 inmates, though it was housing 785 at the time.

By the time the siege had ended, five prisoners lay decapitated. The killers placed the heads on spikes and displayed them on the roof of the prison.

Southern Ohio Correctional Facility, 1993

On April 11, Easter Sunday of 1993, Peggy Vallandingham kissed her husband Robert goodbye in the kitchen as he left for work at the Southern Ohio Correctional Facility, where, for the past two years, he worked as a corrections officer. Robert walked out into the garage, then paused. He turned, then ran back inside his house to do something he had never done before: he kissed his wife goodbye a second time.

She would never see him alive again.

Within hours, he became a hostage under the control of rioting inmates. Four days later, they would strangle him to death and drop his body out a window into the prison yard.

The episode began as a fight but escalated quickly to a "full-scale riot," as one dispatcher at the maximum-security prison described it. There were many causes, including complaints about poor living conditions and a new warden seen as overly strict and unfair. But there was one other cause that was different than the norm: prisoners disagreed with a rule that would force Muslim cons to undergo tuberculosis testing by injection, a procedure forbidden by their beliefs.

While authorities and citizens panels would investigate these and other issues for years after, on April 11 the reasons for the riot were quickly set aside as hundreds of prisoners rebelled, fought one another, and battled the guards. Prisoners captured eight corrections officers as they responded to the disturbance; others were beaten and left bleeding in the yard. Rioters also took fellow prisoners hostage, probably weaker ones to use for bartering with prison officials. State police were able to recapture the yard later in the day and rescue an injured guard, but the situation remained out of control.

Rumors circulated that scores had been killed, fraying nerves among the officials as they negotiated with the inmates. With the ever-present media cameras watching their every move, prison authorities worked in the spotlight as they contended with corrections officers and prisoners hurt, killed, and held hostage. Just when it looked like everything that could go wrong had done so, on the third day of the siege a patrol helicopter malfunctioned and crashed just outside one of the prison yards, injuring the pilot.

On day four, negotiators allowed food and water into the cellblock in exchange for prescription medicine for two of the guards held hostage. On the fifth day, rioters threw the dead body of Robert Vallandingham from a cellblock window just hours before a deal was struck for the release of another guard in exchange for a 15-minute broadcast on live radio by one of the inmates.

The standoff would continue for six more days before the rioters decided to end it and turn themselves over to the authorities. That evening, patrol units began processing prisoners as they gave themselves up one by one. The remaining hostages walked free just before midnight.

When it was over, nine prisoners and one guard lost their lives.

Camp Bucca, Iraq, 2005

Imagine that you're stuck pulling guard duty in a United States-run detention facility in Iraq. First there is the oppressive daytime heat and numbing nighttime cold. Then the lack of quality training, inadequate equipment, a huge language and culture barrier, eyes of every watchdog group in the world monitoring and critiquing your every move, boredom, fear, and the ever-present longing to be somewhere else, especially home.

Then add a riot.

Camp Bucca, a 100-acre compound built from the sand up to showcase the U.S. Army's new detention methods, is one of several detention facilities in Iraq. It's divided into eight compounds, each designed to house 800 inmates. Maximum population is supposed to be 6,000 prisoners; it's near full capacity at this writing.

Though relatively new, Bucca has had its share of disturbances and all-out riots. One of the first occurred in 2004, a result of a fight that broke out between Sunni and Shiite prisoners over a difference of opinion as to how to observe Ramadan, the Muslim fasting month. The clash forced security to place the Shiites in a separate compound.

Two months later, a protest arose over two prisoners sentenced to isolation after they attempted to escape. Prisoners armed themselves with tent stakes and mattresses as shields, but an overwhelming number of troops, guard dogs, and fire trucks got them under control quickly.

In January of 2005, U.S. soldiers entered one of the compounds to conduct a routine search for contraband. The search was completed without incident, but afterwards, a Muslim cleric complained that the soldiers damaged several Korans, a complaint of unknown validity. Nonetheless, it sparked an uprising, and a large mob of chanting and shouting prisoners formed quickly and pressed their mass against the front fence of the compound.

There was concern among the American soldiers, some of whom had only been in country for a couple of months, that the rioters would push the fence over and escape. So the troops began spraying gas, which forced the first two rows back a little. Then the prisoners began throwing chunks of concrete, rocks, and water bottles filled with sand. Some Iraqis had makeshift slingshots and fired missiles into the troops. Within minutes, prisoners from other compounds joined in the riot, adding to the chaos and confusion.

Even the guards in the towers felt overwhelmed as the mobs moved in waves around the compound, targeting each tower. "It was chaotic," one troop said of the hurled debris. "Stuff was coming from everywhere." One tower guard said it was like an upside-down water fountain, with projectiles spewing up and into the towers. Some of the rocks shattered the double-pane glass in the tower houses, forcing guards to crouch and hope they would not get struck with lethal missiles and jagged shards.

In another tower, the guard continuously shouted in Arabic for the mob to stop, but they ignored him. He fired several shotgun rounds of nonlethal rubber bullets but to no avail, as many prisoners had cloaked themselves with heavy sleeping bags. Guards said later that it appeared that the prisoners knew the limited range of the nonlethal weapons. They reported that prisoners would withdraw just enough to avoid getting hit by the rubber bullets or gas sprays, then they would rush forward toward the perimeters.

The intense riot would go on for an hour, ending only when the prisoners began hearing of rioting inmates in another compound getting shot fatally. It was true: four were shot and killed and six others injured. Prison superiors debriefed the two sergeants who fired the fatal rounds, finding their actions within the guidelines of prison policy.

Since then, prison guards at Camp Bucca carry nonlethal weapons that fire at a longer range. Additionally, the camp now has a 1,000-gallon fire truck with a powerful spray to use against rioters.

RACIAL TENSION IN PRISONS

"Race is an immediate and obvious division that provides identity and a sense of security for some offenders," author and veteran corrections author Tom Martin writes in *Behind Prison Walls* (Paladin Press, 2003). "Furthermore, almost all inmates base many of their actions upon expectations of peers from their racial groups. Ignoring this fact of prison life is dangerous, because it prevents a necessary, fuller understanding of prison dynamics."

The complexity of the race issue in prison is illustrated by an incident that took place in the Los Angeles County Jail system in 2006. In February of that year, nearly 2,000 inmates rioted at the North County Correctional Facility in Los Angeles. The facility is a maximum-security complex comprised of five jails on a 34-acre site located about 40 miles from Los Angeles. One inmate died from a beating and more than 100 others were injured. The riot, according to authorities, was racially motivated between black and Hispanic inmates, likely a carryover from feuds between Los

Angels street gangs. Of the 2,000 involved, at least 200 were engaged in what one spokesperson described as "serious fighting." Another called it "massive chaos." At one point during the riot, a long line of 24 ambulances and seven fire trucks waited outside the facility to treat the wounded. Corrections officers managed to regain control of the sprawling facility using tear gas and rubber bullets.

Afterwards, it was necessary to segregate prisoners by race. It's illegal to segregate prisoners except in emergency situations. In spite of this, another riot between blacks and Hispanics broke out in an adjacent jail the next day, injuring another 10 people.

Los Angeles Sheriff Lee Baca told a news conference, "We have a large African-American population that is exposed to an even larger Hispanic population, and the imbalance leads to what we have seen today."

Jody Kent, jails project coordinator for the ACLU of Southern California, showed her naiveté about prison racial issues when she told a reporter, "There isn't enough opportunity for the inmates to do productive things, and that allows for the tensions to rise."

Behind Prison Walls author Tom Martin does not agree that crafts and hobbies will do away with racial tension in prison because the race issue is so deeply ingrained. He writes:

> Welcome to the flashpoint in the field of corrections. Even though it may be politically incorrect to say so, it is a fact that race is an important factor among the inmate population. Some staff members avoid the topic simply because to discuss it requires gross generalizations at some level, and that can be seen as incorrect or offensive. Perhaps others avoid the issue because it is very complex. Whatever the official case may be, race in prison simply cannot be ignored or denied.

In the case of the jail and prison system in Los Angeles, race and gang segregation is an important tool for keeping high-violence-prone inmates under some semblance of control. In short, it prevents inmates from killing each other and helps keep correction officers safe. However, by segregating people, members of particular ethnic groups find themselves in gang-dominated environments, where they must follow the expectations and rules of the gang. If they don't, they are met with severe reprisals. However, when placed into an ethnic group other than their own, they are at risk of being hurt or killed. It's a complex issue.

Some pundits believe that there is greater violence *within* an ethnic group—call it, intraracial gang violence—than there is between ethnic groups. For example, Norteños and Sureños Hispanic gang members are deadly rivals, as are black Bloods and Crips.

Prison staff must deal with the reality of the moment and sometimes, if not most of the time, this means segregating people immediately to prevent more violence and save lives. But what about ongoing programs to offset the constant pressure of gangs, race, and violence on the inmate population?

"Prison made me bitter, not better," says Pernell Brown, a gang specialist with the Community of Colors program in Portland, Oregon. "The mentality of belief that 'once an inmate always an inmate' is alive and well inside the institutions." Brown made these comments at a meeting of the Commission on Safety and Abuse in America's Prisons, coincidentally during the first week of the Los Angeles County jail riots.

Another speaker, Daniel Alejandrez, also a former inmate, asked for jails and prisons to implement more cultural, spiritual, and educational programs. His organization, Barrios Unidos, has been doing just that with gang-affiliated teens and other former inmates. Alejandrez says that acknowledging gangs and gang culture in jails and prisons does not have to mean that prisoners become worse in segregated cells. He said that it was a perfect time after the LA County jail riots to reach out to the inmates with education, counseling, training, and vocational opportunities.

"Over the decades I have seen profound changes in the lives of those afforded even the smallest of opportunities."

PRISON RIOTS: GUARDS' PERSPECTIVES

Other than being individually targeted for assassination by inmates, a prison riot represents the greatest threat to the life of a corrections officer while he or she is on the job. They could be viciously attacked in the initial explosion of fighting, or they could be isolated among the rioting convicts and taken hostage, where their survival depends on the whims of some of the most violent, vengeful people on the planet. Monya LeBlanc and Bill Valentine are two veterans of corrections work who have witnessed prison riots firsthand, and here they tell their stories.

Nevada State Prison, 1996

Retired Sergeant Bill Valentine spent a 20-year career with the Nevada Department of Prisons, many of which were behind the big wall of Nevada State Prison in Carson City, and he has written extensively about life there. Paladin Press publishes his excellent books *Gang Intelligence Manual* and *Gangs and Their Tattoos*.

Sergeant Valentine told of one riotous fight that exploded between two rival Hispanic gangs—around 30 Paisas and an equal number of Aguilas. The two factions, armed with shanks (stabbing weapons) and impact weapons (such as rocks-in-a-sock), slammed into each other in the lower yard, directly under a gun post. The fight was all about power and prestige; the winner would control the yard.

At the time, Sergeant Valentine served as the shift supervisor in an area of the prison called 7 Post, which overlooks the lower recreation yard. He said that he became suspicious that something was brewing just before the riot broke out.

Though it was a warm October day, I noticed the large grouping of Paisas, most of whom were wearing hip-length denim jackets. I presumed, and I would be proven right, that the linings of their coats were stuffed with newspapers and magazines to serve as body armor. In their minds, they figured that they could kill or seriously injure some of the Aguilas before the gun post officer reacted.

The sergeant had no sooner notified the post officer of what he was seeing when it "jumped off," meaning all hell broke loose.

Now, when a riotous crowd out on the street overwhelms the police, the officers can always back off a block or two, regroup, and strategize a new approach. This is not the case in the claustrophobic structure of a prison. I asked Sergeant Valentine if correction officers have a sense that they, too, are incarcerated. "Yes," he said, continuing:

> You learn in the academy that in prison you will not become a bargaining chip if you are taken hostage by the inmates. No gates will be opened. The best you can hope for is that the rescue team coming in after you will do so early, and their aim will be accurate. Anytime something serious jumps off, the first thing that must be done by the officers is to isolate the situation. If this means that one of us gets trapped, then it happens.

Wolf Pack

Tom Martin writes in *Behind Prison Walls* of the response of corrections officers to threats against their own:

Like a wolf pack, the correctional staff fights among itself, sometimes viciously. But when there is an outside threat, such as an inmate attack on a staff member, the full fury of the pack moves into collective, coordinated action. Watching staff members slip from the different units and move down the corridors prior to becoming a swarm is akin to seeing wolves moving through a forest moments before pouncing upon prey. Corrections staff have a more measured response, but watching them respond as a pack to an outside threat is impressive.

This is clearly a powerful incentive for corrections officers to end a volatile situation quickly. The inmates know this, and they know that officers will not hesitate to shoot. Sergeant Valentine describes what happened next:

> The officer in the gun post fired 7 1/2 birdshot into the rioters, which put all 60 of them on the ground. A number of inmates were hit with birdshot. Others sustained cuts and bruises from the brief melee, though had the gun post officer not fired on them to stop the rioting, many of the combatants might have been seriously hurt or killed. After that, it was a matter of restraining each person, sending the injured to the infirmary, and locking them all up.

Since the tension between the two rival gangs had not gone away—each swore vengeance on the other—both factions were isolated and housed away from the other. They were unable even to use the recreation yards at the same time.

I asked how it feels to work in an atmosphere where violence, such as a prison riot, can explode at virtually anytime. Valentine:

> Most officers go to work knowing that anything can jump off at any moment. It is something that is just accepted. Early in my career, I knew that if the inmates wanted to harm me, it would happen. This I accepted, though I learned how to minimize it from happening. Developing informants is a great help, and so is trusting your gut feelings. A veteran officer can detect the many signs that indicate a serious incident is impending, such as increased canteen sales [the inmate shops early since he might end up in lockdown], an increase in inmates being caught with weapons, an unusual number of surly inmates grouping, others trying to get their beds moved, and some reporting for sick call in the hope they would be moved off the yard [the possible battleground] and housed in the infirmary.

While some readers might think firing on inmates to be harsh, one must keep in mind that violence in the form of a prison riot is explosive and deadly. Corrections officers are outnumbered and usually targeted. Birdshot hurts, but not as much as being shanked or slammed in the head with a makeshift club. When I asked Sergeant Valentine what would have happen if the officer had not fired, he answered simply, "Before these shoot-to-stop orders were initiated, Nevada State Prison had suffered a number of violent inmate fatalities, deaths that may possibly have been prevented."

United States Disciplinary Barracks, 1995

Monya LeBlanc is a corrections officer with the Multnomah County Sheriff's Office in Portland, Oregon, where she has worked since 1998. Prior to that, she served with the U.S. Army's Military Police, working in corrections for several years. In 1994, she was awarded Soldier of the Year for 8th Army in the Pacific Region. This is the story of her experience in a military prison riot that occurred in 1995.

It began when one of our MP guards, a private, told an inmate to remove his do-rag [head wrap similar to a bandanna], which is a violation of the prison dress code. Actually, the MP's confrontation with the inmate was probably just the catalyst that set everything off. We'd been hearing rumblings for the past several hours that something was up, so I think his reprimand just set in motion what would have exploded sooner or later anyway. Plus, he wasn't liked by many of the inmates, so that didn't help either.

Monya is talking about a prison riot that occurred at the United States Disciplinary Barracks (USDB), popularly known as "Leavenworth." Located in Fort Leavenworth, Kansas, the prison was established by an act of Congress in 1875 and took more than three decades to build. It continued to incarcerate inmates for more than 80 years and then was completely demolished in 2002 to make way for a new USDB, built a few miles away from the original grounds. When Monya and her husband, David, an MP, served there, everyone affectionately called the aging structure (or not so affectionately, if you were on the wrong side of the bars) "the castle."

> I was a sergeant, six months pregnant, and working graveyard shift in the control room. Think of this room as if it were a brick- and Plexiglas-encased hub of a giant wheel, and the seven housing wings, the spokes. In 1995, we had around 1,700 inmates doing time for every crime imaginable, similar to any civilian prison.
>
> On the night in question, we were especially on guard because we had received a report early in the shift that a couple of inmates had said they were fearful that something was about to happen. Near midnight, I got a call from a guard reporting a "witching hour," meaning that some coordinated event by the inmates was about to happen. Still, we had nothing specific. Then, just as I looked at my watch and saw that it was 11:50, our radio traffic went crazy. Reports were coming in that inmates were padlocking themselves in their cells so they wouldn't get hurt by other inmates, some were setting fires in trash cans, and a mop bucket was found in one cell, which was unauthorized since they were often used as a weapon.

Although prisoners were free to walk about in a common area, Monya didn't feel any immediate fear for herself when the riot ignited. "To get to me in the control room, a prisoner would have to pass through a couple of secure points, which were barred gates with controlled access that only I controlled."

Although she was in a relatively safe location, Monya's initial reaction to hearing the excited garble over the radios and the screams of men coming from 6th Wing sent an adrenaline dump into her body. But then her training, her years of working in the prison system, and her police experience prior to joining the military all kicked in. "I was frazzled for a moment, but then I began keeping a log of the riot, organizing hectic radio traffic, and notifying everyone in authority. And there are many in authority in the military."

Some Control Towers Can Be Breached

In 2004, an inmate at Sam Lewis Correctional Facility in Arizona attacked a guard in the prison kitchen area. The prisoner and another inmate forced their way into an observation tower occupied by two guards, one male and one female.

The hostage situation would last for 15 days. The male guard walked free after one week, but the female remained captive for another eight days as a negotiation team conversed with the captors.

Sometimes in an adrenaline-charged event, an image, a thought, or something someone says burns into one's memory banks. For Monya, it was a sports car. "I notified a captain who said he was on his way. Then for some reason he told me that he would be driving a Corvette. Why he thought I needed to know that I don't know, but it's something that has stuck in my mind."

After the inmate with the do-rag had refused the MP's order to remove it, he punched the guard in the face. Though the MP staggered back from the blow, he managed to trigger his body alarm before other prisoners overwhelmed him. They grabbed his alarm and radio, knocked his much-needed glasses from his face, and then dragged him into 4th Wing, where they held him hostage. The rioters assaulted the first two guards who rushed into the wing, but they managed to break free and escape. In the confusion, the MP who had been taken to 4th Wing broke away and locked himself in a stairwell.

Without his glasses, the young, trembling soldier had to squint through the door's small window, barely making out several figures moving toward him. Good, he thought. Rescuers! He had no idea that a riot was in progress, but he did know he was very happy to be found. He quickly unlocked the door and walked toward his friends.

Body Alarm

In *Behind Prison Walls*, author Tom Martin writes about what happens when a corrections officer activates his body alarm:

Unless it's a very odd facility, when any officer needs assistance, all the staff friction goes out the window. It's Us vs. Them, with Them being the inmates. When help is needed, it's a great feeling to see the swarm of blue, brown, or gray shirts appearing.

But they weren't his buddies, and they definitely weren't his rescuers. When he was close enough to see them clearly, he looked into the cruel faces of several prisoners. He spun around and began to run, but they were on him like wolves on a lone sheep.

The riot was in full swing now as the inmates smashed furniture and jammed the main gate to the wing. They could not get out and the guards could not get in. For the MP hostage, things were about to get especially ugly.

The inmates stripped off his boots and shirt. Then they beat him. They hit him with their fists, they kicked him, and they clubbed him with mop buckets. Just when the MP thought it could not get any worse, the cons got a full coffee pot of boiling water and poured it over his bleeding body. They would continue to torture the young private for the next six hours.

Outside the prison, the administration formed a quick command post. A Special Operations Response Team (SORT), similar to a civilian police department's SWAT unit, waited for orders to force entry. The rest of the prison went into lockdown, and officials notified five other prisons in Kansas of the riot.

(History shows that when one prison riots, others nearby often do the same.)

Before the prison staff could place all the other wings on lockdown status, 6th Wing erupted into violence, though it was short-lived and involved only property destruction. In 4th Wing, where somewhere between 40 and 60 inmates rampaged, they used fire extinguishers to smash out high windows, which allowed the cold, November winds to howl in and quickly freeze everyone. Prison staff underscored the inmates' discomfort by turning off the wing's heat and electricity. (Monya points out that breaking the windows served no purpose. "The inmates couldn't escape from them because they were too high to reach. They broke the glass out just to be destructive. But they forgot that it was winter and they would have to remain in that wing even after we shut off the heat and lights.")

Since Monya was pregnant, she had recently quit smoking. "Not a good time to have done that," she says, remembering the tension-filled night. "Several hours into the riot, our attempt at negotiations broke down. It was time to force entry into the wing."

As the SORT shouted through the heavy metal gate for the inmates to get on the floor, men used blowtorches to burn through the large hinges. With access to telephones, several of the cons inside the wing called their loved ones on the outside to ask them to call the prison and inform them that they were not involved in the riot and were sitting peacefully inside their cells. Some were not telling the truth. When the gate finally gave way, the SORT rushed in screaming commands for the inmates to get on the floor. Anyone who resisted got hit with pepper spray and pinned to the floor with shields.

As a result of the soldiers' professionalism and advanced training, only three inmates were hurt during the retake of 4th and 6th Wings. The MP held hostage and tortured had managed to secrete himself under a stack of mattresses when the SORT secured the area. He would never be the same again.

Video surveillance helped identify the primary rioters, which resulted in 12 of them charged with crimes of riot and assault. The inmate who had refused to remove his do-rag and assaulted the MP would get an additional 12 years. Authorities moved 70 prisoners to federal institutions.

There was a palpable tension among the guards and prisoners the day after the riot. The MPs stood somberly in formation as they received instructions as to how they were going to move dozens of the prisoners to other institutions. I asked Monya if anyone wanted revenge for the MP held hostage. "There was no time for anger or retaliation," she said. "There was a lot of work to do."

On reflection, Monya added, "Looking back on it today, I am proud to have been part of a well-organized and well-trained unit, and proud of the small part I played to end this violent outburst."

• • • • •

Prison is not a weekend at a self-help spa but rather a horrific place that destroys an inmate's self-esteem and fuels him with hard-to-manage, violent urges. When inmates become especially angry and discouraged over the conditions in which they must live, they are likely to act out riotously.

While there is no argument that one must be a bad person to go to prison, the day-to-day stress of just surviving in such a brutal setting increases the likelihood that an inmate will eventually act out violently. For some inmates, hurting other prisoners or guards is a sick way to elevate one's status with others and to themselves. A riot affords the opportunity to vent aggression, to administer payback, and to act out in the moment without regard for, or a total lack of caring about, the repercussions of those actions.

The same psychological elements present in a street riot and sports riot exist in a prison riot. Such elements as groupthink, anonymity, suggestion and imitation, emotional contagion, discharging of repressed emotions, illusion of invulnerability, belief that one is right, collective rationalization of group decisions, out-group stereotypes, and many others serve as enablers for inmates to riot.

Corrections officers are not immune to these powerful psychological factors. It's important, therefore, that officers are educated about them so that they understand and can recognize these influences when they see them displayed by inmates and their fellow officers. Only then will they be able to take appropriate steps to alleviate them.

Sources

"Remembering Attica," by Jennifer Gonnerman, *The Village Voice*, www.villagevoice.com/news/0136,gonnerman,27855,1.html, September 5, 2001.

"The Battle of Alcatraz," author unknown, http://www.alcatrazhistory.com/battle1.htm.

"1980 Prison Riot: A Black Mark on State's History," by Mike Gallagher, *Albequerque Journal*, www.abqjournal.com/2000/nm/future/9fut09-19-99.htm.

"The Southern Ohio Correctional Facility Siege," author unknown, Ohio State Highway Patrol, www.statepatrol.ohio.gov/aboutus/history/socfriot.htm.

"Prison Riots: Why they happen, how to avoid them, and what to do in case there is a riot," by James Topham, http://www.patrickcrusade.org/PRISON_RIOTS.html.

"Prison uprising in Iraq exposes new risk for U.S.," by Bradley Graham, washingtonpost.com, February 21, 2005.

"Brazil: prison riot ends, five headless," author unknown, United Press International, www.sciencedaily.com, June 15, 2005.

"Afghanistan prison riot 'is over,'" author unknown, BBC News, www.news.bbc.co.uk.

"Officials blame racial tensions for California jail riot," by Jean Guccione, *Los Angeles Times*, February 6, 2006.

"One dead, 46 wounded in California race riot," author unknown, www.turkishpress.com, February 05, 2005.

"Race riot?" by Silja J.A. Talvi, In These Times, www.inthesetimes.com, March 27, 2006.

Behind Prison Walls, by Tom Martin, Paladin Press, 2003.

"San Quentin riot prompts lockdown," author unknown, Associated Press, www.msnbc.msn.com, August 9, 2005.

"California Hall of Shame," author unknown, Private Corrections Institute, www.flpba.org.

The Hate Factory, by G. Hirliman, Dell Publishing Co., 1985; iUniverse, 2005.

Chapter 8

World Trade Organization

"The WTO is a rich man's club. It is integral to the global nature of modern capitalism. But it is meeting growing opposition. The Seattle meeting will see tens of thousands of people demonstrating against the WTO in Seattle and hundreds of thousands demonstrating all over the world."

Anarchist News, No. 21, November 1999,
one month before the "Battle in Seattle"

The 135-country World Trade Organization (WTO) is the only global international organization dealing with the rules of trade between nations. It strives for agreements that most of the world's trading nations then negotiate, ratify, and sign in their parliaments. Its goal is to help producers of goods and services and exporters and importers conduct their business.

Advocates of the WTO believe that its work has increased per capita income of the world exponentially. They say that because of its efforts, today's global economy is like a well-oiled machine, and the world's stock markets and the world's people are enjoying the windfall, in particular, a higher quality of living. While some citizens of Third World nations still suffer from inhumane working conditions and governments that are indifferent to their people and environment, the work of the WTO will create, in time, a more civilized and environmentally conscious world.

Those who oppose the WTO, or at least question it (most agree that free trade is beneficial to everyone, but only if it's fair), say that it values the interests of corporate business over democracy. It also violates environmental, labor, and human-rights laws since it has the power to supersede local standards and protections it sees as an obstruction to free trade. The opposition includes such groups as human rights activists, environmentalists, labor unions, people of faith, farmers, social justice workers, students, and teachers. I do not list anarchists among the opposition because most of them just want to wreak havoc and could care less about a cause.

Opponents believe that globalization creates concentrations of capital in great financial and industrial centers, such as Seattle, Washington, where in 1999 the two opposing sides clashed in one of the largest protest riots on American soil since the 1960s. What began as a peaceful demonstration would quickly escalate into a riot involving tens of thousands of people and a state of emergency necessitating help from the National Guard. This well-documented riot warrants its own chapter because of its monstrous scale and because so many of the elements discussed throughout this book were at play. (The event has even been immortalized in a major motion picture titled *The Battle in Seattle*.) Two more WTO meetings—Cancun, Mexico, in 2003 and Hong Kong in 2005—would also have their violent moments, though not on the same scale as in Seattle.

Let's look at these three events to get a sense of the rioters' actions at the WTO meetings and the intensity of their cause.

SEATTLE, WASHINGTON, 1999

Seattle is a beautiful city—large, sprawling, artsy, and known for its laid-back attitude. It's an understatement to say that city officials were startled to see at least 50,000 protestors flood onto their streets four weeks before Christmas 1999 and march against the World Trade Organization's third ministerial conference. To find similar unrest in the Emerald City, "you have to go back to the '60s and '70s, in the days of the Vietnam marches and civil rights marches," Mayor Paul Schell said in a news conference.

By the time the weeklong event ended, there were shattered windows, torched Dumpsters, clouds of tear gas, hails of stinging rubber bullets, human barricades, wanton vandalism, traffic snarls that cost businesses millions of dollars, countless injuries, and assaults . . . many assaults. The police chief subsequently resigned, and the city received an invoice for $3 million dollars, to include expenses for police overtime, expended equipment, and damage to buildings and vehicles. The WTO meeting ended without an agenda for future talks and with Seattle's reputation tarnished for years to come. On the other hand it was a heyday for the protestors, anarchists, and news media.

Let's revisit those momentous three days and nights of passion, police, and protest.

It Begins

They come on the last weekend of November: WTO officials and protestors, thousands and thousands of protestors. They come by plane, car, train, and bus. Most come to be heard and seen lawfully; others come to be heard and seen unlawfully. In the confusion that ensued, it would often be impossible to differentiate the two.

On Monday, demonstrators put on impromptu speeches in front of fast-food restaurants and a march by people wearing, of all things, sea-turtle costumes. No doubt, few of those rushing to work know that the dress-up march is in reference to the WTO abolishing a U.S. ban on shrimp caught from boats that also catch sea turtles. The turtles only block traffic, angering some motorists and amusing others.

Seattle's infamous rain is at full pour Tuesday morning as protestors begin to gather in various locations. This new approach appears to be at least partially organized. Instead of meeting en masse, as is the usual, protestors break into a dozen or more groups, each forming at different intersections, where they link arms to make human chains. Their objective is to block the sidewalks and streets so that the WTO delegates cannot get to their meetings. It works. No matter what sneaky routes the delegates take, protestors block them with linked arms. Soon this scene is happening all over the downtown area. Some of the more aggressive delegates try to force their way through the linked arms, but few succeed.

Star Wars Troopers

Later, much will be made of Seattle police officers' black riot uniforms. More than one observer will say that they looked like something out of *Star Wars*, with their shiny helmets, gas masks, and thick chest, arm, and leg protectors. While some protestors and writers describe them as looking like some futuristic, faceless, Gestapo-like military force, the truth is that this gear has a tremendous psychological effect on lawbreakers, while at the same time providing state-of-the-art protection for police officers who must confront violent resistors.

I can tell you from experience that the impact of bottles, rocks, fruit, trash cans, and firecrackers hurts. It's also nice to have an extra barrier when people throw urine and feces at you. I wish I had been wearing this gear on the many occasions I had to bang chests with violent protestors.

By mid-morning, the protests are in full swing. Most of the large intersections are blocked, delegates are unable to get to their meetings, a labor march of 30,000 people is soon to start, and the police are receiving conflicting orders.

(Actually, the conflicting orders element is just an educated guess based on my experience. Command personnel have a tough job under these circumstances, and they want to do the right thing. They know the chief, city hall, media, and public will scrutinize their orders. An error could mean that, for the remainder of the order-giver's career, his superiors will pass him over for promotion. What often happens then is that orders never come, or if they do, they conflict with another command person's orders.)

A Seattle commander orders the discharge of tear gas. The eye, nose, and throat irritant is emitted into the air at one intersection and probably simultaneously at others. Now people who had been sitting on the pavement are getting shot with rubber pellets. The bullets sting; some hurt like the dickens. The gas and bullets set off a panic in which hundreds of people flee, their eyes and noses burning as if in flames, their throats gagging, and their lungs desperately sucking for air. Some people later claim that the police didn't warn them before they discharged the gas and fired the rubber bullets, while others admit that officers did give them advance warning so that they would have time to leave the area.

"Dominique"

One protestor, let's call him Dominique, said that he and a small group of demonstrators were at an intersection where there were no cameras or media representatives. With the streets closed, the group sat on the pavement as a contingent of police officers in riot gear stood behind them. Dominique said (in what is a perfect example of what was discussed in Chapter 2, "Perceptions") that the police were not carrying their usual clubs but rather what appeared to be baseball bats. (For the record, Seattle officers do not carry bats.) He said that his curiosity about what the police were planning changed to concern when they all began slipping on their gas masks.

Dominique said that several protestors asked the police not to spray them, but officers ignored their request and continued with their silent preparations. Then several more protestors sat down in the street under the curious assumption that if there were more of them, the police would not spray. In fact, that was even more reason for the police to bring out the pepper, especially when the demonstrators locked arms and refused the officers' continuous commands to disperse.

Dominique said that he quickly covered his head with a cloth in anticipation. With eyes covered, he first heard the hiss of spraying gas and then a commotion of people choking, scrambling to their feet, running, and panicking. Then he heard thumps and screams of pain. It was not immediately apparent to Dominique what that was, but when a police baton went *thump* against the side of his head, he made the connection.

He said he was hurting and confused as to why the officers were hitting everyone. Before he could figure it out, an officer yanked the cloth off his head and gave his face a serious dose of pepper spray. Now his head was throbbing, he was hacking up strange colored gunk from his lungs, and he could not see. But he could hear people yelling, the police barking commands, more thumping of batons, people thrashing on the pavement, the sounds of retching, and lots of cursing and name calling. Things like, "You fascists!" "Robots!" and "You pig Gestapo!"

With the help of others, Dominique managed to get to his feet and move a distance away to a place where fellow protestors used bottled water with soda to cleanse his burning eyes. He said the spray was extraordinarily painful, even on his skin. He didn't say if he and the others had considered that none of this would have happened if they had left when officers asked them to, or especially when the officers took a few moments to prepare for the spraying.

Anarchists and Others

The gassing of Dominique and his friends is only the beginning in Seattle. However, as some pundits later hypothesized, this early police maneuver gets the violence rolling. Prior to the pep-

Pepper Spray

In his book *Holidays in Hell*, P.J. O'Rourke wrote about his experience with an early version of pepper spray in a South Korean riot:

Korean riot police use the pepper gas developed during the Vietnam War, which is fast becoming a favorite with busy dictators everywhere . . . the Koreans lay it on in lavish doses, until the air is a vanilla milk shake of minuscule caustic particles. Pepper gas can raise blisters on exposed skin. Any contact with a mucous membrane produces the same sensation as probing a canker sore with a hot sewing needle. The tiniest amount in your eyes and your eyelids lock shut in blind agony. Breathing it is like inhaling fish bones, and the curl-up-and-die cough quickly turns to vomiting.

Today, most police agencies use OC spray, for oleoresin capsicum, an inflammatory agent that causes immediate closure of the eyes, violent coughing, and an explosion of mucous. Its effective on 80 percent of people sprayed, giving most a miserable 30 to 45 minutes until it wears off. Some pepper spray has tear gas in it, too.

pering of the seated protestors, some say that the mood was party-like, albeit with a bit of tension and, based on my experience, probably a let's-get-the-anarchy-started feeling among the partygoers. There is graffiti spraying, too, which isn't a trivial thing if you're the one paying hundreds and even thousands of dollars for its removal. Though it's a party-like atmosphere with a sprinkling of criminal activity, it changes to ugly after the first group of protestors chokes on OC with a dash of tearing agent.

In a move that is either a bad decision by police or simply an example of not having enough law enforcement to do all that needs to be done, the police position themselves between the convention center where the WTO meetings are to be held and the horde of now angry protestors. This tactic leaves a contingent of self-proclaimed anarchists, dressed in black and wearing bandannas to conceal their faces, and those not proclaiming to be but nonetheless acting like anarchists, to have a field day on unguarded property behind the crowd.

They smash out the windows of businesses, mostly owned by big corporations, to include McDonalds, Nike, Planet Hollywood, and Starbucks. The mob inflicts heavy damage on a line of police cars while officers watch from a distance, no doubt unable to move without breaking the integrity of their ranks. They paint their graf-

Police Mind-Set

I don't know what was behind the lack of response by the Seattle police when they witnessed their cars being destroyed, but I have been in similar situations in riots, and I can say that to stand by impotently is gut wrenching for officers sworn to protect lives and property. In my experiences, we were not allowed to respond either because it would have weakened our lines of defense or because a supervisor, usually calling the shots from the safety of a remote command post, didn't want to risk his career by sending in officers to bring the criminals to their knees.

So we watched idly and dumbly as rioters smashed things, threw trash at us, and mocked us. Sometimes they stood nose to nose with us, calling us names and daring us to do anything about it, all while our restrained adrenaline ate away at our stomach linings.

Understand that as a police officer, from day one, you learn, and ultimately become conditioned, to go to the problem. Go help. Go prevent. Go stop. Go catch the bad guy. Go, go, go, while everyone else flees in the opposite direction. So it is pure agony to stand there and watch as rioting criminals taunt you and damage private and city property and not be allowed to respond. It's an insult to the police organization, the individual officer, and to our law-abiding society in general.

Whether you like the police or don't like the police doesn't matter. What does matter is the fact that police officers are the thin blue line that maintains the public order. That, too, is in the officers' minds as they watch people mock that sense of order and destroy what will cost law-abiding citizens, private owners, and taxpayers hundreds and even thousands of dollars—millions, in the case of Seattle.

Therefore, when a squad of officers does get the order to go after the criminals, they move forward on adrenaline that is boiling and bubbling over the brim. Is there a chance one of the lawbreakers might experience a hard drop to the pavement? Maybe, maybe not. It depends on the officers involved and other extenuating circumstances. Should we be surprised when it happens? In my experience on the front lines, I think we should be surprised when it does not. That said, most officers are able to restrain themselves from yielding to their human emotions, but that does not mean it's easy.

fiti on everything, too, including the big letter "A" within a circle, the symbol for anarchy.

Some protestors tried to stop the destruction of property; some were even successful. These people were among those who wanted to voice their concerns about the WTO, march a little, picket a little, and then go home without resorting to breaking things. There were others, however, who supported the anarchists. One anonymous blog writer, who was not an anarchist, wrote:

> The anarchists—an organic community able to take organized, collective and militant action against their real enemies—formed themselves into "black blocks" (so named for the black clothes and masks the anarchists wore) and systematically attacked unoccupied corporate chain stores such as McDonalds, the Gap, Nike, Nordstrom, Levi, and Disney, as well as the notoriously corrupt Bank of America.

Disregarding the question—how can anarchists, by their very name, be "organized and collective?"—this statement shows that while not all of the protestors were engaged in tearing down corporate America, those who did try had support and encouragement. The writer went on to criticize the "moral" nonviolent protestors because they stopped the anarchists and even turned some of them over to the police. It's unknown if this writer and others

A Training Tool for Rioters

Capt. Charles Beene notes in his book *Riot Prevention and Control* that there is a unique training tool available to would-be rioters:

A video game called "State of Emergency" is based on the Seattle WTO riots. It is billed as an urban riot game set in the near future, where the oppressive American Trade Organization has declared a state of emergency. It is up to the player to smash up everything and everyone in order to destabilize the ATO. The game allows the players to earn points by breaking plate-glass windows, punching out police officers in riot gear, and attacking innocent bystanders. Now you too can be a rioting anarchist—and never leave the comfort of your living room.

like him participated in the vandalism or just supported those who did it.

Tuesday Night in the Rain

The clashes continue well into Tuesday night. The police work especially hard to establish order since President Bill Clinton is arriving in the middle of the night. This means that it's mandatory that any area in which he will reside and work must be secure. The police order crowds to disperse and, when they do not, officers lob tear gas and "flashbangs," grenades that explode in a brilliant light and an ear-throbbing bang. No shrapnel, just a concussion that startles and momentarily disorients.

Rick Anderson, a writer for the *Seattle Weekly*, wrote of one police platoon's experience:

> Comprised of five 10-officer squads, D Platoon joined other units clearing Union Street for WTO dignitaries, carving out pathways among some of the 45,000 protesters. As the crowd surged and street fighting erupted, D Platoon was overwhelmed. "One suspect attempted to take an officer's pistol from the officer's holster," [Lt. Kennedy] Condor would write in a report afterward. As reinforcements arrived, they "were fending off punches and kicks and fighting off grabbing hands and tripping legs." Some demonstrators spit on him, others tried to kick him in the groin, says Condor. He was hit in the thigh by a tear gas grenade tossed back into the police lines. For hours, his officers were bombarded with bolts, bottles, rocks, open knives, wrenches, and plastic bottles filled with urine. They were losing.

This continues until police push some of the rioters out of the core riot zone and into a residential area. Neighborhood folks become angry when suddenly awakened by bullhorns, screaming hordes, window-rattling flashbangs, and clouds of tear gas wafting into their bedrooms.

Just Another Day in Riot Town

By Wednesday, it's almost as if police riot squads dashing here and there, masses of people sitting in intersections, squirming people being dragged away by arrest teams, and clouds of drifting tear gas have become as commonplace as Seattle's Best coffee shops. People seem to be dealing with it with a shrug of their shoulders as they make their way to work and proceed through their workday. At least some people do. Others are terrified the entire time. *Seattle Weekly*'s Rick Anderson describes the scene further:

> Then came Wednesday: CS canisters, a no-protest zone, and police retaliation. That night, protesters were driven up Capitol Hill, where some of the more enduring images of an unforgettable week would unfold. Demonstrators were beaten and gassed by cops without ID tags. Some uninvolved bystanders were pepper-sprayed and clubbed. A TV video captured an unresisting man being shot by a cop with a bean-bag gun, then kicked in the groin. It would, to some, become a police conspiracy, the plotted cop assault on a hill where police and residents have clashed before and share an uneasy peace.
>
> Not captured among those WTO images that night, however, is what city investigators say was a withering assault on Lt. Condor and his troops. His story picks up at 8:55 PM, after protesters were repelled by police defending the East Precinct from a perceived attack, but prior to the wider brutal confrontations that included National Guard and county and suburban officers.
>
> "As we inched closer I could see that there were people standing on the [Seattle Central] college campus throwing things at the officers I had left at Harvard and Pine," Condor recalled in his report. "I tell the driver of our Explorer to engage the emergency lights and siren and continue to inch through the intersection in an attempt to get to the suspects.

Not All Is as It Seems

While media cameras captured many of the images discussed here, what occurs most often in these cases is that news clips don't show what preceded a police action. At the risk of looking like I'm defending the officers, just know that a film clip doesn't always show what happened moments earlier.

Yes, the man was not resisting when the camera caught the officer shooting a bean-bag gun at him, but what happened before the camera's lens pointed his way? If bystanders were "uninvolved," why were they there in the midst of a police action? Had the police told them to move? Had the police told them not to interfere? Were they inciting more violence by their shouts of encouragements to those rioting? The camera doesn't show that, and the viewer doesn't know.

People accuse police officers of trying to be anonymous by removing their nametags prior to clashing with rioters. It was not for purposes of anonymity whenever the sergeants and lieutenants ordered my fellow officers and me to remove ours but rather to prevent them from being torn off in a brawl or poked with them should the protective backing come off. More and more, police uniforms have sewn-on nametags for this reason.

Again, I'm not defending the officers but rather pointing out that there is always more to a story, including one captured in part on video.

As we move through the intersection, a man lies in front of our vehicle.

"I jump from the car. As I do so, I note that other demonstrators are grabbing at me and the car. They are yelling 'Kill 'em!' 'Let's get 'em!' 'Kill the cops,' 'Fuck the pigs,' and other menacing words. Given the number of demonstrators, their violent demeanor, and no apparent leader, I felt fear for my life and for the lives of my driver and passenger officer. I walk around the slowly rolling car, pulling and pushing people off the car so that we can escape from what now appears to be a mob. I see a demonstrator throw a smoking object to the east. I look in that direction and see Sgt. Coomes' van. He too is being attacked."

In a few minutes, Condor manages to join other officers,

including a sheriff's department contingent, who are being pelted by flying objects. He recalls tossing a stun grenade at a masked demonstrator who is sneaking behind police lines with a lighted Molotov cocktail. Soup cans, potted plants, and potatoes fill the air, pelting the officers. A group of demonstrators comes from the backside, and Condor readies another stun grenade. It goes off in his hand as he heaves it. The lieutenant is treated in a hospital for a back injury and severe burns to his hand.

Different Views

The police and other Seattle authorities said that troublemakers, especially anarchists from out of town, perpetrated the worst of the Seattle WTO riot. One citizen was quoted as saying that the violence was done by "long-haired, hippie-type losers who in all likelihood had no clue what the WTO really is or what benefits free trade bring to the people they claim to be defending." Critics of the demonstrators wondered how perpetrating violence within residential and commercial neighborhoods would somehow convince other countries to adopt standards of living that are more democratic. Still others noted that some of the protestors, by all appearances, were on the lowest end of the economic and social scale: the homeless, the unemployed, and criminals, who used the WTO meeting as an opportunity to simply act out.

Those on the opposing side said that police resorted to force early and without provocation. Some even claimed the government instigated the rioting to discredit the movement against the WTO. "The police gassed all of downtown," protestors told the press and wrote on Internet sites. They said that some protestors were seen screaming and acting combative at one location but were later seen actually tackling other protestors, which led some activists to believe that these people were really police agents sent in to encourage others to act out violently. They said the police gassed, beat, and fired rubber bullets on peaceful protestors and even uninvolved innocents caught in the area.

Lieutenant Condor's report of what happened to his people on that Wednesday night was quite persuasive to some members of the citizen review panels, who looked at all that happened during the rioting as part of the city council's review of the incident.

Seattle Weekly writer Rick Anderson wrote:

> Some feel it [Lt. Condor's report] offsets prevailing accusations that Capitol Hill violence was one-sided and initiated only by police and will help reviewers produce a more balanced finding. "There's a reality gap among both sides," says a review committee staffer. "No one agrees on what happened. But it seems unlikely that after 12 hours on the streets, Condor would stop to pick a fight with a mob and turn this into what it became. In retrospect, it seems there's more than enough blame to go around."

As I write this, a federal appeals court is still ruling on events at the 1999 WTO in Seattle.

Interview with a Seattle WTO Protester

John Hoffman is the author of *The Art and Science of Dumpster Diving* and *Dumpster Diving: The Advanced Course*. Prior to the 1999 World Trade Organization riot in Seattle, John served in the U.S. Army for four years as a medic with a specialty in psychology. He then went on to earn magna cum laude honors in English writing at Concordia College, Moorhead, Minnesota. After the riot in Seattle, he earned a law degree with distinction from the University of North Dakota, and he is currently working on a Masters of Public Administration at the University of Minnesota, Twin Cities.

A well-known activist in Seattle in the 1990s, John had been arrested twice: once for sitting in front of a bulldozer in defense of homeless encampments, and once for sitting in front of Seattle city hall in defense of homeless who were camping near the building. He was once involved in what he calls a "police riot" on Capitol Hill, and he fought a law against sitting on the sidewalk in Seattle's court with the help of the ACLU Lawyer's Guild. He also sued the Seattle Police Department over its open records issues and false arrest.

John graciously agreed to answer questions about his experience at the WTO riots.

Loren Christensen (LWC): Why did you attend Seattle's WTO?

John Hoffman (JH): If there is a protest, I'm there, and this looked to be the biggest protest in quite a while. I can gauge how big a protest will be by stuff I see prior to the protest: leaflets, talk in the news media, and who is involved in the organizing. The reading on my gauge for this protest was off the scale. I knew it was going to be huge, and I wanted to be part of it.

LWC: What was your function?

JH: Due to signing separation papers with my wife on November 30, I wasn't involved until December 1. I saw that many of the leaders had been arrested and people in the streets on December 1 needed leadership. I just leaped into the stuff happening in the streets and tried to make the protests as effective as possible. When I met up with the union folks, I slipped into my role as a union member. I often saw my role as a bridge between unorganized street protesters and union members, but it was a role I carved out spontaneously.

LWC: Where were you when the riot started, and what were your first thoughts?

JH: On Tuesday, November 30, much to my dismay, I was in my apartment in the University District, signing a separation agreement with my ex-wife. Word of what was happening downtown was on the television. My thought was, "Holy shit, it's huge and I have to get into it as quick as I can before it dissipates."

LWC: Did the power and scope of the protest and riot surprise you?

JH: Yes, even though I knew it was going to be huge, how big it was shocked me. I'm still shocked that such an important event happened and that I was able to be involved and play a role.

LWC: What were the first few hours like for you?

JH: *Existential.* No, seriously. I had just put my soon-to-be ex-wife on a plane with my little child and I headed downtown into the mess. It was early December 1. The first part of it was a desperate desire to find the very heart of the disturbances and not be left out. Once I found what seemed to be the heart of things, it was like I became one with the disturbances. In my core, I was empty and torn. My whole life was falling apart. But suddenly the protest filled me with meaning. I felt an opportunity to let loose a cry of frustration and rage and have my own feelings become part of the useful driving force of the event.

So my pain was meaningful and useful, not my own private burden to bear in dark loneliness. When I saw the first police line and a group of protestors, I felt like a lost tribesman who suddenly finds his tribe, a lost soldier who reunites with his unit in the heat of battle. I felt a wild, fierce joy. I felt my life had meaning.

I would like to add that I noticed a few folks who were in a similar situation. For example, one of the Lesbian Avengers who was playing a powerful role in the protests was told by her girlfriend, "It's either me or the sea turtles. Choose!" And she replied, "Sea turtles" and walked out the door. Going to the protest was so important for some people that they threw aside their life and brought it to the protest, bringing along their hurt and pain. Going to the event was more important than a lover, or one last desperate chance to reconcile with a spouse taking a little child to the wastelands of North Dakota on a jet plane.

LWC: What are your thoughts on the police response?

JH: They were feeling helpless, offended, and overwhelmed. They were angry and frustrated, and they took it out on us. I know the awful truth: they weren't getting any from their wives or girlfriends, so they wanted somebody to fuck over, and we were an opportune target.

LWC: What are your thoughts on the violence and vandalism that occurred?

JH: I'm very frustrated by the way the media turned a little vandalism to a Starbucks into some kind of iconographic moment. I'm frustrated with the people who were dumb enough to wear masks and smash that Starbucks but, on the other hand, that radical action was galvanizing and, frankly, Starbucks deserved everything it got. Starbucks has looked inside itself and reformed its policies, so smashing their window was all for the good.

I don't care for the tagging; I think it's stupid. Painting slogans would have made more sense. Unfortunately, a protest is like a war; you go to a protest with the protestors you have, just like an army goes to war with the troops it has. If the violence and vandalism made everybody think really hard about how opposed many people are to the WTO, then that's all for the good. A few windows and a few damaged surfaces are a small price to pay for all that consciousness raising. But stupid vandalism put out a message which was very difficult to spin by the folks who actually had a fucking clue what they were doing.

LWC: What are your thoughts regarding the anarchists?

JH: The anarchists brought energy and courage, and a willingness to do something. People distance themselves from the anarchists but, when it comes down to it, the anarchists served a useful role. They are willing to go very far to the front and take round after round of tear gas and rubber bullets. Things would not have gone down the same way without them. The anarchists are like that one guy who gets up to a microphone at a public meeting, blurts out the truth in unvarnished terms, and then sets off the whole room . . . some of whom will distance themselves from the heat and expression of his sentiments.

Thus, we both need the anarchists and we need to distance ourselves from the anarchists after the fact. I just wish the anarchists could be more

media savvy. Like, if you're going to smash a window, you need to leave
an articulate flyer explaining why it is tactically necessary. And maybe
that requires some thought and planning, and careful selection of targets
instead of joyously acting in the violent spontaneity of the moment, but
you know what? *Fucking grow up, people, and be more effective.*

All the same, for the record: I am in unity with the ultimate decision
to smash those windows. It was politically necessary, though it could
have been pulled off with a hell of a lot more finesse, wisdom, and media
savvy. People who have the guts to do something along those lines are
rare, and also quite young, so you cannot expect them to be perfect or
well-practiced.

LWC: Do you wish there had been more violence?

JH: I wish we had managed to penetrate the police barriers and get
inside the WTO meeting itself. I wish we had managed, at the very least,
to get inside the Westin, get into the rooms of the delegates, and seize
records revealing their evil and illegal actions. I really wish that when the
police hit us with gas on December 1, that we had known that was their
last stock of gas . . . they were running out . . . and we had not faltered
and gone sideways in scattered groups, but pushed forward. It is a difficult
thing to wish for more violence, and I certainly don't wish for violence
against human beings, but the things I listed above are what I wish for.

**LWC: Some protestors could care less about a cause. Instead,
they come for the excitement of the event and to act out. Your
thoughts.**

JH: Yes. You have to figure out who those people are, harness them,
and make them useful.

**LWC: Was there ever a point where you thought the protest/riot
was more about clashing with the police than about the WTO?**

JH: Well, it's the police you have in front of you, not the WTO, so
you are forced to focus on the police. And many people have issues with
the police, arguably even more than they have with the WTO, and they're

there because of those issues with the police, but that's not MOST of the people, at least not at the WTO event.

I think there is a certain number for whom it is mostly about clashing with the police and they are taking an opportunity to clash with the police. And again, you have to figure out who these people are and encourage them, because it's the police who stand in the way of your goal in this particular case, and people who have issues with the police can be useful to the rest of the group, just like people who can make cool signs and banners can be useful to the rest of the group.

LWC: Did your feelings about the police change during the course of the three days? Remain the same? Why?

JH: Word came of bad actions by the police. So my opposition to the police—their actions and mind-set—increased. On the other hand, I was impressed that they never used lethal force. In that sense, I thought they were good and had discipline, and I had a grudging respect for them. Getting hit by a rubber projectile half an inch from my left nut also made me respect their marksmanship, though it's quite possible that was a projectile which wasn't, in a sense, aimed. I guess getting gassed and hit by a projectile made me respect, more than ever, the violent force they were capable of unleashing. If I feared them before, I now feared them more than ever, because I was aching and coughing from gas.

LWC: Sometimes police officers are uncomfortable in their role because they agree with the protestors. Your thoughts.

JH: I'm aware of the discomfort officers can have with their role and, yes, I have been at protests like that. Officers who agree with the protestors can play a useful role by restraining themselves to the greatest degree possible. For example, I was arrested once for sitting in front of a bulldozer on Seattle's Duwamish Greenbelt in the summer of 1994. It was pretty clear those officers DID NOT agree with me because of the way they hurt my arms and dragged me over some blackberry brambles. Officers who agreed with me could have avoided inflicting that, even if they had to play the role of arresting me.

In my opinion, officers who whine about their "discomfort" with their role are being self-indulgent little wimps. You think you're uncomfortable? Try wearing handcuffs. Feeling a twinge of remorse doesn't make you a good person, it just makes you a pig with issues. Restraining yourself is useful, but it would be far more useful if such conflicted officers would play a more supportive role instead of whining about their precious widdle feelings.

LWC: Did your mind-set change about the WTO, the police, or the protest at any point during the three days?

JH: Well, when we stopped getting gassed and there was less civil disobedience, I thought, well, now it's just a regular protest. And it wasn't nearly as much fun, nor did I feel it was having as much of an impact.

LWC: Were you or anyone you know ever in a position where it was just you or them vs. one or more cops?

JH: No. It was always group against group. I've been in situations like the one you describe before, but that did not happen at the WTO, at least not to me or anybody that I knew. I was aware of a large group of people arrested and in jail, and I'm sure they had that experience, but I cannot say I knew them well, so I cannot speak to it. Some folks I knew fairly well who worked at a socialist bookstore were arrested, but I don't remember talking to them about this one-on-one thing.

LWC: Were you ever frightened? Anxious? Hyped?

JH: When I was sitting on top of a bucket with my back deliberately turned on a police line just a few yards away, speaking to a crowd, getting them riled up, knowing I could be grabbed at any moment . . . when I had opportunities to speak to the crowd and the crowd responded in a positive way . . . yeah, I was hyped. I've never done heroin, but I suspect it was a lot like that feeling. I was anxious and frightened a number of times, such as when it looked like I could be captured and arrested in the running street battle. Also, when some of us got inside the Labor Temple and avoided arrest but we thought the cops might get inside and arrest us.

LWC: Were there periods where you felt everything was so out of control—actions of the police, actions of the protestors/rioters, the continuous violence on both sides, an overwhelming sense of unreality—that you thought that everything was total anarchy?

JH: No, I never felt "total anarchy." I always felt that in this place where I am, things are out of control, but I always figure that control is coming back, or things are controlled in nearby buildings and that control will, soon enough, wash back over things. I heard other folks express the feelings of "total anarchy" but, for me, I always felt like I could have influence on events happening around me, and so I never felt like things were out of control . . . rather, you're in the middle of a conflict, and the conflict has its own logic, its own control.

LWC: Sometimes people acting in a violent mob feel anonymous, just another person in a mass. This often allows them to act out even more. Have you ever felt that? If so, did it alter your actions?

JH: No, I was extremely well-known to the Seattle police due to my activist efforts between 1994 and 1999, so I never had the luxury of being anonymous. I'm pretty sure other people around me felt that way, though. In fact, if you know people feel that way, you can channel that feeling in a particular direction and encourage them to do things they wouldn't normally do.

LWC: In a race riot there is a phenomenon called "impersonality," meaning that a person sees all members of a certain race or group as being all good or all bad. Did you see that in others? In yourself?

JH: I would have to say that I saw the protestors as "all good," at least in the aggregate, and the police as "all bad," at least in the aggregate. It is certainly an "us against them" kind of feeling.

At one point, we had the Sheraton half surrounded and I was trying to scrounge some supplies. I ran into a guy who said he needed to get past the police, but they wouldn't let him. He had a beard and seemed like a professor type. I thought he was trying to help the protests and felt like he needed to get past the police line and get inside the Sheraton. I told him I couldn't get past it either. As we talked, we suddenly figured out who the other was. With my short hair and manner of dress, he had mistaken me for someone on his side. With his professional beard, I had mistaken him for someone on my side. In fact, he was playing some kind of role with the WTO, and I was playing a role with the protests. We both had different motivations for wanting to get past the police line and into the Sheraton.

His mouth dropped open and he stared at me, wide-eyed as this realization struck both of us. I said, "Oh gee, sir, it would appear we are on different sides. Look, uh, if you're playing a role with the WTO, I suggest you stay away from my group over there. They are pretty hyped up right now."

"You're . . . you're with them!" he said. "Oh my god . . ." He backed away and then dashed off.

It was this weird moment where we met in the heat of battle and we talked to each other like human beings. Then we abruptly figured out we were on different sides. But because he was a human being to me, I couldn't, like, turn to my group and start shouting, "We got one! Right here!"

I sometimes wonder who he is and where he might be right now. Maybe he's telling the other side of this story.

LWC: In a mob, there is a powerful instinct to follow the actions of others? Did you see any of this on either side?

JH: Yeah, I felt that, though often I was hoping to do an action and have others follow me depending on that feeling. One of the most powerful manifestations of this instinct is to run with the group, like a herd. But I want to point out that saying "follow the actions of others" is an overgeneralization. People can support a behavior in complex ways, which don't always mean doing the same exact behavior.

The most vivid manifestation I saw would be when me and a small group decided we would run ahead to see if the Labor Temple was open so we could get inside and avoid arrest. Our plan was to run back to the group, but we saw that the group got surrounded and grabbed. A few folks who saw us run began running with us, thinking that we knew where we were going. These were the only people who managed to get inside the Labor Temple with my group. They literally ran because they saw us running and thought that they would, too.

LWC: Did you see any cops act out in a way as if they were having a good time?

JH: Not in person. I remember images later from TV, but honestly, I would have to say I didn't see it. They were black, masked lines who moved in unison from my point of view.

LWC: Did you see any cops act out beyond their authority?

JH: Since they were apparently authorized to shoot the gas and rubber bullets, I'd have to say that I never personally witnessed cops acting beyond their authority. I did, however, see some dramatic injuries to the back of a 16-year-old woman. She was apparently shot several times at close range in the back with some kind of beanbag or rubber bullet gun. So I did see direct evidence of cops who were probably acting beyond their authority when I saw that. But I didn't see the act itself.

LWC: What were some of the erroneous perceptions the public got from the riot?

JH: The public thinks that the Starbucks window thing was somehow the point or the main event of the protests when, in fact, it was a small, tangential happening which just got spun and played too much in the media. Consequently, everybody who was in the event has to position themselves vis-à-vis for what should have been an obscure moment with little relevance to the event.

LWC: Is there anything else on which you would like to comment?

JH: I see a riot as being a meeting where the actions are the words, and people are involved in getting a kind of consensus. Only the situation is fluid, not static, so they have to get fluid consensus in a rapidly developing environment. There are definitely people who are leaders, but they have to have a certain humility and ability to play to the crowd and fill its needs or their leadership will be rejected.

A riot is certainly not a random event without principals and psychology. People who have experience in riots and protests can play a major role in convincing people to go in a particular direction and do particular things. I certainly learned lessons from the Broadway Police Riot of September 1994 and other protests, lessons I applied during the 1999 WTO. Also, formal training and professional experience is useful, such as in psychology and the military. Anything where you can learn to deal with the psychology of large groups. Even salesmanship can be useful.

There were a few things that I felt the police did wrong on December 1. When they met us with gas and rubber bullets, they used a bullhorn thing on a police car, like the commander's van or something. The voice broadcasts went something like this: *"This is the Seattle Police Department. Disperse immediately or we will be forced to use chemical agents."*

What's weird is that I head that same exact voice saying the same exact thing in September of 1994. So it was either a recording or the same exact cop saying the same exact thing. His voice was so angry and demanding that it cannot help but be defied by a crowd in that kind of mind-set, a mind-set that should be fairly obvious by the circumstances. [A mind-set that has the crowd] running toward [the police] who are holding weapons. That's a red flag indicator of that mind-set.

So it's like, do you [the police] say those words because they actually want us to disobey? Or haven't you [the police] figured out that what you say and the way you say it is part of the reason the crowd acts in the defiant way that it does?

Words that would have worked here: *"This is Commander (his real full name) of the Seattle Police Department. We're here to negotiate with you. Please hold fast and do not cross our line. We do not want to use force against you. I've ordered my men to turn their weapons to the ground. But please do not cross our line because we have orders to use force if you do."*

These words would have radically changed the situation. The crowd would have stopped short and engaged in an argument about what to do, what it wanted, who should speak to the police, or whether it should go forward. The violent mind-set of the police actually feeds into the needs and desires of the crowd when it's in a certain riotous mindset.

Like Notches on a Six Shooter
John Hoffman tells of one proud protestor who used a Sharpie marker to add slash marks on his back each time the police gassed, struck him with a baton, or shot him with a rubber bullet. It's unknown how many he acquired

Getting gassed and shot with rubber bullets is a mark of distinction, a fucking honor. If I had not been gassed or shot, I would have felt less important and less vital in my role. When you gas me, when you shoot me with a rubber bullet, you are playing into my game even as I take sincere steps to avoid being gassed and shot.

Police seem to think there are no words that will change the action of the crowd, or that the words they are saying are the right words, but, 1) there are words you can say that will change the situation, 2) the words the police use are generally the wrong words.

CANCUN, MEXICO, 2003

The government of Mexico promised in early 2003 that it would guarantee the safety of everyone attending the fifth WTO ministerial conference and that it would foster an atmosphere of openness and tolerance. They said they would not permit violent protests and if anyone tried, the authorities would deal with them quickly.

As the weeks grew near, hundreds of soldiers and police kept watch over the preparations for the September meeting. Meanwhile, the National Union of Autonomous Peasant Organizations of Mexico said that their groups in Cancun would derail the ministerial conference and loudly protest against unjust globalization and the WTO's power. When the meetings began, they held true to their promise.

From the back of the main hall of the convention site, dozens of activists chanted "Shame!" and held up signs. They shouted that the WTO was obsolete and undemocratic, their voices nearly drowning out a speech by Mexico's foreign minister.

Outside, the protestors numbered in the thousands, most of whom were farmers shouting that they wanted agricultural protections kept as they were. One vegetable farmer from South Carolina said, "This is a battle of the rich against the poor. And no one is poorer in the United States than the farmer."

Nude Protest
In another oddity, 29 activists stripped naked under the blazing Cancun sun and lay down on the sand in such a way that their bodies spelled out "No WTO." One observer noted, "Hey, whatever it takes to get the press focused on you, though it's hard to imagine the fully dressed WTO delegates giving up, saying, 'We just cannot go on. Naked protestors don't want us here.'"

While there are many protestors who use the WTO to draw attention to their particular political causes, and there are protestors legitimately concerned about the power of WTO, it's a safe bet that no one is more feverish about it than those in fear for their family, work, and property. And farmers believe that this is the fight of their lives.

Case in point: Moments after farmers arrived at a large police barricade, a Korean man, a 54-year-old farmer named Lee Kyung Hae wearing a sign around his neck that read, "WTO kills farmers," scaled the fence. Then, for the world to see, Lee rammed a knife into his heart. Several people came to the man's aid, picked him up, and carried him through the throng. He later died from his injuries.

Some reports say that Lee intended only to wound himself but he stabbed too high. Other South Koreans said that his suicide was an act of sacrifice to show his disgust at "how the WTO was killing peasants around the world." We will never know for sure, but his act certainly points out the intensity many of the protestors share.

The situation turned even more serious and violent at midweek when between 2,000 and 5,000 protesters came to demonstrate. First, dozens of women used wire cutters to make holes in a tall chain-link security fence, and then two dozen rioters squeezed through the openings to attack the police near the tourist section of the beach. Like a scene from a war movie, one protestor used a loudspeaker to blare, "We're going in! We're going in!" as a way to psyche and encourage rioters to charge through the hotel beach property and fast-food eateries.

At another clash a day later, the police dodged and sometimes didn't dodge thrown sticks, rocks, metal bars, bottles, even raw sewage. Protesters rolled out a battering ram made from garbage cans and a tree trunk, promising to "tear down the barriers of imperialism." Officers sprayed them with tear gas and thumped their heads and bodies with batons.

Although the Cancun riot had its intense moments, people were hurt, and one protestor died by his own hand, the violence never reached the level of the WTO riot in Seattle.

HONG KONG, 2005

In early 2005, Hong Kong police began training for several months in preparation for the WTO's sixth ministerial conference in December. Since it had been many years since Hong Kong law enforcement had dealt with civil unrest perpetrated by large numbers of protestors, their preparation turned out to be a wise move, considering the tradition of violent protests that had been a big part of WTO gatherings in Seattle and Cancun.

Hong Kong police tried out their new skills on hundreds of South Korean farmers (some news reports estimated the number at

900) who came organized and ready for violence. The farmers were fearful that if their domestic agriculture markets opened under a new WTO treaty, which would allow for more imports of rice, their biggest cash crop, they would not be able to compete and thus lose their livelihood and even their land. Although the police outnumbered the protestors two to one, the Koreans, Southeast Asian groups, and activists from Europe and the United States would force the officers to earn their money that week.

The farmers' early tactics ranged from graffiti ("No Bush" and "Down WTO" in red letters on the U.S. Consulate) to vandalism, sit-down protests near the conference center, and minor scuffling with police. Protestors tried a new twist when dozens of men donned life jackets and jumped into the Victoria Harbor in an attempt to get media attention. They got it.

Observers were impressed by the coordination behind the protests. For example, after the protestors jumped into the water, one of them gathered all of their shoes and met them where they climbed out farther down the dock. Others in their party held up a large banner to shield the swimmers as they changed back into dry clothes.

At another location, protestors formed a human wall to prevent journalists from getting hurt while other protestors clashed with riot police. During that scuffle, many rioters were able to wrestle officers' shields away, only to return them later as a contingent of Koreans cleaned up the debris from the clash.

The most violent event at Hong Kong's WTO weeklong event occurred when a thousand protestors broke off from a prearranged route and moved toward the conference center. At one point the protestors turned riotous as they attacked police with bamboo sticks, metal rods, and a metal gate, which they used as a battering ram when charging officers.

The police struck back with their batons and even managed to grab a few of the poles and return the favor by whacking some of the protestors on the head. Some Koreans and their supporters threw stones and water bottles while others tried to overturn police cars. Police struck back further with water cannons. When that didn't work, they resorted to pepper spray, which left many demonstrators staggering blindly as helpers poured bottled water on their burning faces. Additional police arrived, ending the madness, at least for a while.

In the end, 140 protestors and police officers received injuries and 1,000 protestors went to jail. The police were criticized for overreacting with indiscriminate use of pepper spray and water cannons, while the press was accused of creating a climate of fear and tension about the demonstrators (especially the Korean farmers) in the months leading up to the event. And the WTO struck a deal to end farm export subsidies, dashing the hopes of the Korean farmers and their families.

• • • • •

At this writing, no city has yet to ask to host the next WTO ministerial conference, which is supposed to occur every two years. The task is a daunting one, with organizing, providing accommodation, and providing for the security of thousands of delegates, journalists, and campaigners. It took Hong Kong, for example, 18 months to prepare and diminish a tremendous volume of resources. Then factor in the risk that the talks might collapse and that the inevitable protests might disrupt the host city, all of which costs tens of thousands, if not millions, of dollars. Then there is the tarnishing of the city's reputation. The violence that ripped up Seattle hurt its image nationally and globally and tapped the city coffers to the tune of $3 million in damages, while the cost to commercial businesses from vandalism and lost sales has been estimated as high as $25 million.

Finding a venue is likely to be a continuous problem every two years, unless the protests suddenly stop. Fat chance.

Sources

"Riot Journal," by Eric Scigliano, *Seattle Weekly*,
www.seattleweekly.com/features/9948/features-scigliano.shtml.
"World Trade Organization—Seattle Protest," by Stephanie
Zimmerman, Zmedia.org, www.newmediaphoto.com/
WTO.html.
"Protests rage as deadlocked WTO go to wire," by Sophie Walker
and Dominic Lau, Reuters, www.alertnet.org.
"Suicide mars WTO talks," author unknown, CNN.com/World,
http://edition.cnn.com/2003/WORLD/americas/09/11/cancun.
wto/
"Protestors swarm the streets at WTO forum in Cancun," by
Ginger Thompson, *The New York Times*, www.nytimes.com,
September 14, 2003.
"One Cop's WTO: The blue side of the Capitol Hill riots," by Rick
Anderson, *Seattle Weekly*, www.seattleweekly.com/news/0032/
news-anderson.php, August 9, 2000 (quotes used with author's
permission).
Holidays in Hell, by P.J. O'Rourke, Atlantic Monthly Press, 1988.

Chapter 9

Miscellaneous Riots

Let's briefly explore those riots that don't fit into the sports, prison, and racial categories. As you shall see, they too can be spontaneous, destructive, injurious, and deadly.

POLITICAL RIOTS

We begin with a short look at a few of the big riots that happened during the tumultuous 1960s and early 1970s in the United States, followed by a major series of riots that erupted worldwide in 2006.

Madison, Wisconsin, 1967: Antiwar Riot

During the 1960s, the University of Wisconsin–Madison gained a reputation as one of the nation's most radical campuses. Protests began at the university around 1963, when students opposed the government's support of Ngo Dinh Diem, South Vietnam's president. Two years later, the campus began its first antiwar events, mostly teach-ins about what was occurring in

Vietnam and about what actions students could take to show their concern. Protests against the war increased in 1966 and into 1967, especially against Dow Chemical's (maker of napalm, a jellied gasoline used in the war) attempts to recruit on campus.

The first protest against Dow Chemical at Wisconsin occurred in February of 1967, when students staged a sit-in. That one was uneventful, but another sit-in in October when Dow returned to the campus turned violent. This time, the protestors roosted in a long hallway of one of the campus buildings.

Twenty campus police, backed by 20 off-duty Madison officers, gathered to try negotiating with the protestors. When the students refused, 30 more city officers roared to the scene, helmets on their heads, nightsticks in their hands. The police were ready to rumble; all they needed was the green light to go. It was Chancellor William Sewell's school, so he called the shots. "Clear them out," he told the officers.

A booming bullhorn gave the students two minutes to leave, but the only response were jeers, curses, and insults.

What happened next depends on who is telling the story. Some say the police smashed through the doors right after the two-minute warning. Others say the police gathered their forces outside, honoring it. Either way, when they did enter, a surging wall of students slammed into them. In the end, the protestors lost to flailing police batons.

Once the students had been beaten out of the hall, a larger group of around 1,000 formed outside. Some chanted, others beat drums, and mimes danced about. (I have also encountered mimes at protests, and I have never understood their role at these things. Whatever it is, at least they are quiet about it.) Tear gas wafted, batons slammed heads, and students fought back. In the end, 19 police officers would go to the hospital along with 47 students.

In the aftermath, everyone had an opinion as to who was right and who was wrong. The students stood up to the police, but some say the police were untrained and undisciplined to know how to handle the resistance any other way than with force.

The clash made the evening news and people took notice, especially students across the country. Looking back, one can argue that the University of Wisconsin was the forerunner of an antiwar movement that would soon involve millions.

Chicago, 1968: Democratic National Convention

On Thursday, August 22, four days before the 1968 Democratic National Convention in Chicago officially began, city police shot and killed a 17-year-old boy after he had pulled a gun on them. Protestors held a memorial march for him later the same day, which no doubt kindled the flames for them to do battle with the police, although in the latter part of the 1960s it didn't take much.

On Saturday, two days prior to the convention's start, protestors, police, and 6,000 National Guardsmen trained in separate locations for their inevitable clash. The protestors, who were mostly associated with an organization called National Mobilization Committee to End the War in Vietnam (informally known as "Mobe"), practiced karate and crowd protection techniques, while the Guard and police platoons trained in crowd-control tactics.

Things began to heat up Sunday when thousands gathered to hear music at Lincoln Park and officers told them that they could

Many Issues

The Democratic National Convention took place during the last week of August 1968, but national and world events of the previous two years fueled the violence that bloodied the streets just outside the convention hall. To list a few:

- An escalating war in Vietnam, to include the Tet Offensive, which experts believe was the turning point in public support for the war.
- The assassinations of Martin Luther King and Senator Robert Kennedy.
- Race riots throughout the United States.
- A hard line against protestors by Mayor Richard Daley, who ordered the police to shoot to kill arsonists and shoot to maim looters.

not use a flatbed truck as a stage. The people ignored the police order and within minutes, fights erupted all over the park between the protestors and the cops. As quickly as it had started, it ended, but with a shaky calm. Shaky and short-lived.

(As a former cop, I can imagine what the officers felt like wading into the midst of thousands of people, most of whom hated the police, to tell them not to stand on the back of a vehicle. In situations like that, it's best to choose one's battles with wisdom. In my opinion, the order to send in officers was poorly thought out. It was dangerous for the cops, with little to gain.)

Near midnight, police again clashed with about 2,000 protestors congregated on the streets outside the park. It's unknown what started it. If the demonstrators were damaging property or hurting innocents, then the police should definitely have moved against them. However, if they were merely congregating, as some news reports indicate, one must again question the wisdom of the order to move against such a mass of volatile people. Whatever started the riot, once it got going, the police let their batons do their negotiating as they beat protestors, reporters, and photographers.

On Monday, Mayor Richard Daley officially opened the convention. The first few hours were uneventful, but near midnight, a lone police car nosed into a barricade that demonstrators had erected earlier in Lincoln Park. Now, I was not there and therefore don't know all the details (I was watching it on television with fellow soldiers from where I was based in the Florida Everglades), but a lone police car bumping a barricade erected by protestors seems a little like poking a wild beast with a stick. This wild beast began stoning the car.

As if the police had anticipated the mob's reaction, a mass of officers immediately moved into the park, preceded by a cloud of eye-stinging, throat-burning tear gas. This clash would be far worse than the one on the previous night, as club-wielding cops not only thumped protestors but attacked residents on their porches who were only watching the fracas. Then officers went after the reporters again, attacking more of them on this night than at any other time during the convention.

Compared to the night before, Tuesday was a relatively quiet day. There was a 1,000-person march, which the police managed to stop without resorting to force. Maybe by now they were learning to pick their battles more carefully. The marchers formed a picket line and refused to disperse, remaining there until the next morning when officers used force to remove them. There were other gatherings throughout Tuesday, at which various celebrities spoke out against the war.

That evening, 200 clergy and church members, some of whom carried a 12-foot cross, joined forces with 2,000 protestors in Lincoln Park. When they remained past the mandated curfew, police again used tear gas and clubs to move them from the park.

On Wednesday, around 15,000 protestors gathered at Grant Park to participate in an antiwar rally sponsored by Mobe. More than 600 police officers surrounded the rally as National Guardsmen positioned themselves on rooftops. When someone tried to lower the American flag to raise a blood-splattered T-shirt, the issue of knowing when to pick battles showed itself again.

If there are only 600 of you and 15,000 of them, do you really want to take action because someone is switching flags, no matter how offensive that might be? Chicago's police did, and Mobe's marshals promptly confronted them. A clash ensued, and officers managed to beat them back with batons. The cops eventually prevailed, but only because the mass of people didn't turn on them. We can assume, though, that the incident didn't help police/protestor relations.

Rally organizers quickly directed the crowd to begin moving to the convention site, but no sooner had they set out than police and Guardsmen blocked their route. Some protestors managed to sneak through, while others spread out in pockets of large groups. Police leaders ordered the crowds to clear the street. When they ignored the command, waves of officers moved in with tear gas and batons, striking down anyone in their path, including bystanders.

Protestors fought back, much of it caught on film by TV crews positioned around the Hilton Hotel. While not the most violent clash that week, the film footage has been shown in many documentaries and at least one motion picture.

On Thursday, protestors tried several times to march, but each time the police moved in quickly to stop them. When protestors resisted, they got hit with a wall of tear gas.

When the convention officially ended on Friday at midnight, 668 people had been sent to jail, 1,000 received injuries that were treated by medics on the street, and an additional 111 went to area hospitals. Police reported 192 officers injured, with 49 needing to go to the hospital.

On a national level, the actions of the Chicago police would impact police/public relations for years.

Kent, Ohio, 1970: Kent State

Kent State, often portrayed as a peaceful, quiet place before the infamous 1970 shooting, had had its share of demonstrations and controversy during the 1960s. In 1968 and 1969, the Students for a Democratic Society (SDS) and the Black United Students (BUS) had demonstrated against police recruiting on campus, the school's Reserve Officers Training Corps (ROTC), and a law-enforcement training program.

Students held a large demonstration at Kent State University

Fear of the Draft

In April of 1970, many people were beginning to think that the Vietnam War was grinding down. However, on April 30, President Richard Nixon announced in a televised speech that a massive American and South Vietnamese troop offensive had been launched into Cambodia. He said, "We take these actions not for the purpose of expanding the war into Cambodia but for the purpose of ending the war in Vietnam, and winning the just peace we all desire."

A war-weary public had heard it all before. Many were enraged, and draft-age men were especially concerned. College campuses exploded in protest across the country, one of them Kent State University.

---

the day after President Richard Nixon's announcement that American troops were moving into Cambodia. Their signs and chants demanded, "Bring the war home." Protestors and police clashed violently that night, both on campus and in the streets of downtown Kent, where at least one bonfire was set, dozens of windows smashed, fire hoses slit, and police cars vandalized. The police responded with tear gas, but the rioting raged on.

On May 2, Mayor Leroy Satrom declared a state of emergency and asked Governor James A. Rhodes to send in the National Guard. By the time the troops arrived, the ROTC building was in flames, as hundreds of protestors cheered. When firefighters moved in to put out the fire, the crowd threw rocks at them, cut their fire hoses, and attacked responding police officers. With heads tucked to avoid thrown missiles, firefighters managed to extinguish the fire, only to have the building set ablaze a second time. Again, firefighters put out the fire and again protestors set it to flames. (Kent State's ROTC building was one of 30 burnt nationwide in the first days of May.)

The National Guard moved into action. The troops used tear gas, made mass arrests, and even resorted to fixed bayonets. One student was bayoneted in the leg. Eventually, the troops and police officers pushed the rock-throwing protestors back into campus buildings.

May 3 was a relatively quiet during the day. Governor Rhodes, running for U.S. Senate on a "law and order" platform, gave a speech in which he said the demonstrations were the product of an organized band of revolutionaries. He said that the individuals were "the worst type of people we harbor in America, worse than the brown shirts and the communist element . . . We will use whatever force necessary to drive them out of Kent."

That evening, a National Guard commanding officer told his troops that Ohio law gave them the right to shoot if necessary.

Later that night, a large crowd gathered in an area of the campus called the Commons and refused to budge when the

National Guard announced immediate enforcement of a new curfew. Guard officials read the Ohio Riot Act to the protestors, and when that didn't work to disperse them, troops fired tear gas from hovering helicopters.

Angry students moved toward the town to protest there, but Guardsmen cut off their path. When they sat in the road and demanded that the mayor and the university president speak with them, authorities told them that officials would meet them back at the campus. After the students returned to the school, not one official showed up, though swooping helicopters did and sprayed gas, forcing them to take cover in their dormitories. Helicopters with searchlights crisscrossed the campus all night, as if it were some Vietcong-entrenched valley in South Vietnam.

By 11 AM on May 4, more than 200 students had gathered on the Commons. While some officials believed that the governor had declared martial law, he would not take such official action until May 5. Still, the National Guard decided to disperse all assemblies on the campus grounds.

By noon, 1,500 protestors and spectators had gathered. An army jeep drove to the front of the crowd; a soldier dismounted. Using a bullhorn, the army man gave the crowd an official order to disperse, but students only jeered at him. In response, troops quickly formed a skirmish line and began advancing toward the protestors, lobbing tear gas canisters before them. Some protestors threw the tear gas back at the oncoming troops.

After clearing the Commons, the Guardsmen marched over a hill, firing tear gas to scatter protestors into a small area of trees and brush. The troops then marched down the hill onto a football field, where soldiers and protestors engaged in an almost silly confrontation of throwing tear gas canisters and stones at each other. However, the situation was about to turn grim, bloody, and deadly.

Troop G, positioned on the field, knelt and aimed their weapons at students in a nearby parking lot. What happened next remains controversial to this day. Some say there was a verbal command to fire; others say the troops fired on their own volition. Whichever it was, for the next 13 seconds, a dozen troops fired 67 rounds, killing four students and wounding nine others.

Former student Dean Kahler, shot in the lower back and left paralyzed, said this to CNN news 30 years after the event:

> I just jumped on the ground and covered my head and prayed that I wouldn't get shot. I was shot . . . and then I was praying that I wouldn't get shot again. After the shooting, there were the screams and the tormented voices of the students that I heard. And last, but not least, lying on the ground looking up and seeing the students' faces. The shock, the disbelief, was just unbelievable.

Bob Carpenter was news director at the campus radio station then. He said 30 years later:

> There isn't a day in my life that goes by that I don't wake up without some conscious thought of this. I was in Vietnam twice before. I did not have the fear that I had on this campus—helicopters swooping down, tear gas, bullets. It was a scary thing. I get goosebumps talking about it right at this moment.

Ironically, only one of the four killed had actually been participating in the protest; one of the three who was not involved was a member of the campus ROTC. The closest wounded student had been 71 feet from the Guardsmen. Of those killed, the closest was 265 feet away.

Protestors were enraged, shocked, frightened. The National Guard warned faculty members that the students must disperse immediately, but the students' anger was at full boil. One of the professors, Glenn Frank, now deceased, took desperate command. Recorded by a radio reporter, Frank pleaded in a voice that cracked with deep emotion. "I don't care if you've never listened to anybody before in your life. I am begging you right now, if you don't disperse right now, they're going to move in. It will only be a slaughter. Please, listen to me. Jesus Christ, I don't want to be part of this. Listen to me."

The country split in opinion as to whether the Guard acted appropriately and legally. Many adults supported the Guard's actions, while students saw it as a slaughter of innocents.

In the four days that followed the shooting, more than one-third of the nation's campuses went on strike, about 100 per day. One hundred thousand marched on Washington, D.C. to protest the Vietnam War and the Kent State killings. In New York, protestors clashed violently with hundreds of construction workers. It was a galvanizing event for the antiwar movement and one that epitomizes the emotion and turbulence of the Vietnam War era.

Worldwide, 2006: The Cartoon Riots

In the early months of 2006, street riots broke out in dozens of countries around the world after a newspaper in Denmark published cartoons lampooning the Prophet Mohammad. Many Muslims consider any depiction of the prophet to be sacrilegious.

A Danish newspaper first published the cartoons in September of 2005, but in early 2006, newspapers in Europe and elsewhere republished them as a way to demonstrate freedom of expression.

The impact was near catastrophic as massive protests erupted across the Muslim world. As violent riots, bloodshed, and deaths spread, the cartoonists remained free, though there exists in Denmark a blasphemy statute that can garner heavy fines and prison terms for violators. The law is simple: don't demean a recognized religious community. The law is simple in other countries, too, where authorities have charged writers for using slanderous words against Islam and Muslims.

In Germany, France, Norway, Italy, and Austria, some newspapers and magazines republished the cartoons in question to make a point that people who might be offended cannot dictate restrictions on free speech. This set off rebukes and calls for responsibility and restraint by Western officials. It forced editors into hiding, caused the firing of others, and resulted in some resigning over the issue. One newspaper in Malaysia lost its license to publish.

Outraged and offended Muslim demonstrators and rioters took their rage to the streets in Afghanistan, Libya, Pakistan, Indonesia, Turkey, and Nigeria, to name just a few. Each passing day the clashes grew in intensity, with an ever-increasing body count. With far less restraint than is used by the police and the military in the United States, law enforcement in places like Pakistan and Nigeria fought the riotous crowds with tear gas and deadly bullets.

In Islamabad, Pakistan, thousands of police and paramilitary forces—some riding in armored personnel carriers, others positioned behind sandbag bunkers—deployed around the capital to block a rally organized by a coalition of hard-line Islamic parties called the Muttahida Majlis-e-Amal (MMA). Intensely angered by the cartoons, this dangerous group sympathizes with the former Taliban regime of Afghanistan. Eventually, the leader received permission to protest with a few supporters, but when hundreds of others tried to join in the rally, police fired tear gas and warning shots over their heads.

In Istanbul, Turkey, thousands joined the Islamic Felicity Party to protest the insult to the Prophet. Protest leaders shouted over loudspeakers for people to "resist oppression" and chanted slogans against the United States, Denmark, and Israel. Throughout the rest of the country, thousands demonstrated in the streets, burning European flags and effigies of Danish Prime Minister Anders Fogh Rasmussen. A Muslim teenager shot and killed an Italian priest as he prayed in his Black Sea coast church. According to Turkish media, the 16-year-old suspect told interrogators that he killed the man to avenge the publication of the drawings.

Thousands more demonstrated in India, and 20,000 protested in Bangladesh, where Prime Minister Khaleda Zia demanded an apology for the "extremely arrogant" drawings.

In the Philippines, hundreds of Muslims set fire to a cardboard Danish flag outside a Manila mosque. They demanded an apology from Denmark's prime minister and insisted that Philippine President Gloria Macapagal Arroyo speak out against the caricatures.

In Gaza, protestors threw stones, burned tires, and tried to force their way into the European Union (EU) building. Outside, protestors tore down the EU flag and replaced it with the Palestinian flag. From there they went to Germany's representative office and commenced to break out windows with hammers, vandalize the courtyard, and tear down the German flag and set it ablaze.

In Malaysia, 3,000 demonstrators chanted, "Destroy Denmark! Destroy Israel! Long live Islam! Destroy George Bush! Destroy America!"

In Africa, violent protests killed 11 people in Libya and 16 in Nigeria the next day. Most of those killed in Nigeria were Christians, after rioting Muslims set fire to churches, retail stores, and vehicles. Some lost their lives inside the churches. The Christians retaliated by destroying Muslim homes, burning their mosques, and attacking them with machetes. At least 85 more died.

What about the cartoonists? They are still alive, much to the disappointment of many who want their heads. One artist said his inspiration for the pictures was "terrorism," which, he says, receives its "spiritual inspiration" from Islam. He said he drew them under freedom of expression and freedom of the press. Another artist noted, "I didn't think anyone outside the newspaper's readers would see the cartoon, and now a billion people have. It's a surreal situation."

LABOR RIOTS

For more than 100 years, workers around the world have marked May 1 with rallies, picnics, demonstrations, and riots. It's a day that provides an occasion for workers, especially those in Europe, to express their unity, passion, and dedication to social change.

Those of us with grey in our hair remember those Cold War images of tanks and missile launchers parading before the Kremlin and May Day riots in Europe. In recent decades, socialists and communists have adopted the day as their own. In Germany, for example, an assortment of radical groups (including neo-Nazis) use May Day to demonstrate for their causes, often leading to violence between people on different ends of the political spectrum, as well as with law enforcement.

Few Americans realize that the celebrations of labor, violent protests, and all-out rioting that have occurred overseas on May 1 actually mark events that took place in the United States in the 1800s. While the U.S. now celebrates Labor Day in September, in the latter part of the 1800s, most states observed it on May 1. In time, the special day moved to September to take advantage of the waning days of summer and to distance itself from an event that played out the first week in May of 1886.

Chicago, 1896: The Haymarket Riot

On May 1, 1886, approximately 340,000 workers went on strike across the United States to protest 10- to 12-hour workdays and six-day workweeks for little pay. In Chicago, where an estimated 80,000 went on strike, it would lead to violence.

Although previous strikes had resulted in shorter workdays, some employers refused to comply with the strikers, among them the McCormick Harvesting Machine factory on the west side of Chicago. Not only did the factory bosses not comply, they added insult to injury by hiring "scabs," non-union workers. This angered union workers, to the extent that the police were called in on several occasions to restore peace between the two groups. But that was only a warm-up. On May 3, the situation was about to turn especially ugly.

It began when striking workers outside the factory grounds attacked the scabs as they left the facility. When the strikers provoked the responding police officers, the officers fired rounds over

Two-Year Effort

Two years earlier, the Federation of Organized Trades and Labor Unions (predecessor to the American Federation of Labor) began a nationwide movement to fight for a change in the number of hours workers spent on the job. They asked all American employers to adopt as a standard an eight-hour workday, instead of the 10- to 16-hour workdays they had had for far too long. They gave employers two years to abide. Those who didn't would be subject to a nationwide cease-work strike on May 1, 1886.

their heads, but even that failed to disperse the hostile crowd. The strikers, now a riotous mob, knew what they wanted, and they were not about to leave. In fact, they wanted a piece of the cops.

The May 4 edition of the *Chicago Herald* reported what happened next:

> The officers wavered for a moment before the onslaught, and then leveled their revolvers at the crowd. The barrels of the weapons glistened in the sunlight, there was a flash, and then an explosion followed that startled the horses in the car barns two blocks away.

That time the police officers' "crowd control technique" quelled the disturbance, but at the cost of six protestors' lives.

The next night, striking workers called what they hoped would be a mass meeting to protest the officers' actions the night before. They expected 20,000, but bad weather reduced the crowd to 2,500. The city's business leaders considered the three planned speakers to be "dangerous agitators" and "anarchists," but the mayor issued a parade permit for the gathering anyway, believing there was no cause for concern. Business leaders didn't agree and encouraged a police inspector to call up reserves to position themselves nearby. The inspector did exactly that, calling in 700 of them.

Still thinking that the meeting was going to be no big deal, the mayor ordered the inspector to send his men home. The inspector not only refused but, two hours into the event, ordered his men to disperse the crowd.

Within minutes, formations of officers began advancing toward the crowd as police leaders barked commands for the crowd to disperse and go home. With the cops watching the crowd and the crowd watching the cops, it's unknown if anyone saw the pipe bomb arc through the air from the entrance of a nearby building. It exploded in the midst of a 200-man police column, killing one officer instantly and wounding six others so severely that they would die later.

The explosion stunned the police for a moment, but they recovered quickly, drew their weapons and began shooting into the fleeing crowd of laborers. Fear, anger, and a need for revenge kept them firing for a solid five minutes.

In spite of the mayor's plea for calm, the police inspector and other police leaders initiated a desperate search for the person or persons responsible for the bomb. The press called the hunt a "reign of terror" as police ignored and even stomped on what few rights Chicagoans had in those years. They arrested hundreds of suspects and beat and interrogated them for hours. Officers hammered out false confessions from people thought to be anarchists or sympathizers of the labor unions.

Authorities subsequently tried and sentenced eight people on conspiracy charges to incite violence that led to the deaths of the police officers. They sentenced seven to hang, and the eighth received a 15-year prison sentence. On November 11, 1887, four went to the gallows. One died later in an explosion of some kind, and the others had their death sentences commuted to prison terms. Police never found the person who actually threw the bomb.

The trial and sentences of the Chicago workers stirred labor groups to protest around the world. In 1889, the Socialist International declared May 1 as a day of demonstrations, and since 1890, it's been recognized annually by a variety of labor movements worldwide.

Controversial Statue

On May 4, 1889, Chicago erected a statue of a police officer in Haymarket Square, the first of its kind in the nation. For many years after, people saw the police as martyrs in the event of May 4, 1886, but as time passed and big labor unions grew, that perception would change. During the 1960s, vandals defaced the statue and blew it up twice. Repaired each time, the statue was eventually moved to the Chicago Police Training Academy.

Boston, 1919: Police Riot

As noted throughout this book, the police are always the first responders to a riot and, if the situation is violent enough, they ask for assistance from the military. But what if it's the police who need to be controlled?

On September 9, 1919, 1,100 members of the Boston Police Department, the majority of whom were Irish-born or American-born men, walked out on strike. For years they had worked for low pay, as much as 98 hours a week, with one day off every two weeks. During the few hours they did have off, they were always on call.

The officers complained, but to no avail. Making the issue even more complicated and thick with tension was that the upper echelon of the police department consisted of Protestants who ruled with an iron fist over the Irish-Catholic street officers. Although the Protestant elite enjoyed tremendous power and authority, and they had worked hard for decades to keep the Irish down, there was an increasing Irish presence in politics and a growing Irish middle class, with thousands on the public payroll.

In that summer of 1919, officers felt that their only hope for better pay and working conditions was to join with the American Federation of Labor (AFL), the nation's largest labor organization. But it was a risky move, given all that was going on. World War I had just ended, and many employers, in an effort to keep the profits they had enjoyed the past few years, were reneging on wartime concessions of higher pay and good working hours. On the other side of the issue, 4 million workers across the country were striking to keep the gains they had made during the war. Many in the nation saw labor unions as dangerous, even communist. Thousands of labor leaders found themselves arrested.

The Boston police commissioner ordered officers not to join a union, so when 19 violated his order, they found themselves suspended. The policemen's union called a meeting and voted unanimously to strike.

It began on the evening of September 9 and, within minutes, Boston's lawless figured out that fun times could be had. First, they gambled openly in the street. Then several men kicked in the door of a tobacco store and looted it, which encouraged hundreds more to follow suit in a crazed frenzy of smashing windows, looting stores, and attacking people in the streets. When they tired of that, they turned on the cops. They first harassed the unarmed striking officers, then turned their attention to those who remained on the force but were dangerously outnumbered. With only a quarter of the police department on duty but unable to respond, the looting and rioting spread quickly to all quarters of the city.

The next day, politics reared its head as the mayor first refused blame for what was going on, then called out the military, known then as the "state guard." Governor Calvin Coolidge put out the word that he was in control, not the mayor, and that he would save Boston.

Harvard students and a few young businessmen were brought in as volunteers to help the police, but the crowds quickly turned on them, chanting, "Kill the cops." For their protection, the students stayed inside the stations. When the replacement officers did dare to go outside, large crowds immediately confronted them, taunting and harassing.

When the first of the military arrived, they quickly went to work to save the cornered officers, which angered the crowd and set them off on a stone-throwing spree. It was a struggle for the troops until they brought in horsemen with swords and additional soldiers willing to shoot the rioters. The army set up machine gun units near the Park Plaza Hotel and shot around 25 people, killing five of them.

Eventually, authorities stopped the riot and brought the chaos under control. When the new police union asked to reinstate the striking officers, Coolidge refused and hired an all-new police department, drawing on recently returned World War I veterans. The Protestant elite cheered the governor's action.

Governor Coolidge would be reelected two months later, and a year after that he would be vice president. When President Warren Harding died in office, Coolidge became the president of the United States. It's a safe assumption that none of the fired officers voted for him.

Today, it's illegal in all 50 states for police officers and firefighters to strike.

Xizhou, China, 2005: Worker Riot

Let's flip through the calendar to present-day China and visit a textile factory in the city of Xizhou, where police officers lead three prisoners—their hands and feet chained, heads shaved, wearing gray pajamas—to the entrance gate of the Futai Textile Factory. The officers order them to stand motionless and then snap a few pictures. The purpose of this bizarre episode is to intimidate the factory's workers as they arrive for their shift—men and women who, along with these three shamed prisoners, had clashed violently with police a week earlier.

The issue was about salary or, if you were to ask the average Futai worker, the lack of sufficient salary for their 11-hour workdays. The problem began when workers received their monthly paycheck and found that their usual $60 to $100 checks had been reduced to $50, $40, and even lower in a few cases.

The Chinese government does not allow an independent organization to hear workers' grievances. Therefore, many workers,

You Think Your Job is Tough?
Millions of workers in China work under conditions that would be considered intolerable in the United States. Most are 18- to 22-year-old women who toil on assembly lines more than 60 hours a week, sometimes 90 hours a week, for wages that are equivalent to about $120 a month. Most live at their factories in company-provided dormitories and eat in company cafeterias, and then have to pay the companies a third of their pay for food and their meager living quarters.

increasingly frustrated and with nowhere to turn, are willing to take the chance and fight against what they feel is a corrupt system. However, to protest in China is to risk a prison sentence. Still, a dependent and hungry family is powerful motivation for people to take chances.

The workers were not a happy a group when they went back to their weaving machines the next day. They griped, they weighed their options, and they considered the risks. After a while, the workers who had received the greatest reduction in pay scooted back from their machines, stood, and with arms hanging at the sides, did nothing. A few minutes passed and then others stood; they, too, did nothing. Some continued to work, but those protesting began to harass them for doing so. By noon, half of the factory's 3,000 sweater makers had stopped working.

They formalized their complaint in a letter regarding the abrupt salary reduction and asked that the foremen show it to the management. They heard nothing back. Actually, management called for a meeting of executives for the next day to discuss raising salaries, but no one informed the workers of this. But even the next day there was no word from management. As one striker said later, "If there had been a response, there would not have been a strike."

Not long into the shift, workers in one group began chanting, "No raise, no work!" Soon another group joined in the chant. Then someone from a third group shut off the electricity, making every weaving machine in the factory inoperative. When a foreman shouted that the work was over, everyone filed outside, where they gathered in an intersection to continue their chant for higher pay.

Traffic began to jam on the streets that intersected with the impromptu demonstration, and angry motorists leaned on their horns and shouted epithets at the protestors. This lack of support didn't bide well with the already angry strikers, so they snatched melon rinds from under nearby fruit stands and hurled them at the cars. Just as they began throwing rocks at the motorists, a half-dozen members of Xizhou's unarmed Security Protection Personnel pulled up to the chaos on their motorcycles and began to push the strikers with long sticks.

This was not the wisest tactic, since the workers didn't like the security guards anyway. The community paid the officers to keep order and protect buildings, but the guards often harassed the workers and shook them down for money. In addition, the officers had apparently misread the indicators that these strikers were serious—very serious.

"People's anger was exploding like fire," one striker said. The workers turned on the officers and bombarded them with stones, forcing them to flee and leave their motorcycles behind. That would prove to be the officers' second error, as the strikers set about smashing the bikes with stones and setting one ablaze.

A van full of regular police pulled up, but before the officers could get out they found themselves in a hailstorm of stones. Within minutes the riot was in full swing, with thousands of workers stoning the police van, angry motorists caught in the middle of it all, and officers thumping rioters with their batons. Several hundred camouflage-wearing riot policemen roared to the scene and commenced beating people and firing tear gas. When the beatings subsided, dozens of rioters were arrested and hauled away.

Police set some free after a day of intense questioning, although others remained incarcerated for weeks without visitors or a change of clothes.

A week later, officers displayed the aforementioned shaved

and chained prisoners at the entrance gate to intimidate workers against further striking and rioting. However, most of the workers had already arrived and were busy weaving and hoping that their protest had forced management at least to listen to them.

The managers never held their meeting, though they did pledge to improve pay.

WILD PARTIES

As a cop, I never liked responding to wild party complaints since often the merrymakers were already volatile and out of control by the time the police walked into the environment. Imagine the setting: partygoers dancing, singing, chugging beers, and jumping clothed or unclothed into the pool. Then the police walk in and inform the crowd that the fun is over. Talk about unwanted guests! I cannot recall any rowdy party I responded to where the drunks took that order kindly.

In the first type of party call, everyone is having a rowdy and fun time when the cops show up. That type is hard enough for officers to deal with. Then there is the kind that erupts into chaos and violence before the police show up. With this one, the fun part has already come and gone, and now everyone is mean-drunk and violent. *Then* the cops walk in.

Whenever there is a big, drunken blast with a wrong mix of young people, some uninvited, and some wanting to fight and tear up things, the handwriting, as they say, is on the wall.

Portland, Oregon, 1974

My partner and I had been rushing from hot call to hot call all evening: bar fights, family brawls, a fatal car accident, a foot chase. Typical sweltering summer evening, full-moon activity. About 10 PM, a "code zero" from the downtown core area blared out on the radio, a rare emergency call for all cars in the city to respond. In this case, the call was regarding two officers down, both shot, the gunman still armed and running through the blocks.

We were working on the east side of Portland, and by the time we got halfway to the city proper, radio canceled the code. We learned later that other officers had cornered the suspect and he had subsequently shot himself to death. The incident had begun when two officers had confronted a man wanted on a murder warrant. The suspect overpowered the officers, disarmed one, and shot them both. One would survive his wound, but the suspect had stood over the other and pumped several more rounds into his chest, killing him.

The news shook my partner and me because the dead officer had been a training coach for both of us. He had been a good man, a super cop, and devoted husband and father. We finished the call right at quitting time and then headed to the precinct, both of us quiet, hurt, and a whole lot angry.

Most of us from the afternoon shift were in the locker room changing into our civilian clothes to go home when a sergeant's voice boomed over the PA system.

"Afternoon officers, get back in uniform. We got another code zero, this one at 67th and Center. Night officers are on the scene of a large, out-of-control party that's turned into a riot." We got dressed quickly, piled into cars, and roared to the scene.

The sergeant's "out-of-control" description grossly understated the situation. The party had begun when 175 young adults tried unsuccessfully to squeeze into a two-bedroom house for a beer blast. Although the place could hold only 20 people inside, and others had to hang out in the yard, that didn't prevent everyone from getting drunk—out-of-their-minds drunk.

As the evening wore on and the empty bottles increased, the partygoers grew combative with each other and then with the first four officers who responded to a loud party call. More officers were called in, and more after that. But more were needed, and that was when my afternoon shift was ordered back out.

The scene looked like a mini version of the Battle of

Gettysburg. Cops and drunks fought in a yard to our right, in front of the big house to our left, in our headlights to the front of us, and on the sidewalk a ways down the street.

Someone ran out from between two houses and kicked our passenger door, and a couple of seconds later a full can of beer bounced off our hood. Mobs of people lining the sidewalks screamed "police brutality!" as others ran off between the houses. Neighbors in bathrobes watched from their front windows; brave ones watched from their porches.

The mayhem lasted another 15 minutes before we got some semblance of order, mostly through attrition by arrest or because some rioters made the wise decision to flee the scene.

One drunken man about 22 years old was especially venomous with his curses and name-calling as my partner and I struggled to cuff him. We had him bent over the hood of our car yelling at him to stop with the kicking and spitting, when another drunk yanked my partner away, leaving the spitter and me to go at it one on one. I was already on the verge of getting really annoyed with the man when he said something that pushed me over the edge.

"I heard about those pigs getting shot tonight," he spat. "I'm glad the one died. Fuck him. I'm glad he got killed. Too bad the other one didn't get . . ."

I dumped him onto the pavement, hard.

He cried out in pain. "Hey, you can't do—"

"I just did, asshole," I said. That is when all the stressors of the evening exploded within me. "In fact, I quit." I ripped my badge off my shirt and threw it on the ground. "Now it's just you and me. Two citizens. That means I no longer have rules to follow."

A bit Hollywood, I admit. But I was pissed.

He was not too drunk to realize he had made a big mistake. "I'm sorry man," he cried as I dribbled him all over the pavement as if I were in the NBA and he was the ball. "I didn't mean what I said. Owwwww!"

Just as I was about to slam dunk him, a couple of officers

pulled me off the man. A third one easily handcuffed the now limp, whimpering suspect.

"Here's your badge, Christensen," one of them said quietly. "Put it on, take a breath, and go help your partner over there."

Good advice. I followed it, and the rest of the event went without major incident. No one ever said anything to me about what I did, and the young man didn't complain.

Sometimes it's hard to stay emotionally uninvolved.

Boulder, Colorado, 2004

A huge Halloween street party was held on University Hill in Boulder, Colorado, in 2004. When police first responded to a rowdy party call around 9 PM, they learned that one of the residents had a permit to hold a block party. The officers told everyone to quiet down and then left, believing that was the end of it. However, officers had to return a while later in response to another complaint from neighbors of rowdy behavior. That time they wrote several tickets for underage drinking.

All was relatively calm until police began to break up the parties that were spread among several houses. Revelers grew angry, no doubt fortified by copious amounts of alcohol, and within minutes, more than 1,500 partygoers filled the streets, transitioning into a riotous mob. They hurled rocks and bottles at officers, set fires in the street, and overturned cars.

Overwhelmed, officers called for reinforcements from their department, SWAT included, as well as officers from surrounding jurisdictions. The rioters again were ordered to disperse, and again the mob refused. The police then escalated their level of force with the aid of discharged tear gas. A good whiff of that and the rioters ceased and dispersed.

Police charged several adults with inciting a riot, criminal mischief, engaging in a riot, obstruction, and arson.

Interestingly, the city had issued the permit to hold a block party for the hours of midnight to 2 AM. Not too hard to recognize the warning signs with several parties involving hundreds of young people, a university area, a late night on Halloween, and a boatload of booze. If only all predictions were this easy.

New Windsor, New York, 2003

Your teen is going to a dance party at a local skating rink. Music, roller skates, punch, and chips. Should be fun. Should be safe. That was what most parents thought as they dropped their kids off at the rink.

The party began as just another teen event, but before it was over, it would turn into a riot that few of the 150 present would forget.

The problems started with an exchange of insults, but when the kids deemed their words not antagonizing enough, one 15-year-old boy pulled a knife (though security guards had supposedly searched everyone prior to entering the place) and slashed people under the funky light of a spinning disco ball. Within seconds, two partygoers were cut and bleeding, others began fighting each other throughout the building, someone sprayed Mace into the crowd, and several kids ripped fire extinguishers from the walls and sprayed each other.

Into this the police walked.

"It was total mayhem," one officer said of the 150 rioting teens. They called for additional officers from two nearby jurisdictions as well as the state police. It took them a while to restore order and make arrests, including apprehending the knifing suspect as he attempted to flee.

This riot is a clear example of how a gathering can go from 0 to 60 in mere seconds. One moment the partygoers are having fun and in the next they are fighting, vandalizing, and rampaging. Was this riot predictable? According to the police, there had been similar incidents at this particular skating rink, which records show gets more police calls than any other business in the town. It also employed four security guards and four others who help during the evening. That certainly implies something. Did the parents know this before allowing their kids to go there for a party? If not, why?

Greeley, Colorado, 2001

Many times, people complain that they were "victims" of police pepper spray when all that they were doing was observing the actions. "I was an innocent bystander," they say (or claim).

One solution to not being involved in a riot is to leave as soon as things turn ugly. Call this decision a common sense one. If you should choose to stay when, say, a party moves from being a gala event to a destructive rebellion, the chances of you being involved, even when you're just watching, are pretty darn good.

But what if the riot comes to you? Such was the case in Greeley, Colorado, when another university party turned bad. As one witness said, "It started as a group of people having a good time and then they became a crowd. Then the crowd became a mob, and you cannot control a mob; that's when it's a riot."

The party, hosted by three students, began around noon in one house in a quiet suburb. It was a simple affair, with drinks and conversation. However, by 9 PM, the number of partygoers had swollen to 1,000, their mass spreading down the street until 500 people were milling about in various front yards.

What if this was your neighborhood, and when you looked out the front window you saw nothing but heads? That is exactly what one neighbor reported, and it was the reason why he dressed quickly in only his pants and shoes, then grabbed a can of pepper spray and his sword.

Yes, sword. The man was a 35-year veteran kendo instructor. He did call the police before he got dressed and gathered his weapons, but they told him to get out of the neighborhood. He didn't want to. He wanted to go out into his yard and order every-one off his property.

The crowd wisely obeyed this shirtless man who clutched a can of pepper spray in one hand and a sword in the other, but they didn't go far, nor did they go away peacefully.

The swordsman watched from his lawn, at least for a short while, as the mob ripped down street signs and began burning them in a bonfire in the center of the street. Then he went into the street and grabbed some of the signs to drag into his yard to protect them. Two rioters who really wanted to burn them came after the man to get the signs back. The man's first sword strike broke one of the rioter's arms, but a second blow to the man's neck broke the sword.

The swordsman said later that the rioters were like mad dogs as they burned, trashed, and fought one another. When the drunken wilders tried to loot the man's home, he fought them until someone clunked him in the back of the head with a bottle.

The rioters were in full swing by the time the police, dressed in full battle regalia, marched down the street in formation, their shields forming a wall. The rioters met them head on, throwing bottles, chunks of concrete, and rocks. Then they set fires, at least 10 of them. The police responded with tear gas and rubber bullets.

When it was over, no one seemed to know why it happened. There was no sporting event, and it was not a holiday. There was, however, much alcohol and too many rowdy students in a small space.

And one angry neighbor with a sword.

San Bernardino, California, 2006

Between 1,500 and 4,000 punk rock fans spilled out into the streets during a concert in San Bernardino, California, in March of 2006. The riot began when someone stabbed at least one skinhead during a confrontation that erupted after other skins began chanting "white power" during the concert. Before it would end, it would take 190 officers from 10 surrounding police agencies to quell the violent disturbance. Officers and fans suffered injuries, and many people caught in the riot choked on tear gas inside and outside of the concert hall. Rioters broke windows in surrounding businesses, vandalized cars, set fires, and threw bottles. Fifteen people would go to jail.

I scanned a few online blogs to see what fans were saying about the incident and found their responses quite revealing as to how they view the police, the act of rioting, their responsibility, and how they think in general. Here are a few of the comments.

- "Fucking pigs." This writer went on to comment on his dislike for the police and that it was their fault that the riot occurred.
- "Nazi bastards." While the uninformed eye might not be able to differentiate between a punk rocker and a skinhead, there is a difference, and the two factions are hugely aware of it. This person, a punk rocker, blamed the skinheads for the problems that erupted.
- "Man, I so wanted to be there." While most try to escape the violence of a riot, this person lamented about missing out on it.
- "You people are idiots." The writer was angry with other punkers for seizing the opportunity to vandalize local businesses. She feared that those in authority would not permit future punk concerts at the same location. She was also upset because she felt that she already lived in a bad neighborhood and now, because of the rioting and vandalism, it was even worse.
- "Damn! I wasn't there!" Another disappointed because he missed the riot.
- "My daughter was frightened." A 39-year-old woman took her young daughter to the concert and was upset because her child had been frightened during the chaos.
- "The cops were chicken." This concert fan claimed that the police were afraid, but he didn't elaborate how he knew that.
- "Damn pigs!" a 16-year-old blog writer flamed, then went on to blame the police for the damage and the tear gas in his neighborhood.

A police lieutenant commented to the media that punk shows draw "an interesting crowd." He said, "Given the choice, a punk rock concert probably is a good one to pass up. The antisocial lyrics as well as the physical abuse during their dancing just fires up the emotions and builds into a frenzy that is ripe for assaults and property destruction."

"It looked like a miniature version of the Los Angeles riots," one business owner complained. "This should have never happened. The city should have taken better care of us."

HUMAN STAMPEDES

While some might not define a human stampede as a riot since it doesn't involve criminal vandalism and some of the psychological elements we have discussed in this book, its dynamics fit the *Merriam-Webster*'s definition of a riot as "public violence . . . a tumultuous disturbance of the public peace by three or more persons assembled together and acting with a common intent."

Here are two "tumultuous disturbances" that occurred during the course of this writing. Both events involved thousands of people fighting for their lives in desperate disregard for the lives of others.

Saudi Arabia, 2006

On January 12, 2006, tens of thousands of Muslim pilgrims in Saudi Arabia were heading toward Al-Jamarat, three pillars representing Satan. Muslims journey to the pillars to throw stones at them in the belief that the act rids them of sin. There is one point along the way that for years has been a bottleneck for the masses that attend the Hajj, the pilgrimage to Mecca. In 1990, 426 people were killed at the same place, and 244 died there in 2004.

As the massive throng hurried to the pillars on January 12, those in front tripped over luggage and other personal effects they were carrying, causing those behind them, thousands upon thousands of people, to stumble, fall, and crush those who had already fallen. Panic followed as people jumped over each other, fought, and screamed in terror and pain.

"The bodies were piling up," one witness said. "I couldn't count them. There were too many."

Before it was over, 1,000 received injuries and at least 345 lost their lives.

Baghdad, Iraq, 2005

During another religious procession, this one in Iraq, hundreds of thousands of celebrants—some reports estimated the number at a million—snaked slowly through the streets from the center of Baghdad toward the Kazimiyah shrine in the northern section. The jammed procession is an annual event that honors Musa al-Kadhim, a ninth-century imam and revered Shiite figure.

No doubt many of the participants were thinking of the year prior when crowds of worshippers were bombed at Shiite mosques in the city, killing 181 people. This year, tensions were high. Iraqi security forces had shut down many of the streets to prevent attacks on the procession by the Sunni-dominated insurgency, while other troops conducted pat-down searches at random locations. Earlier in the day, mortars hammered the procession near another religious shrine, killing seven and injuring dozens. No doubt this confused and concerned the thousands of marchers in what was an already tense, war-torn city.

At one point along the way, the multitude of people had to cross a bridge that spans the Tigris River. Thousands of them pressed onto the structure, their advance slowed by security forces checking marchers at the front. With nerves already frayed, a rumor began at the checkpoint that someone in the crowd had a bomb wired to him. When another began yelling that a suicide bomber was amongst the throng, it ignited a riotous panic that set in motion a horror that would "leave a scar on our souls," as President Jalal Talabani noted in a televised address.

The multitude at the front turned and charged into the crowd of people crossing the bridge toward them. Deadly panic ensued: a collision of men, women, children, and the elderly, all of them pushing, shoving, and screaming in a tangle of terror and flailing limbs. A metal fence that ran along the edge of the bridge to protect people from the swift waters below ironically became a deadly wall that crushed the masses.

Then the railing gave way.

Hundreds of people spilled over the sides to tumble 90 feet through the air and into the churning, muddy Tigris River. Others deliberately jumped to avoid the crush but then drowned or landed on people already in the river, injuring and drowning even more.

It was a riot for survival on the bridge as the panicked horde frantically pushed one another, screamed in desperation, clawed, kicked, and punched against the suffocating crush.

The dead began to stack up on the bridge's span.

Parents had a horrific decision to make with only seconds to do it. Should they throw their children off the bridge and risk them drowning or keep them on the bridge and risk the crowd crushing them to death? Those who decided their chances were better in the murky water launched their screaming children into space. Some survived; many drowned. Those people—children, women, and the very old—who didn't fall, jump, or get thrown to their deaths were knocked down onto the bridge's surface. A gruesome stampede trampled scores to death.

One particularly shocking news photo of this tragedy shows the bridge covered with thousands of shoes lost during the riotous stampede. Not shown were the kindhearted people underneath the bridge pulling the dead from the river.

The death toll would reach 1,000. The number of injured, likely uncountable.

WILL IT EVER END?

As this book went to press, the news continued to churn out story after story about riots, protests, and unruly crowds all over the world. Here are three examples from California alone.

San Diego

A brawl erupted on a San Diego beach on a hot Memorial Day in 2007, forcing police to darn riot gear and confront a bottle-throwing crowd. Many in the mob of 500 had been drinking, which no doubt played a part in the violence. Around 70 officers formed a skirmish line along the boardwalk while an overhead police helicopter circled, ordering the crowd to disperse. Officers made 16 arrests.

San Francisco

In August 2007, rioters shut down the Southland Mall in Hayward, just outside of San Francisco. It began in the mall parking lot, where bleachers had been set up for spectators to watch a basketball game. After the game, several young people started fights and then stormed into the mall to overturn displays, kick merchandise, vandalize kiosks, and frighten customers and employees. Thousands of shoppers fled the mall property in their cars and on foot before several jurisdictions of officers were able to regain control.

Los Angeles

On May 1, 2007, in Los Angeles, a pro-immigration rally at MacArthur Park ended in chaos after police moved in on the demonstrators, firing rubber bullets. Organizers had purportedly obtained permits for the event, but soon people began to illegally block the streets. When people began throwing rocks, bottles, and other debris at officers, the police declared the rally an unlawful assembly and told the crowd to disperse. The order was also given from police helicopters circling above, police cars, and handheld bullhorns as lines of cops dressed in riot gear moved into the park. The police fired 146 foam-rubber projectiles, hitting marchers and members of the media. News footage and clips on youtube.com show the police using their batons to strike people who, though not combative, were nonetheless in the area after the orders to disperse had been give. More than 50 lawsuits have been filed at this writing.

Sources

"Chicago '68: A Chronology, by Dean Blobaum, www.geocities. com/Athens/Delphi/1553.

"Rights in Conflict: The violent confrontation of demonstrators and police in the parks and streets of Chicago during the week of the Democratic National Convention of 1968," by Daniel Walker, www.geocities.com/Athens/Delphi/1553/ ricsumm.html.

"Aftermath," J. Gregory Payne, Ph.D, www.may4archive.org /aftermath.shtml.

"Kent State: May 1–4, 1970," by May 4th Task Force Members, www.cs.earlham.edu/~paulsjo/KentState.html.

"Peace-loving' Protesters: Kent State Revisited," by Steve Farrell, NewsMax.com, www.newsmax.com/archives/artcles/2003/3/9 /021116.shtml#4a, 2003.

"Kent State shooting survivors gather for 30th anniversary," by Gary Tuchman, www.CNN.com, May 4, 2000.

"Two Days in October," PBS, www.pbs.org/wgbh/amex/twodays/ peopleevents/p_veterans.html.

They Marched into the Sunlight: War and Peace, Vietnam and America, October 1967, by David Maraniss, Simon and Schuster, 2003.

"Deadliest cartoon riots kill 16 in Nigeria," by Tume Ahemba, www.reuters.com, February 18, 2006.

"Bodies burned in open after Nigeria riots kill 138," by George Esiri, www.reuters.com, February 23, 2006.

History of the Chicago Police from the Settlement of Community to the Present Time, by John J. Flinn, Police Book Fund, www.chipublib.org/004chicago/timeline/haymarket.html, 1887.

"The Haymarket Square Riot: A Journey into Chicago's Past" by Troy Taylor, www.prairicghosts.com/haymarket.html, 2000.

"Hibernian Chronicle: Chaos follows Hub police strike," by Edward T. O'Donnell, The Irish Echo online. www.irishecho. com/newspaper/story.cfm?id=15188.

"Boston police strike of 1919," by David Wieneke, Boston History and Architecture, www.iboston.org.

"A Chinese riot rooted in confusion, " by Edward Cody, *Washington Post*, www.washingtonpost.com, July 18 ,2005.

"Boulder block party turns into a riot," by Ryan Delaney, 9News.com.

"Teen party at Upskate turns violent," by Ben Montgomery, *Times Herald Record,* www.recordonline.com.

"Man with sword defends home against rioters," by Brian D. Crecente, FreeRepublic.com, April 30, 2001.

"Riot sets community on edge against punk," by Megan Blaney, www.sbsun.com, March 9, 2006.

"Fight breaks out over riot damage," by Joseph Ascenzi, www.thebizpress.com, March, 13, 2006.

"345 dead in stampede on last day of haji," by Salah Nasrawi, Associated Press, www.breaitbart.com.

"US party turns into melee overflow crowd in Berkley riots, nearby stores looted," by Henry K. Lee, *San Francisco Chronicle*, www.sfgate.com, October 16, 2000.

"Nearly 1,000 Shiites killed in stampede over bomb rumors," by Rick Jervis, *USA Today*, www.usatoday.com, August 31, 2005.

About the Author

Loren W. Christensen began his law enforcement career in 1967 as a military policeman in the U.S. Army and then joined the Portland (Oregon) Police Bureau in 1972, retiring in 1997. During his years on the PPB, he worked street patrol, gang intelligence, dignitary protection, as a defensive tactics instructor, and in riot control.

Loren Christensen on crowd-control duty with the Portland Police Bureau (fourth helmeted officer from left).

As a freelance writer, Loren has authored 36 published books on a variety of subjects, written dozens of magazine articles, and edited a newspaper for nearly eight years. He was honored recently to coauthor an article, "The Evolution of Weaponry," with Lt. Col. Dave Grossman for the *Encyclopedia of Violence, Peace, & Conflict* published by Academic Press.

Loren began training in the martial arts in 1965 and continues to this day. He has written several books on the subject and has starred in six instructional DVDs.

Retired from police work, Loren now writes full time, teaches martial arts to a small group of students, and gives seminars on the martial arts, police defensive tactics, and verbal judo.

Loren Christensen today.

To contact Loren, visit his website at www.lwcbooks.com.